D0565614

PUT 'EM UP! FRUIT

Put 'em Up! Fruit

A PRESERVING GUIDE & COOKBOOK

Creative Ways to Put 'em Up, Tasty Ways to Use 'em Up

Sherri Brooks Vinton

PHOTOGRAPHY BY JENNIFER MAY PHOTOGRAPHY, INC.

Storey Publishing

The mission of Storey Publishing is to serve our customers by publishing practical information that encourages personal independence in harmony with the environment.

Edited by Margaret Sutherland
Art direction and book design by Jessica Armstrong
Text production by Theresa Wiscovitch and Jennifer Jepson Smith

Cover and interior photographs by © Jennifer May Photography, Inc.
Food styling by Jessica Bard
Prop styling by Raina Kattelson
Author's photo by © Chris Bartlett
Icons by Dan O. Williams

Indexed by Christine R. Lindemer, Boston Road Communications

© 2013 by Sherri Brooks Vinton

All rights reserved. No part of this book may be reproduced without written permission from the publisher, except by a reviewer who may quote brief passages or reproduce illustrations in a review with appropriate credits; nor may any part of this book be reproduced, stored in a retrieval system, or transmitted in any form or by any means — electronic, mechanical, photocopying, recording, or other — without written permission from the publisher.

The information in this book is true and complete to the best of our knowledge. All recommendations are made without guarantee on the part of the author or Storey Publishing. The author and publisher disclaim any liability in connection with the use of this information.

Storey books are available for special premium and promotional uses and for customized editions. For further information, please call 1-800-793-9396.

Storey Publishing
210 MASS MoCA Way
North Adams, MA 01247
www.storey.com

PRINTED IN CHINA BY R.R. DONNELLEY
10   9   8   7   6   5   4   3   2   1

Library of Congress Cataloging-in-Publication Data on file

FOR MY FAMILY
— *past, present, and future* —
who have shared, celebrated, and will
carry forward the joy and tradition
of the dinner table.

CONTENTS

FOREWORD

Sherri Brooks Vinton is a talented cook and food preserver, and I have been a fan of her culinary skills for many years now. It's actually hard to believe that we met nearly a decade ago, when she was traveling around the country doing research for her book *The Real Food Revival,* and I was in the midst of publishing *Edible Ojai,* the first "edible" magazine in the network that has become Edible Communities, a collection of nearly 80 regional food magazines published in various food communities across North America. It was during that first meeting that Sherri left a lasting impression on me that has endured all these years: not only was she writing a book that would help readers navigate confusing food labels and help them to find "real food" wherever they shopped, her personality was such that you felt good just being around her. To this day, it's rare to meet someone as warm or as kind as Sherri is (not to mention, as hard working)! That day, I found myself imagining how great it would be if we lived closer to each other and what it would be like to hang out in her kitchen over a cup of tea every now and then.

That feeling of camaraderie has now come full circle with *Put 'em Up! Fruit,* and I feel honored to have been asked to write this foreword. With it in hand, all of us have, in a way, been invited to hang out in Sherri's kitchen. Trust me, you are going to love your time with her.

Preserving fresh, seasonal foods has been a lifelong love of mine. Ever since my grandmother — the eldest of 17 siblings from a farm family in upstate New York — showed me how to make Concord grape jelly when I was four, I have been smitten with the process. I still remember the first time I watched Nana hang that grape-filled cheesecloth sack from the knob on her kitchen cupboard and how I held my breath as she placed a heavy rock on top of the fruit so that it dripped slowly into a bowl that was waiting to collect the juice on the counter below, certain the whole thing would come tumbling down at any moment. In the decades that have passed since that event took place, the act of canning and preserving foods has evolved from a tradition born out of necessity for some homemakers, into a full-fledged, modern-day, do-it-yourself food movement that is resonating with almost everyone who cooks or cares about where their food comes from. Whether for economic reasons, a penchant toward thriftiness, or having a sincere interest in sustainability, nothing else feels quite as rewarding as a well-stocked pantry full of home-preserved foods.

Whether you are new to canning or an old pro, *Put 'em Up! Fruit* will make you think about the range of fruit preserves in a new, refreshing way. Sherri has covered everything from various jellies and jams to poached pears in wine, dried cranberries, smoky tomato salsa, whole dried lemons, fruit cheeses, and even gastriques. Whatever recipes from this book become your favorites — and I know there will be many — be sure not to miss Sherri's recipe for Classic Concord Grape Jam on page 141. Thankfully, it doesn't require any cheesecloth or heavy rocks and tastes just as wonderful as Nana's did several decades ago!

Tracey Ryder
Cofounder, Edible Communities

Orange + CUMIN Chutney

GREEN GRAPE and Moscato Jelly

SMOKY TOMATO SALSA

Jar suitable for refrigerator storage; not approved for canning

CLASSIC ·PEACH· JAM

PLUM & PRUNE CONSERVE

Thyme HERB JELLY

Poached Quince

Whole Dried LEMONS

BLUE-BERRY SYRUP

Introduction

Over the past few years, home food preservation has been dusted off and prettied up. It's no longer sniffed at as that old-fashioned chore from your grandmother's time, like using hand-cranked laundry presses and coal-heated clothes irons (though it wouldn't surprise me to see these popping up in hip Brooklyn households sometime soon!). Home food preservation is being rediscovered for what it is — a practical, economical way to enjoy seasonal foods all year round.

The fervor for putting up your own food isn't just a trend. It's not just for hip, tattooed kids trying to push the culinary boundaries or back-to-the-landers living off the grid. Moms wanting better control over what they feed their families, gardeners looking to use up their backyard bounty, groups of friends looking for a new kind of "stitch and bitch" session, home cooks looking to further economize on their grocery budget — food preservers come from all walks of life and have varying motivations for getting back into the swing of putting food up.

I've always said that the food movement has something for everyone — you can be an anarchist, an environmentalist, or a hedonist. Whether you are looking to reclaim the food chain from corporate control, use your food choices to save the planet, or just have a great-tasting meal, you can find it all in the real food revival. And so it is with food preservation. A dedication to local farms, desire for wholesome ingredients, or love of hand-crafted flavors — any one of these would be a terrific reason to put up your own food.

Not Fancy, Just Food

Food preservation is driven by economy, resourcefulness, and a desire not to waste fresh food. Preserving can showcase a home cook's ingenuity at its finest — the ability to make something gorgeous out of something you would normally throw away, such as turning citrus rinds into glittering candies. And it soothes our little lizard brains to see the stores of food lined up on the shelves as the wind howls outside our doors.

You can see the necessity and beauty of food preservation across cultures and continents, from many of which I pulled inspiration for my own recipes. Colonial American blueberry shrub, membrillo from Spain and South America, Moroccan tagines, black lemons from the Middle East, Asian spring rolls, and stuffed grape leaves from Turkey — it has been inspiring and informative to rediscover some of the old traditions of food preservation and to attempt to carry these traditions and flavors forward.

LAMB TAGINE WITH POACHED QUINCE, PAGE 218

CARROTS WITH PLUM GLAZE, PAGE 212

I generally don't preserve food as a way of supplanting my seasonal diet. I have very little interest in corn in the middle of January. I don't yearn for handfuls of berries in the winter. What I do crave, though, is a little treat, a little break from my dietary routine. Preserved foods give me that. A little fruit chutney to go with my low and slow cooking. A dram of infused tipple to sip by the fire. Something to perk up my plate and palate.

That's what preserving food does for me and what I hope this book can do for you. Not to blur the lines of seasonality, but to offer a few ideas for preserving abundant seasonal produce and then some suggestions for using those lovely creations to supplement your larder in fun new ways. Yes, berry jelly is a fun thing to make. But you needn't save it just for your bagel. You can whisk a spoonful into a vinaigrette. Poached quince are sweet as candy straight out of the jar and bring just the right fruity note to an exotically spiced lamb tagine. Cherry jam is wonderful on a scone, but good as well when used in a pan reduction sauce. Plum jam turns a piece of whole wheat toast into a little slice of luxury and brings the same luscious touch to sautéed carrots. In these ways and more, you can bring the flavors of summer into your kitchen, not enough to scramble the calendar, but just enough to feel the sun on your face, if only for one brief moment.

Part One

Jar suitable for refrigerator storage; not approved for canning

Getting Started

I know that the fruit waits for no one, and if you are as impatient as I, you want to jump right into your next project. But take just a minute to look through this next section. It gives you some pointers for getting the best results, some definitions of terms used in the book, a little rundown of the processes we'll be using, and a troubleshooting guide to make sure we keep the train on the rails. That way we can make the most of your gorgeous produce and your time spent in the kitchen.

Your Keys to Success

Like the first *Put 'em Up!, Put 'em Up! Fruit* is arranged by produce item so that you can look up the food that you have in abundance quickly and easily, and then plan what you would like to do with it.

For each produce item, there are a number of preserving recipes that utilize a variety of techniques for extending the life of the food. Some are very simple and take only a few minutes to accomplish, while others are more what you might consider "project cooking," so you can pick the one that suits your day and tastes.

Each preserving recipe is accompanied by a "Use It Up!" recipe, a suggestion for using the preserve in your cooking. Many of these recipes can be used with a variety of preserves, so don't hesitate to mix and match the "Put 'em Up!" recipes with the "Use It Up!" recipes — there are endless combinations and I have listed some alternatives to try as well.

You can also try the "Use It Up!" recipes with preserves you have made using recipes from other books, preserved foods you have been gifted, or even those you have bought at the market. The "Use It Up!" recipes allow you to work with the preserved foods you have on hand in fun and creative ways.

Do not, however, make substitutions within "Put 'em Up!" recipes unless a recipe specifically notes that it is okay to do so. Home food preservation is not hard, but it is not very tolerant of improvisation. A jam recipe designed for one fruit may not give you good results when used with another. Some processes work really well with certain fruits but will give you abysmal results with other produce, so you can't always just trade apples for oranges.

FOLLOW THE DIRECTIONS

The weights and volumes of produce and other ingredients have been carefully calculated to give you consistent, wholesome results. Use the measurements indicated, cut to the sizes indicated, and always add the ingredients to the pot in the order given. For reasons explained throughout the book, adding sugar and then berries will give you very different results than adding berries and then sugar, so try to stick to the playbook for consistent results.

That's not to say that you cannot make these recipes your own. The hand of the cook is very apparent in fruit preservation. I am sure that old hands can attest to the fact that every turn at the jam pot has made them that much more adept. If you're new to home food preservation, you will find your own style as you go. No matter your level of experience, the skill and attention you bring to your jam, jelly, infusion, or chutney will make every nibble and sip that much more delicious.

BUY GOOD FRUIT

The first step to making any good-tasting preserve — or anything edible — is to start with excellent locally grown ingredients. Shop at a farmers' market or farm stand, or glean from your backyard or that of your neighbor (after begging "please" of course). Food destined for home food preservation should always come from as local a source as possible for peak ripeness and to minimize the amount of bacteria that will naturally develop from the time it leaves the farm until it is in the pot.

Buying directly from local growers also means that you will avoid the topical fungicides and waxes that are often applied to grocery store produce to extend its shelf life. Leaving aside the issue of whether these treatments are safe or not, food that has been treated will simply not be able to absorb the syrups and brines that often give preserved foods their flavor and keep them safe on the shelf. Untreated produce is best for preserving.

This book is organized by fruit so that, rather than finding a recipe you want to make and then searching for the ingredients to make it, you are free to respond to the market and what is in season, grabbing what looks good and putting it up. Not only does shopping this way guarantee that you are getting food that is of the best quality, but the sensory experience — enjoying the sights and smells of the harvest as it becomes available — is part of the fun. What's going in your canner this weekend? Well, only the most tempting, gorgeous things — the fruits that are so enticing you just can't stand the thought of passing them by. If you have your heart set on making something specific, say putting up many quarts of tomatoes, talk to your farmer about when they will be at their peak. Buy too early and you will be paying top dollar; too late and the fruit may be overripe. Work with your farmer to get fruit at its best and at its best price.

There is a misguided notion that food destined for preserving should be of inferior quality, and many canners look for "seconds" at the market — those items that aren't good enough to display and can be purchased for a discount. If this means that they just aren't pretty, that's fine, but badly damaged or rotting fruit is not. If you want wholesome, terrific-tasting preserves, you have to start with food that is already good enough to eat. No amount of simmering, freezing, or drying is going to resuscitate a gasping, half-dead thing back to vigor. And rotten food means food that has picked up a lot of bacteria — not a good place to start your preserving project.

When you are selecting fruit for preserving, look for produce that has been allowed to mature on the vine. These vine- and tree-ripened fruits will have the most flavor. Avoid overripened fruits, however, as their lower pectin levels can make it hard

The orchard fruits at Silverman's Farm and the gorgeous, organic produce at Sport Hill Farm are two of the best reasons to live in Easton, Connecticut. Eat good food: support your local growers!

TOO FAR GONE —
this fruit is good only
for compost.

A LITTLE PAST
THEIR PRIME — trim
and freeze this fruit.

A MIX OF PERFECTLY RIPE
AND ALMOST READY —
this is what you want
in the jam pot.

to achieve the desired gel stage. In fact, it's smart to include a portion of slightly underripe fruit in your preserving recipe. A good rule of thumb is that about 20 to 25 percent of the total volume of fruit should be a bit shy of full ripeness. Not green and immature, but strawberries with a bit of white shoulder showing and peaches that are still rather firm, for example, will have more pectin than fully ripened crops, making it easier to achieve a good gel.

Once you select your fruit, it should have a quick trip from harvest to processing. Some delicate fruits, such as hand-picked strawberries, will show signs of deterioration in as little as a day, even under refrigeration. Even hardier fruits, such as apples, will give you your best results if you preserve them soon after picking. For the best preserved foods, find lovely local things, buy them at their peak, and put 'em up!

SO, TO SUM IT UP:

- Secure locally produced foods directly from the grower or your own backyard.

- Avoid supermarket produce, which may have been treated with fungicides and protective waxes that interfere with the preserving process.

- Use only wholesome, fresh fruit.

- Include up to 25 percent slightly underripe fruit for the best textures and gelling qualities in your recipes.

- Process food soon after picking.

Definitions

What's the difference between a compote, a conserve, and a preserve? While they all denote sweet fruit spreads, these terms have been used historically to indicate subtle differences in style and preparation. Modern cooks take a good bit of creative license with these terms. Tomato marmalade, for example, is something that I've seen more than once, but anything described as marmalade, technically speaking, should contain strips or bits of citrus peel in obvious profusion. Just sayin'. I've not run so grandly afoul of the culinary classifications, but I am probably guilty of bending the rules a bit myself. Although most preserved food spreads are ubiquitously labeled "preserves" and no one seems to be blushing at the error, here is a list of the terms and their meanings to use as you will.

CHUTNEY

In flavor, chutneys lie somewhere between preserves and pickles; even though they are often made with fruit as their main ingredient, they utilize vinegar for its preserving power. Chutneys are made with all kinds of fruits simmered with spices and savory flavorings such as garlic and onions. Some common ones include mango, tamarind, cilantro, and onion chutneys.

COMPOTE

Compotes contain large pieces of fresh or dried fruit gently simmered in sugar syrup. In a compote, care is taken to maintain the shape of the fruit so that it remains intact and suspended in a clear liquid. The syrup can be a simple combination of water and sugar, or it can be flavored to enhance the taste of the fruit.

CONSERVE

Chunkier than a preserve but not as full of whole fruit pieces as a compote, conserves are thick mixtures of fruit cooked gently in sugar syrup so that large pieces of fruit remain. Raisins or nuts are frequently added to conserves.

CURD

Sweet and creamy, curds are spreads made with eggs, butter, and citrus juice. Curds can be a challenge to master as they require precise attention to the quality of ingredients, cooking times, and temperatures. Although the most popular flavor is lemon, lime and orange curds are equally delicious.

FRUIT CHEESE

Fruit cheeses are nondairy pastes made out of fruit, lemon juice, and sugar that have been cooked down to a very dense texture. When cooled, they should be firm enough to be sliced with a knife.

GASTRIQUE

Gastriques are pungent vinegar-based sauces that are heavily reduced to take on a thick, syrupy texture. The base of the gastrique is a combination of vinegar and sugar that is cooked down and used as a canvas for a featured flavoring such as berries or citrus juice. Because of their intense flavors, gastriques are used in small amounts to accent the flavor of dishes.

INFUSION

Typically made with vinegar or a high-alcohol spirit, infusions take on the flavor of a featured fruit, vegetable, spice, or herb. The flavoring agent is submerged in the base liquid and allowed to steep until it has "infused" the liquid with flavor.

JAM

Probably the most popular fruit preserve, jams are sweet spreads made with mashed fruit or fruit that has been cooked until it has fallen apart. Jams rely on either natural or added pectin to achieve a gelled consistency that is thick enough for a spoonful of the spread to hold its shape.

JELLY

Sweet, clear spreads made from fruit juice alone, jellies are firmer in texture than jam but not as firm as fruit cheese or paste.

KETCHUP

What makes ketchup, ketchup? In my view, it's the familiar combination of flavors and spices that support the fruit in a smooth, pourable sauce. While we most often associate ketchup with tomatoes, other fruits, used with a similar range of spices found in the typical version, can offer subtle twists on this familiar condiment.

LEATHER

Typically made out of fruit, leathers are dried sheets of puréed produce. The purée can be lightly sweetened, and then it is spread out on a flat surface to dehydrate. Leathers are typically eaten as a snack but can be used in recipes that call for dried fruit.

LIQUEUR

Add sweetener to a spirit infusion and you have a liqueur. They are often potent and, as such, are served in small amounts, typically after a meal.

MARMALADE

Marmalades are thick spreads made from seeded citrus fruit. The peel, which is sliced thinly, minced, or shredded, is a necessary element, bringing both texture and flavor to the spreads. Because of the high pectin level of citrus fruits, marmalades can be made without added thickeners. Simply sugar and fruit cooked down to a gel will give a lively marmalade.

PICKLE

Fruits or vegetables that have been acidified to prolong their shelf life are called pickles. Two kinds of pickles are featured in this book. Vinegar pickles, such as Sweet Pickled Plums (page 206), use bottled vinegar to help cure the fruit. Lacto-fermented pickles, such as Pickled Grape Leaves (page 150), create their own preserving liquid. In this case, the leaves are submerged in a salt solution and allowed to ferment, creating the lactic acid that preserves them.

PRESERVE

The word "preserve" is often used to describe any fruit that has been cured to protect its flavor and texture. However, it does have a specific definition, which is fruit that has been cooked into a thick spread, with large pieces of fruit suspended in a gelled syrup.

PURÉE

A purée is a slightly thickened sauce that has been mashed or blended to a smooth consistency.

RELISH

While often thought of as a pickled cucumber condiment for topping hamburgers and hot dogs, relish can be made with any fruit or vegetable. It contains uniformly cut pieces that retain shape and texture when cooked and are suspended in a flavored sauce.

SALSA

Salsa is the Spanish word for "sauce." Although we may think of it as a red dip for tortilla chips, the term can actually be applied to a wide range of piquant sauces that can be smooth or quite chunky and that utilize fruits and vegetables equally.

Smoky Tomato Salsa

Jar suitable for refrigerator storage; not approved for canning

VINEGAR

Vinegars are fermented liquids. Natural bacteria have acted on these liquids, such as wine or apple juice, to digest their natural sugars and convert them into acetic acid. Any fruit juice can be converted into a vinegar as long as the beneficial bacteria are allowed to propagate.

Preserving Pointers

Food preservation is one of my favorite types of cooking. The intersection of craft and science is fascinating — harnessing microbes for fermentation, watching a jam pot full of fruit and sugar set up into a spreadable delight — these processes are magical. Here are pointers that explain the mechanics of preserving. A peek behind the curtain, so to speak, that takes some of the mystery out of the process of preserving fruit.

BOILING-WATER METHOD BASICS

If you can boil water, you can can your own food. The most popular method of canning, also known as the boiling-water method, requires very little specialized equipment and can be done in as little as 10 minutes.

BOILING-WATER METHOD EQUIPMENT LIST

To can the recipes in this book, you will need only two specialized items: canning jars — the thick glass jars with two-piece lids (like Ball and Kerr jars) — and a set of canning tongs (you cannot substitute regular tongs). You can get these things at your local mom-and-pop hardware store, or you can order them online. Grocery stores often carry them as well. The canning jars are important — the extra-thick glass keeps them from breaking during processing, and the two-piece lid helps form a vacuum seal that keeps your food safe on the shelf. The special design of the tongs allows you to move the jars into and out of the boiling water safely and easily.

BUBBLE TOOL

CANNING TONGS

LADLE

CANNING FUNNEL

LIDS IN A HEATPROOF BOWL

LID LIFTER

CANNING RINGS

To can your preserves, you will also need the following common kitchen items:

▶ A LARGE POT WITH A LID. Your pot must be at least 3 inches taller than the tallest jar you will be using, but it does not need to be a canner. Any pasta pot, stockpot, or lobster pot will do.

▶ A FALSE BOTTOM FOR THE POT. You will need something that will raise the jars up off the bottom of the pot to allow boiling water to circulate beneath the jars. This can be a canning rack, a cake cooling rack, or even a layer of the rings that come with the canning jars.

▶ A "BUBBLE TOOL." A thin, non-metallic tool, such as a plastic knife, wooden skewer, or chopstick, allows you to remove trapped air bubbles from your filled jars without scratching the inside of the glass.

▶ A CANNING FUNNEL OR SMALL LADLE. With either utensil, you can neatly fill your jars. If you don't have a canning funnel, you can cut the bottom off a regular plastic funnel to get a v-shaped cone that will help you fill your jars.

Why Do You . . .
sterilize some jars and not others?

Sterilization is an important step for ridding your equipment of lingering microbes that could contaminate your recipes. Any jar that is processed for 10 minutes or more using the boiling-water method is effectively sterilized by virtue of being submerged in boiling water for that period of time. You do not need to pre-sterilize these jars. Jars that are processed using the boiling-water method for less than 10 minutes must be pre-sterilized to ensure that all microbes are eliminated. Similarly, any jar that will not be heated at all as part of the preserving process — such as for infusions — is best sterilized before being filled to kill any lingering microbes that might interfere with your results.

To sterilize jars, submerge them in boiling water for 10 minutes. You can turn the heat off after that, but keep them in the water until you are ready to use them to keep them microbe free. If you can't submerge the jar you are going to fill, you can swirl several washings of boiling water in it and then give it a rinse with vinegar or potable alcohol, such as vodka.

▶ A LID LIFTER. This magnet-tipped plastic wand is used to lift lids, one at a time, out of their bowl of hot water. You can use rubber-tipped tongs to do the job, or quickly reach in with your fingers if you dare. Just be careful to avoid scratching the lids' white coating, which would expose the metal and could lead to rust during storage.

▶ A NONREACTIVE POT FOR PREPARING YOUR RECIPE. All recipes that use the boiling-water method to preserve them have an acidic pH. This acid is necessary to keep your food safe on the shelf. It can also interact with the pot in which you prepare your recipe. Reactive metals such as aluminum and uncoated cast iron can leach minerals into the food, discoloring it and giving it a metallic taste. For the best results, use a nonreactive pan or pot made of enamel-coated cast iron or stainless steel when preparing food for canning.

THE BOILING-WATER METHOD, STEP BY STEP

1. **Wash.** Wash everything with hot, soapy water and arrange it on a clean towel near the stovetop, if possible. Separate your lids from your jars, washing them as well, and put the lids in a small heatproof bowl.

STEP 2

2. **Load the canner.** Put the rack (or whatever "false bottom" you're using) in the pot, add the glass jars, and fill with enough cold water to fill and cover the jars. Set the loaded canner on your burner, cover it, and bring the water to a boil. If the water in the pot starts to boil before you are done preparing your recipe, just turn it off and keep the lid on it. You can bring it back to a boil as you near completion of the recipe. You never want to have to wait for your canner to heat up — always have it ready and waiting for your recipe to be complete.

STEP 3

3. **Prepare your recipe.** Now is the time to cook the recipe you will use to pack your jars.

4. **Remove the jars.** Using canning tongs, remove the jars from the boiling water. Add the boiling water in the first jar to the bowl full of lids to soften their rubber gaskets. Empty the water from the rest of the jars back into the canner and set the jars, right side up, on your work surface for filling.

STEP 4

5. Ladle the hot food into the jars. Use a canning funnel or small ladle to keep things neat. Fill the jars as indicated in your recipe — each will specify the necessary "headspace," the distance between the top of the food and the top of the jar. Be sure to allow the proper headspace to ensure that the jars seal well.

6. Release trapped air. Swipe your bubble tool around the inside of the jar to release any trapped air. Top up, as necessary, to maintain the correct headspace.

7. Clean the jars. Use a dampened paper towel to wipe the rims of the jars. A clean rim will give your lid a better chance of sealing properly.

8. Lid the jars. Lift lids from the hot water, one at a time, and center them on the jars.

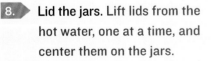

9. **Apply the rings.** Screw the rings on the jars until just fingertip-tight, meaning that you use just your fingertips to twist on the rings. Do not wrench the lids on any more than this or you will prevent the venting action of the two-piece lid that is necessary for a good seal.

STEP 9

10. **Process the filled jars.** Submerge the filled jars in the boiling water; they should be covered by at least 2 inches. Put the cover on the pot. Keep the jars submerged in boiling water for the amount of processing time indicated in the recipe.

STEP 10

11. **Rest the jars.** When the processing time is over, turn off the heat, remove the lid of the pot, and let the jars sit in the hot water for 5 minutes.

12. **Remove the jars.** Using canning tongs, remove the jars from the hot water to a towel-covered surface. Allow the jars to cool for 24 hours.

STEP 13

13. **Check the seals.** Check the seals on the jars by removing the rings and gently pushing up on the edge of the lids. Alternatively, you can turn the jars upside down, over a bowl if you prefer. If the lids stay secure, the seal is complete.

STEP 13

14. **Store.** Wipe the jars and store, without rings (which can trap moisture), in a cool, dark place for the amount of time indicated in your recipe.

Altitude Adjustments for Boiling-Water Processing

If you are canning at high elevations, you have to increase your processing time to compensate for the lower boiling point of water at increased altitudes. Make these adjustments to ensure safe, consistent results.

IF YOU ARE AT AN ELEVATION OF	INCREASE YOUR PROCESSING TIME BY
1,001–3,000	5 minutes
3,001–6,000	10 minutes
Over 6,000	15 minutes

THE ROLE OF ACID AND SUGAR IN PRESERVES

Many home food preservers believe that sugar is the critical ingredient in making a shelf-stable jam. While sugar can play an important role, it is the acid in the recipe that makes canned jam — and any food preserved by the boiling-water method — a shelf-stable product. That's why jam and jelly recipes often include a bit of lemon juice — it gives the spread the pH oomph it needs to be canned safely.

The proper level of acidity is also critical to gel formation. If there is too little acid, the gel will never set; if there is too much acid, the gel will weep, over-tightening and pooling liquid on the surface of the spread.

There is a bit of debate among canners over the use of bottled versus fresh lemon juice. The USDA recommends that bottled lemon juice be used for all preserving recipes. That's what I use and I'll tell you why: the amount of lemon juice called for in many recipes is about ¼ cup — about the juice of one lemon. Lemons vary in their pH level; some are a little more acidic, some are less. Bottled lemon juice, on the other hand, has a more consistent pH, giving me the same result every time I use it. I also find it easier to keep on hand than fresh lemons. There are a lot of good lemon juices on the shelf these days, including some that are 100 percent organic and preservative free. I don't think I'm sacrificing anything in quality by using the bottled stuff, but I gain reliability in one of the key ingredients in good home food preservation. However, in my classes I have met a number of home canners who swear by fresh lemon juice — particularly those who are lucky enough to have trees in their own backyards and have reliably good results.

Sugar does a different job. Most important, it protects texture, a property that you can use to great advantage. Sugar toughens the cell walls of produce. The earlier it is added to a recipe, the tougher those walls become. If you want to have big chunks of fruit in your recipe, whole strawberries for example, you can even combine your fruit with the sugar in your recipe and let it macerate overnight. In the morning you will have what looks like some deflated fruit and a lot of fruity syrup. Fear not! Although the fruit may look worse for wear, this extended sugaring shores up the cell walls of the fruit and will give the produce its best chance of maintaining its shape during cooking. On the other end of the spectrum, if you want a smooth jam or are trying to make a smooth sauce, such as applesauce, then you want to add your sugar after the fruit has broken down. Simmer your fruit with a little water until it falls apart, and then add your sugar to get a smooth result. And if the middle ground is where you are headed, add the sugar and the fruit together at the time of cooking and you will get some texture, but not big chunks. Got it, sugar?

Sugar also gives a lovely, glossy sheen to the spread and protects color. Batches of low-sugar spreads lack the high-gloss finish of their high-sugar counterparts, and their hue will fade more readily in storage than those that get a high dose of the sweet stuff. These differences, however, are purely aesthetic and do not affect the safety of the jam.

Where sugar acts as a bit of a preservative is after the jar is opened; it extends the refrigerated shelf life of the jam. Why do commercial jams last so long in the refrigerator and mine don't? It's a popular question, and I'll tell you that at least one of the reasons is sugar. Large amounts of sugar reduce microbial activity in an opened jar of jam. If you look at the ingredients label of grocery-store spreads, you will see that sugar is often the first or second ingredient. Even many homemade recipes call for equal amounts of sugar and fruit, and you will notice that these sugar-heavy preparations do last longer in the fridge. Lower-sugar recipes will give you about 3 weeks to enjoy them once they are opened.

TYPES OF ACIDS IN PRESERVED FOODS

Acid is the key to successful home food preservation. Any food preserved using the boiling-water method must have a pH of 4.6 or less. But you don't need to test for the pH yourself, as the recipes have all been formulated to yield this pH. This is a good reason never to substitute the kind or amount of acid indicated in a recipe; you could jeopardize the success and safety of your results.

▸ ASCORBIC ACID. Also known as vitamin C, ascorbic acid is used in home food preservation as an anti-browning agent. It is available in crystal form or as tablets. Each teaspoon of the crystals contains about 3,000 mg of ascorbic acid, the equivalent of six 500 mg tablets. The crystals or crushed tablets are mixed with water to create an acid bath that protects the color of fruits such as apples, apricots, peaches, and pears.

When my recipe calls for both blanching and an acid bath (common in recipes involving peaches, for example), I often combine the two processes by adding ascorbic acid to my ice bath. It saves space, time, and cleanup. Blanched fruit goes into the acidulated ice bath to cool and is then peeled and returned to the same bath to seal its color.

▸ CITRIC ACID. The most important role that citric acid plays in home canning is to lower the pH of recipes, such as whole canned tomatoes, below a pH of 4.6 so that they can be safely preserved with the boiling-water method. Often such recipes call for either citric acid or lemon juice; the two can be used interchangeably to achieve the same effect. Never reduce the amount called for in a recipe because, even though you may not be able to taste it, it is a critical element in safe home food preservation.

Citric acid can also be used as an anti-browning agent, though it is not as effective as ascorbic acid.

▸ LEMON JUICE. Lemon juice contains both ascorbic and citric acid, but in lower concentrations. While it doesn't pack the acidic punch of ascorbic and citric acid powders, it offers terrific flavor that can bring an essential brightness to your preserves, particularly for long-cooking spreads that can dull in their time on the stove.

▶ ACETIC ACID. Acetic acid is the pucker power you find in vinegar. It can be an important element in a recipe destined for the boiling-water method, as it can effectively lower the pH to a level safe for canning. However, its strong flavor means that it will always play more than a supporting role, as it often dominates the flavor of the preserve. This can be used to great effect in making pickles, of course, and when balanced with sugar and other flavorings, acetic acid can make for great-tasting chutneys and sweet/sour pickled fruits such as pickled plums.

▶ LACTIC ACID. Lactic acid is created during fermentation. Essentially, it is controlled rot. It might sound off-putting but it tastes delicious! Lactic acid is produced when fresh produce is submerged in a brine; the salt keeps pathogens at bay while beneficial bacteria act on the fruits and vegetables, digesting the sugars and converting them to lactic acid, which gives the food the acidic pH that keeps it safe on the shelf.

ALL ABOUT PECTIN

Pectin is the natural compound found in produce that, under the right conditions, gives spreads their gel. Pectin levels vary greatly — apples and citrus fruits have the highest levels, while other vegetables and fruits, such as rhubarb and raspberries, have very little. To achieve the desired gel with low-pectin produce, many recipes call for added pectin.

You can test for pectin content by combining 1 teaspoon of simmered fruit with 1 tablespoon rubbing alcohol. Place the alcohol in a small dish, add the cooled fruit, and stir. High-pectin fruits will form a solid mass, while low-pectin fruits will break apart into small globules.

The ease with which a fruit gels is determined not only by the amount of pectin in the fruit, but also by its acidity. Rather than giving a list of high- and low-pectin fruits, the box on page 27 groups fruits by how easily they gel, which takes into account both their pectin and their acid content. Keep in mind that just-ripe fruit has more pectin than overly ripe fruit. To boost its gelling ability, use slightly underripe fruit in combination with full-flavored ripe produce.

I am often asked why I use Pomona's Universal Pectin and not one of the more readily available powdered or liquid pectins on the market. Not to sound like an ad, but the main reason is that, unlike other pectins, which rely on copious amounts of sugar to gel, Pomona's Universal Pectin uses calcium powder (included with the pectin) to achieve a gel. So I can use much less sugar and even alternative sweeteners, such as honey, stevia, and agave nectar, in my recipes and still get a good set.

To use Pomona's Universal Pectin, combine the sugar with the pectin and combine the calcium powder (included in the kit) with water before proceeding with the recipe.

Fruit Gel Levels

HIGH GELS READILY	MEDIUM WILL GEL, GIVEN TIME AND ATTENTION	LOW HARD TO GET A SET WITHOUT ADDED PECTIN
Sour apples/crab apples *	Blueberries	Apricots
Citrus *	Cherries	Pears
Concord grapes	Peaches	Raspberries
Cranberries	Ripe apples	Rhubarb
Plums	Strawberries	
Quince		

have the strongest gelling power

REACHING THE GEL STAGE

Knowing when to take your jam pot off the heat is key to successful jam making. For added-pectin jams, the math is simple: you add the pectin, make sure it's dissolved, and load up your jars. The added pectin will ensure a good set.

But for long-cooking jams, it's not always so simple. You have to cook the spread until you reach the gel stage — that magical moment when the ideal texture is achieved. A few minutes shy of the gel stage and you have syrup. The same recipe cooked too long will give you the equivalent of jam tar. Not that these results are failures; syrup can be poured over pancakes, and jam that is a bit too thick can often be heated and used in savory recipes or puréed into smoothies. The goal, however, is to cook up a preserve that will be thick but spreadable after it has been processed and cooled. Being able to recognize when the gel stage has been reached while the jam is still in the pot is the key to achieving it.

Experience helps, of course, but you'll be surprised at how quickly you come by it. With just a few batches under your belt, you will start to get the feel of the jam pot — the magical moment when its contents shift from fruit soup to an unctuous, inviting confection. You will see the bubbles grow in size from a small, boiling froth to large, marble-size orbs. In no time at all, interpreting the feel of the spoon as you drag it through the thickened mixture will be second nature.

There are also several tests you can use to determine whether you have reached the gel stage.

▶ TEMPERATURE. Jams gel at 220°F. This should be a black-and-white test — either you are at 220° or you are not — but I find this to be the least reliable indicator of doneness. By the time I get the temperature reading, my jams are often too stiff. But I do find temperature to be a helpful sign of when I'm getting close to the "zone," and then I verify with one or both of the tests that follow.

▶ SHEETING. The test that gets the most "Huh?" responses from students when I introduce the idea in class, sheeting is hard to visualize, but once you see it you'll get the picture. It's essentially when two drops become one, a marriage, if you will, of drips off the spoon. Huh? Indeed. Here's how it works: Stir your almost-done jam with a wooden spoon. Lift the spoon sideways from the pot. In a too-thin jam, the drops will stream off the bottom edge of the spoon. As you get closer to the gel stage, the hot jam will drip. When you are right on the money, the drops will join, forming a sheet, before falling into the pot. That's sheeting. Give it a shot and you'll see what I mean.

▶ WRINKLE TEST. This is my favorite test. It is the easiest and the one that I find most reliable. The test is done like this: Put a clean plate in the freezer to chill while you're preparing the recipe. When you think your jam might be ready, dribble a few drops of hot jam onto the plate's cold surface, give it a minute to cool, and then push on the little spot of jam with your finger, like you are trying to wipe it off. If the smudge of jam wrinkles when you start to push against it, the jam is ready. If it is thick but does not wrinkle, you need to cook it a bit more. (And if you are like me and forget to freeze your plate, just dribble the jam on the bottom of an ice cream carton. That will do the trick.)

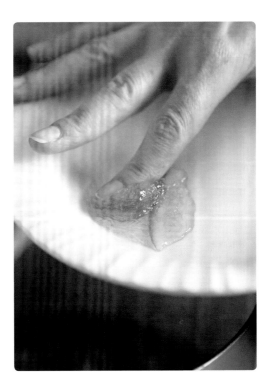

MARMALADES

There are a number of ways to make marmalade. Some you can accomplish in one session, and others ask you to return to the kitchen for short stints over the course of several days. The goal of all of these methods is to wind up with a spread that is pleasingly bitter and tart but also balanced by enough sweetness, and to ensure that the peels have enough tooth to be noticeable but are soft enough to be enjoyable. Having enough water in the pot is critical to this last aspect of your marmalade. When you are cooking preserves, water can buy you time. If you don't have enough water in the pot, the marmalade will gel before the peels have had a chance to soften. Never start with a dry marmalade; when in doubt, add a little extra water to the pot at the beginning of cooking, and the taste and texture will be better for it.

Cutting off the tops and bottoms of the citrus fruit greatly reduces the amount of bitter pith that makes it into the final product. The end result is fruit that has just enough of an edge to balance the sweet flavors of the spread without overwhelming you with pucker power.

Finally, scrub! Marmalade uses the peel of the fruit, so it's important to scrub the fruit thoroughly before you begin your recipe. Dirt and residue can easily be trapped in the mottled texture of the skin. Clean up even homegrown fruit for wholesome results.

Lemon Ginger Marmalade, page 153

CHUTNEYS AND RELISHES

Chutneys and relishes take fruit preservation in a decidedly savory direction, and I adore them for it. The combinations of sweet fruit and aromatic vegetables and herbs bring intriguing flavors to the table and look terrific in the jar, so they are always welcome gifts to bring to lucky hostesses. They often require a bit of time in their preparation. Don't skimp here. It's important to chop and dice the ingredients exactly as indicated in the recipe. Uniform prep ensures that your ingredients cook completely and evenly. And make sure that you cook them long enough to make them tender, but don't dry them out.

If you are simmering along and you realize that your produce needs some extra cooking time to achieve the right texture, you can safely add a bit of water without affecting the pH level that keeps your food safe on the shelf. When you ladle a finished chutney or relish into jars, it should have a nice layer of liquid floating on top. This will keep the top of the produce from drying and darkening during storage, making every bite wholesome and delicious.

Savory Cranberry Relish, page 116

WHOLE FRUIT

Whole fruits can be canned in water, fruit juice, or syrup. When canning whole or halved fruit, it is imperative that the fruit be firm so that it maintains its shape during the process. Choose fruit that is well formed, and trim or peel it carefully — every flaw shows in these preserved fruits.

Sugar syrups protect the flavor and texture of the whole fruits that you can. You can use as light or heavy a syrup as you like, but if your recipe calls for acid, be sure to add it — that's what keeps your food safe on the shelf.

Mild-flavored honey can be used to replace as much as half of the granulated sugar called for in a canning syrup recipe. Honey may add flavor and color to the fruit, depending on the type of honey you use. Maple syrup can be used to replace up to one-quarter of the sugar in a recipe, but it will affect the natural flavor and color of the fruit.

Syrup Preparations

DESIRED SYRUP CONSISTENCY	FOR EVERY 1 CUP WATER, ADD THIS AMOUNT OF SUGAR
Very light	2 tablespoons
Light	¼ cup
Medium	½ cup
Heavy	¾ cup
Very heavy	1 cup

Grapefruit Sections in Lavender Syrup, page 134

GASTRIQUES

Gastriques may not be a tool in your repertoire, but they are one worth acquiring. Don't let what might seem like an unfamiliar technique put you off, because they are super easy to make. Boil down a little sugar and water until it colors slightly, add an equal amount of vinegar, reduce the mixture, and add the flavoring of your choice — there you go, gastrique! A small amount stashed away in the cupboard, fridge, or freezer can bring the kind of plate-gracing flourish that raises your dish to dinner-party ready. Caramelizing the sugar takes a little practice (actually more patience than skill), but it's nothing you can't handle. See page 157 for a step-by-step description of making gastriques.

INFUSIONS

When in doubt, infuse it. Infusions are becoming all the rage, and it's easy to see why — they're easy to make. Start with high-proof spirits, such as vodka, or neutral-flavored vinegars, such as white distilled vinegar, and add small amounts of fruits and herbs to imbue the liquids with flavor and hue. Infusions add zest and variety to your kitchen pantry and allow you to experiment with the flavor combinations coming out of your garden or market.

Because you don't need to cook the finished product to preserve it, it's best to start with a sterilized container to ensure that only good things are in your jar. Just dunk your infusing or storage bottles into a pot of boiling water and let them boil for 10 minutes (see the box on page 19).

DRIED FRUIT

Drying fruit is one of the most straightforward food preservation methods. It requires little hands-on time and can be a very low-tech process. Using a food dehydrator, of course, is one way to dry your fruit. But I find that the oven or even, in the proper circumstances, good air circulation can get the job done. Because I don't dry large amounts of food, oven drying is the path I take and the one I suggest for those just starting out.

Although drying food is a simple process, there are still obstacles. The most serious complication is that the outside of the fruit will toughen before the inside is dry. This condition is called "case hardening," and in addition to slowing your drying time, it can threaten the quality of your preserved food. Case hardening can create the same kind of anaerobic, nonacidic environment that can lead to botulism in canned goods.

To avoid case hardening, be sure to dry your fruit slowly at a low temperature. While it may seem counterintuitive, high temperatures will not speed the process but will create the case-hardened leathery surface that you want to avoid. Use the temperature indicated in the recipe or in the dehydrator's manual for best results.

Some drying recipes call for blanching the fruit or cutting or pricking the skin, also called "checking" the fruit, to speed the drying process. While the wet process of blanching may seem to be heading in the opposite direction of drying, this step is necessary to soften the skin, making it more air-permeable. And like checking the fruit, blanching can split the fruit's skin, allowing moisture to escape during the drying process.

Dried Cranberries, page 125

PREPPING PRODUCE FOR PRESERVING

Prepping fruits, vegetables, and herbs is often the most time-consuming part of home food preservation. Enlisting some extra hands to help with the work is always a good idea. Get some friends over, break out your canner, share the work, and then share the wealth. Throughout the book, I'll give you pointers on how to prep specific fruits. But here I explain prep terms that you'll find throughout this book and in other cookbooks as well. In addition to explaining what each term means, I include tips on the easiest ways to achieve the desired sizes and shapes.

▶ JULIENNE. Firm food cut into fine matchsticks is julienned. The process is time consuming but makes for a really lovely presentation. To do it, trim your produce and cut it lengthwise into planks that are ⅛ to ¼ inch thick. Stack the planks and slice them lengthwise into sticks that are ⅛ to ¼ inch thick. In the case of an already thin food, such as citrus peel, use a vegetable peeler to shave off fine, thin strips, and then slice the strips into slivers. That's julienne.

▶ CHIFFONADE. Leafy food, such as basil, cut into thin ribbons is chiffonade. To do it, stack your leaves on top of each other. Roll them, lengthwise, into a tube. Cut the tube, crosswise, into fine slivers, no more than ¼ inch wide. As you slice, the slivers will fall off the knife in the "little rags" of a fine chiffonade.

▶ MINCE. Cutting food very finely, almost to a paste, is mincing. Garlic and ginger are two foods that recipes often indicate should be minced. The easiest way to do this is to begin by cutting small pieces of the product: coins for ginger, halves for garlic cloves. Lay the pieces on a cutting board, set a chef's knife flat over the food, and whack the side of the knife with the heel of your hand, smashing the ginger or garlic. You can then turn your knife to the normal cutting position of blade against board and rock it back and forth over the smashed pieces to reduce the food to a very fine mince.

▸ CHOP. When a recipe calls for food to be chopped, it is generally not a precise direction. The goal is to break down the produce so that it cooks more quickly and is easier to work with. Typically, the "chop" direction is followed by a size suggestion; 1-inch or 2-inch pieces are common. If a recipe calls for produce to be simply "roughly chopped," size is not critical.

▸ DICE. Cutting food into small, even squares is dicing. The dice size can vary from a small dice of about ¼ inch to larger cubes. Dice size is important. It needs to be as consistent as possible so that the chopped produce looks good in the dish and cooks evenly. To cut dice of a solid food, such as an apple, first trim and peel it as directed in the recipe. Then cut the food into planks of the thickness indicated. Stack the planks and cut them into batons (long strips) of the width indicated. Finish off by turning the batons 90 degrees and slicing off squares to make cubes of the size indicated by the recipe.

Troubleshooting

Even the most experienced home food preservationist will turn out a less-than-perfect batch of goods now and again. Some preserves might be a smidge too thin, others a bit too thick, and sometimes you might get a jar or two that is just plain ugly. Most often you can cover up your errors with a little repurposing; loose jam makes fine syrup, if that's what you call it. But whenever you are working with food, it's important to know the difference between "not pretty" and "not safe." Here are the top challenges of preserving your own fruit and the best ways to avoid them.

THE DREADED FRUIT FLOAT

If you've ever processed gorgeous produce only to find that the contents of your jars have separated into distinct bands, with solids at the top and liquid at the bottom, you have experienced the dreaded fruit float. While it can occur in any recipe, fruit float is most pronounced in jars of canned whole fruits that contain a high proportion of liquid by nature and in jams, jellies, and preserves, where the gelling process sometimes suspends floating fruit as the spread sets, rather than letting it disperse throughout the mixture. Jars of whole canned tomatoes — picture-perfect going into the canner — come out clotted, with a dense layer of tomato bobbing atop inches of tomato water. Fruit float will turn a ready-for-its-close-up jam into a two-layer concoction of too-thick jam over clear jelly. While less common, fruit float may also manifest as a thin layer of liquid at the base of blended items such as barbecue sauces and mixtures such as salsas.

The good news is that fruit float is harmless. It won't win you any blue ribbons, but it does not affect shelf life or safety. And while unsightly in the jar, fruit float can often be remedied by giving the contents of the jar a quick stir upon opening it.

Avoiding Fruit Float

Even the most skilled and experienced canner gets sideswiped by fruit float on occasion, but there are some things you can do to limit your jars' susceptibility to this malady.

COOK YOUR RECIPE THOROUGHLY. Cooking breaks down the cell walls of your produce and gives the air that is normally housed there a chance to escape. If you are hot packing your recipe, be sure to cook it for the full amount of time indicated. But don't overcook your recipe. Pectin, the natural compound found in fruit that allows it to gel, will break down when cooked for too long, losing its gelling properties.

ALLOW COOKED RECIPES TO REST for 5 minutes or so to let any air bubbles in the mixture settle out before you fill your jars.

DO NOT OVERPROCESS YOUR JARS. Boiling your filled jars for longer than indicated in your recipe is called overprocessing, and it can force some of the liquid in your recipe out of suspension.

FLIP YOUR JARS. Once your jars have sealed, but while they are still a bit warm (but not hot), you can turn them over and let them settle for about half an hour to give the rising fruit a chance to redistribute throughout your jam. Then you can store them right side up.

BE PATIENT. After a few weeks whole fruits, such as tomatoes, will often release the air trapped within them and descend back into the liquid.

IGNORE IT. Be proud that you got your good food into the jars safely, and know that it will be just as delicious, fruit float and all.

FRUIT FLOAT

PRESERVES TOO FIRM

One minute you have luscious fruit bubbling away in the pot; the next minute it has turned to tar. It can happen in an instant, particularly with marmalades, which, with their high pectin content, can seize up in a heartbeat. The trick is, of course, not to over-cook the spread. But as long as you haven't scorched the fruit, you can usually loosen it back up a bit by adding a splash of water. This will thin the spread enough to give it a more agreeable texture. Be sure to return the spread to a boil for a minute or two before canning to make sure that it is hot enough for your processing time to hold true.

SIPHONING

When liquid is lost from jars during processing it is called "siphoning." A small amount of siphoning won't affect the safety of your product, but a large amount of siphoning, as shown here, exposes your food to too much air for it to be considered wholesome. Even if you get a seal on the jar, you should refrigerate it and use the contents within three weeks.

Avoiding Siphoning

ALWAYS CLEAN YOUR JAR RIMS THOROUGHLY. Any trapped food particles or spices can prevent good contact between the lid and the jar and lead to siphoning.

NEVER OVER-TIGHTEN YOUR JARS. Doing so will cause the pressure to build up and the contents to be forced out of the jar.

AVOID OVER-FILLING YOUR JARS. The food can press up against the lid and cause the contents to leak out into the water.

SIPHONING

PRESERVES TOO THIN

Keep in mind that pectin can take a while — up to several weeks — to fully form a gel, so don't pull the trigger too quickly. The jam or jelly that looks a bit thin 24 hours after canning may be perfectly set in a few weeks' time. If your preserves are still too thin after that grace period, try using them as a syrup for pancakes or ice cream. You can also remake thin preserves and can them again (see below). Here are some frequent causes of thin preserves and some tips for remedying them:

▶ NOT ENOUGH TIME. The most common cause of a thin preserve is undercooking. If you take a classic spread, one that doesn't use packaged pectin, off the burner too soon, it will not have had the chance to reach the gel stage. It is important to follow the visual signals of the preserve — watching how it behaves in the pot — and not the clock. Use the cooking times indicated in recipes as guidelines, knowing that they will be affected by the water content of your fruit, the power of your burner, and the size, height, and thickness of your pot. You are the best judge of your preserve's doneness.

▶ TOO LITTLE ACID. If you did not add the lemon juice called for in the recipe, or if you are using fresh-squeezed lemons that are a little light on acid, you may have a hard time getting a gel. Acid acts with the pectin to produce a good set, so make sure to use the full amount indicated in the recipe. You can add a bit more lemon juice to the pot to encourage a gel.

▶ OVERCOOKING. Pectin will break down if cooked for too long, particularly if you have cooked your preserves over low heat — low and slow is more likely to break down your pectin than a lively boil. If the natural pectin in your produce has broken down, you will have to add powdered pectin to encourage the spread to set.

▶ NOT ENOUGH PECTIN. Even fruits that are commonly believed to have enough pectin to gel can fall short of adequate thickening from time to time. You stir and stir but the mixture never wants to reach the gel stage. Most likely the fruit was too ripe. You will have to add a bit of powdered pectin (or a bit more if you were already working with an added-pectin jam) to the pot.

▶ NOT ENOUGH SUGAR. If you are making what I call a "classic" spread — one with no added pectin — then the sugar is part of the magic formula that helps you achieve the gel stage. Think of it as "candying" the fruit. If you are having a hard time getting a gel in such a recipe, you can try adding a little more sugar to achieve your goal.

To remake preserves without adding pectin, empty all of the contents into a large pot, bring the mixture slowly to a boil, and add a "remedy" from those described above, whether it's more sugar, more acid, or simply more time. Check frequently to see if this second round has passed the gel test.

To remake preserves that contain Pomona's Universal Pectin, empty the contents into a pot and bring slowly to a boil, as above. Add 1 to 2 teaspoons calcium water (from the Pomona's Universal Pectin kit) to your reheated jam, and then slowly sprinkle in a sugar/pectin mixture (½ cup sugar combined with 1 to 2 teaspoons powdered pectin should do it). Stir to dissolve. (Spreads that use added pectin will thicken as they cool.)

Whichever method you use, you can reprocess these jams just as you did the first time, using the boiling-water method, or you can store them in the refrigerator and use within 3 weeks.

CLOUDY JELLY

Cloudy jelly is usually caused by cloudy juice. Boiling the fruit or pressing on the jelly bag as the fruit hangs will produce cloudy juice. The cloudiness will not affect the flavor or quality of the jelly; it is just a cosmetic difference.

However, if your jelly starts out clear in the jar and then clouds as it sits on the shelf, you may have another problem. This kind of cloudiness may indicate contamination due to insufficient processing or a broken seal. Discard jelly that clouds over time.

MOLDY FERMENT

White film or mold blooms may appear on the top of a crock of fermenting produce. As long as the mold is not touching the food (which should be submerged beneath the liquid), it can be scooped off and all will be fine. Mold should never be allowed to progress, however. Skim regularly to keep the food wholesome.

MOLDY PRESERVES

I have had more than one seasoned canner tell me that when they were growing up, sure, some of the jam from their open-kettle processing or paraffin-sealed jars would have a layer of mold on top when they opened up a jar, but they would just peel this off and eat the jam anyway. I am glad that they have lived to tell me the tale, but this is not something that I recommend. If your canned food has mold on it or in it, discard it.

Keep in mind as well that home-canned products that do not contain artificial preservatives will not last as long as store-bought items that do. You can expect your homemade canned items to last 1 year unopened and about 3 to 4 weeks under refrigeration once you have popped the lid. After that, they will start to deteriorate.

COLOR CHANGE

While sugar does not prevent good food from going bad in the jar, it does protect color and texture. Low-sugar spreads will dull or darken sooner than high-sugar preparations. If the spreads appear normal in all other ways — no foul smell, bulging lid, or bubbling — then the color change is not a symptom of spoilage, merely of age. To minimize color changes in your jar contents, keep them in a dark storage space if you can, and certainly away from direct sunlight.

CONTAMINATION

The most serious form of contamination and the one most associated with canning is botulism, a potentially life-threatening illness. The toxin that causes this condition only thrives in nonacidic environments, so it is rarely associated with fruit preserves, which are acidic by nature. To avoid any risk of botulism, always follow your recipe, and never skimp on the amount of acid — in the form of vinegar or lemon juice — or alter the amount of produce in the recipe. Careful attention to tested recipes will ensure that your preserved foods have the proper acid balance that keeps them safe on the shelf.

Part Two: RECIPES

page 70

DRIED ORANGE ZEST

page 176

CLASSIC CHERRY JAM

page 112

LEMON RED ONION and OREGANO JAM

page 159

PEACH MELBA COMPOTE

page 188

CRANBERRY -QUINCE- PRESERVES

page 122

Quick Apricot Jam

page 68

PEAR JELLY

page 194

Blueberry Ketchup

page 235

page 96

Bottle suitable for refrigerator storage; not approved for canning

Apples

At the peak of the season, orchards and farmers' markets are bursting with such a wide variety of apples. Thanks to the increased popularity and support of heirloom varieties, the availability continues to broaden for the "vintage" apples our ancestors ate, such as the Newtown Pippin, Gravenstein, and Northern Spy. They look very different from the shiny, perfectly symmetrical (and often perfectly tasteless) pommes you find in the supermarket and can come in a wide spectrum of colors — bright red, green, pink, mottled brown. The differences aren't in the peels alone. Heirloom fruits such as apples are the direct descendants of varieties that have been grown for generations. Each variety has its own unique set of characteristics and thrives in its specific range of growing conditions.

Unlike commercial apples, which are grown for uniformity and shelf stability, heirloom apples can vary widely in their flavors and textures, making them more "recipe-specific" than you might think. Pie apples are tart and hold their shape. Try Cortland or Empire. Want an apple that is crisp and tastes great eaten out of hand? My favorite is the Macoun. And want a pantry of pommes to last you through the winter? Then stock up on Winesap, an excellent "keeping apple." Ask your local farmers about the different kinds of apples in their orchards and get a taste of biodiversity.

APPLE AND PEAR SAUCE

Makes about 6 cups

What fruit preservation book would be complete without an applesauce recipe? You can use all apples or all pears for this sauce, but the combination tastes great and is just a beat apart from other fall fruit sauces you may have tried. Use a few different "saucing" varieties of apples and pears for the most complex flavor. The spices are optional but offer a fitting bass note to the tangy, light flavors of the fruit. Sugar sets the color and adds gloss.

INGREDIENTS

- ½ cup water
- ¼ cup bottled lemon juice
- **2** pounds apples
- **2** pounds pears
- ½ cup sugar
- ½ teaspoon ground cinnamon (optional)
- ¼ teaspoon ground cloves (optional)

PREPARE

1. Pour the water and lemon juice into a large nonreactive stockpot. Roughly chop the apples and pears, adding them to the pot with the lemon water as you work to prevent browning. Bring to a boil, reduce the heat, and then simmer, covered, until the fruit is tender, 10 to 20 minutes.

2. Pass the mixture through a food mill to remove the seeds and skins. Return the sauce to the pot and add the sugar and the spices, if using. Simmer, stirring, until the mixture is thickened and a dollop of sauce on a plate doesn't weep liquid, about 20 minutes. Remove from the heat.

Refrigerate: Cool, cover, and refrigerate for up to 5 days.

Freeze: Cool, then transfer to freezer containers, cover, and freeze for up to 6 months.

Can: Use the boiling-water method as described on page 20. Ladle into clean, hot half-pint jars, leaving ½ inch of headspace between the top of the sauce and the lid. Run a bubble tool along the inside of the glass to release trapped air. Wipe the rims clean; center lids on the jars and screw on jar bands until they are just fingertip-tight. Process the jars by submerging them in boiling water to cover by 2 inches for 10 minutes. Turn off the heat, remove the canner lid, and let the jars rest in the water for 5 minutes. Remove the jars and set aside for 24 hours. Check the seals, and then store in a cool, dark place for up to 1 year.

VARIATION:

Apple & Pear Butter

Fruit butter is just fruit sauce that has been cooked down a bit further. You can make your Apple and Pear Sauce into Apple and Pear Butter by continuing to simmer it over low heat for another 30 to 40 minutes, until it's thick and rich. Be careful to mind the pot, however, as the thickening mixture burns easily.

USE IT UP!

Potato and Cheese Pierogi with Apple and Pear Sauce

Makes about 3 dozen, serving 6-8

I grew up eating pierogi, delicious Polish dumplings. I can still picture my Granny Toni rolling out the dough on her kitchen table and pressing out the rounds with a water glass. With a quick flick of her finger off her kitchen spoon, she would portion out the perfect amount of filling on each round. It was a visual and taste memory I will never forget.

When I moved to New York City, homesick days would find me plunked down at one of the fabulous Polish diners in the East Village getting my fix. They sure would do the trick, too. Pierogi are the ultimate comfort food.

Now I make my own with my filling of choice, potato and cheese. I boil them until they are just tender, so that the dough still has some tooth to it, and then fry them up with some caramelized onions. Serve with Apple and Pear Sauce (page 46) and a cold glass of beer. Na zdrowie!

DOUGH INGREDIENTS

5 cups all-purpose flour

5 eggs

1 cup milk

¼ cup sour cream

1 teaspoon salt

Recipe continues on next page →

Potato and Cheese Pierogi with Apple and Pear Sauce, continued

FILLING INGREDIENTS

- **3** pounds russet potatoes, peeled and quartered
- **6** tablespoons butter
- **2** ounces cheddar cheese, grated
- **2** ounces cream cheese, softened
- **1** small onion, grated
- **1** teaspoon salt

  Freshly ground black pepper

  Apple and Pear Sauce (see page 46), for serving

  Sour cream, for serving

PREPARE

1. To make the dough, combine the flour, eggs, milk, sour cream, and salt in a large bowl. Use your hands to blend and mix until the dough comes together. Turn it out onto a floured work surface and knead until the dough is elastic and smooth, 10 to 12 minutes. Return the dough to the bowl, cover, and let rest for about 1 hour.

2. While the dough is resting, make the filling. Put the potatoes in a large pot and cover with cold water. Bring to a boil and cook until the potatoes are tender, 15 to 20 minutes. Drain and transfer to a large bowl. Using an electric hand mixer or potato masher, blend the potatoes and 4 tablespoons of the butter until smooth. Let the potato mixture cool and then blend in the cheddar cheese, cream cheese, onion, salt, and pepper to taste.

3. Divide the dough in half, and keep one half covered. Roll out half of the dough on a lightly covered surface to a thickness of about ⅛ inch. Use a 3-inch cookie cutter or a glass to cut out circles of dough. Set aside the scraps and cover.

4. Moisten the edge of each circle with a little water. Place a scant tablespoon of filling in the center of each circle. Working one at a time, fold each circle in half and pinch the edges together to encase the filling. Remove the filled pierogi to a baking sheet as you go.

5. Repeat with the reserved dough, and then combine all the dough scraps and repeat once more.

6. Melt the remaining 2 tablespoons butter and pour into a serving dish. Set aside.

7. Bring a large pot of water to a boil and add a handful of salt. Drop the filled pierogi into the water, about eight at a time. Boil gently until they are cooked, 5 to 7 minutes; they will rise to the top when they are done. Scoop the pierogi out of the water with a wire spider or slotted spoon. Toss with the butter in the serving dish to prevent sticking. Repeat with the remaining pierogi.

8. You can serve the butter-coated pierogi as is or fry them with onions that have been browned in butter. Serve accompanied by Apple and Pear Sauce and sour cream.

APPLE CIDER

1 quart of cider for every 4 pounds of apples using the hot pressing method,
or about 8 pounds of apples using the cold pressing method

Homemade apple cider is hard to accomplish without a press. You need the pressure of the mechanism to squeeze the juice out of the pulp. But if you are just absolutely flush with apples and want to give it a go, you can manage some small yields by straining your fruit. You will get a much higher yield using the hot pressing method, as described below.

INGREDIENTS

Any quantity apples

PREPARE

1. Set a colander lined with a double thickness of dampened cheesecloth over a large bowl or pot. (Make sure that there is enough distance between the bottom of the colander and the bottom of the pot for the juice to drain. A stockpot is usually tall enough for the job.) Shred your apples either in a food processor or on a box grater.

2. For cold-pressed cider, simply scoop the shreds into the draining setup.

3. For hot-pressed cider, which will give you a greater yield, scoop the shreds into a large nonreactive pot and gradually bring to a simmer over medium heat. Transfer the heated shreds to the straining setup.

4. Place a plate on top of the cold or hot shredded apples and put a weight, such as a gallon jug of vinegar or another pot filled with water, on top of the plate. Allow the shredded apples to drain for 3 to 4 hours. Eight pounds of apples will yield about 1 quart of cider using the cold-press method, and 4 pounds of apples will yield the same amount if you heat the pulp.

5. To pasteurize your cider, transfer it to a pot and heat it until it reaches 160°F on a candy thermometer. Stir the cider occasionally while heating to ensure that the temperature is the same throughout, not just hot on the bottom of the pot.

PRESERVE

Refrigerate: Cool (if necessary), cover, and refrigerate for up to 5 days.

Can: Use the boiling-water method as described on page 20. Bring the cider to a boil, and then pour it into clean, hot pint jars, leaving ¼ inch of headspace between the top of the juice and the lid. Wipe the rims clean; center lids on the jars and screw on jar bands until they are just fingertip-tight. Process the jars by submerging them in boiling water to cover by 2 inches for 10 minutes. Turn off the heat, remove the canner lid, and let the jars rest in the water for 5 minutes. Remove the jars and set aside for 24 hours. Check the seals, and then store in a cool, dark place for up to 1 year.

→ Whether you pasteurize your cider or not is up to you. The USDA recommends pasteurization to prevent contamination from pathogens such as *E. coli* O157:H7 and requires that unpasteurized cider be labeled as such. Contamination is of particular concern if the cider is made from apple "drops," fruit that has fallen from the tree and is harvested from the ground for pressing. Such apples are much more likely to come in contact with pathogens than those that are picked straight from the tree.

USE IT UP!

Braised Bangers (English Pork Sausages)

Serves 4–6

Oh, let me tell you there is nothing quite so good as a heap of bangers and mash on a cold, rainy day. I cook mine up with apples and onions and then braise them in apple cider to make a hearty gravy. I did not invent this idea — I nicked it off my English in-laws. It's standard pub fare in old Angle Terre and firmly in place on my family's list of favorites. It's also a great trick to have up your sleeve for pork chops. Serve it up with some whipped potatoes to soak up all of the lovely gravy goodness.

INGREDIENTS

- **1** tablespoon olive oil
- **2** pounds English-style bangers (or any thick pork breakfast sausages)
- **2** tablespoons unsalted butter
- **1** onion, chopped
  Salt and freshly ground black pepper
- **1** tablespoon all-purpose flour
- **1** cup Apple Cider (see page 50)
- **1** apple, peeled, cored, and diced
  Hot mashed potatoes, for serving

PREPARE

1. Heat the oil in a large skillet over medium heat. Add the sausages and sauté until brown on all sides, turning as necessary, 5 to 7 minutes (sausages will not be cooked through). Remove from the pan and set aside.

2. Melt the butter in the hot pan. Add the onion and a pinch of salt and pepper. Sauté until the onion is translucent, 5 to 7 minutes. Add the flour and whisk to make a paste. Add the cider and whisk until smooth.

3. Return the sausages to the pan and add the apple. Cover, reduce the heat to low, and simmer until the sausages are tender and cooked through, about 20 minutes. Remove the cover and, if necessary, simmer to thicken the sauce. Serve with mashed potatoes.

APPLE CIDER VINEGAR

This recipe makes about 2 cups of vinegar, but once it is thriving, you can add small amounts of apple juice to the jar to keep yourself well supplied. The active vinegar will readily "digest" the juice.

Fermenting fruit juice is a long-established method of home food preservation. After all, wine is nothing more than a carefully controlled fermented grape juice. There is one significant factor: air. Want wine? Cut off the air supply of your ferment. Want vinegar? Aerate it. To speed the process, you can submerge a little aquarium "bubbler" in the juice and it will turn to vinegar more quickly. Or take my route and add a little raw organic vinegar to get it going — a vinegar jump-starter.

INGREDIENTS

3 cups preservative-free apple cider, such as the Apple Cider on page 50

½ cup raw, organic vinegar

PREPARE AND PRESERVE

1. Sterilize a 1-quart canning jar by submerging it in boiling water for 10 minutes. Remove it from the water, and then pour the cider and vinegar into the jar. Top the jar with a layer of cheesecloth secured with a rubber band to keep out dust and pests. Set aside in a corner of the kitchen where it will enjoy the warmth of the space but not be disturbed.

2. After 3 to 4 weeks, a gelatinous film will begin to form at the top of the liquid. This is the mother — the colony of beneficial bacteria that turns sugar into acetic acid. Think of it as the engine of the vinegar. It will continue to grow thicker as the vinegar matures. A thick layer of sediment will form at the bottom of the jar; this is a natural part of the process.

3. After another several weeks, the mother will thicken and the cider will take on the characteristically tart flavor of vinegar. When it reaches your desired strength, carefully scoop out the mother and set it aside. Strain the vinegar through a double thickness of cheesecloth, cover, and refrigerate for up to 6 months. Because this is a living food, it will continue to grow and change as it ages. Refrigeration will slow this process considerably but will not halt it. Vinegar that smells strongly of acetic acid (similar to nail polish remover) is past its prime and should be discarded.

→ You can use the mother to start another batch of vinegar by adding it, along with a bit of the vinegar, to a quart of fresh cider.

USE IT UP!

Ideas for Using Cider Vinegar

Apple cider vinegar has long enjoyed a reputation as a health elixir. It has been drunk as a tonic since ancient Roman times and is still believed to aid everything from weight loss to diabetes. I am no doctor but I do get a jolt when I knock some back — and that's always good for you.

Here are a few ways to enjoy yours:

- Add a few tablespoons to still or sparkling water for a refreshing beverage.

- Use in salad dressings.

- Add a few tablespoons to a cup of water and use to deglaze the pan after pan-roasting meats. The reduced liquid makes a delicious gravy.

- Add a splash to sautéing greens to brighten their flavor.

- Sprinkle over steamed vegetables in place of lemon juice.

Cultivating a Vinegar Mother

Vinegar mothers may not be pretty, but they get the job done. This red wine vinegar mother formed as it converted the wine into vinegar. A piece of the living mother can be added to a new batch of wine (or in the case of Apple Cider Vinegar, apple cider) to start a new jar of vinegar.

KITCHEN HOW-TO
Prepping Apples

PEELING THE FRUIT

You don't need any special tools to prepare apples for your recipes. A sharp knife will do for peeling and slicing out the cores. If you find yourself staring down a quantity of apples on a regular basis, however, you might want to invest in a couple of tools that can tackle the task more efficiently.

An apple corer is a small, cylindrical hand tool with a serrated end that easily punches through the fruit from stem to blossom end to remove its seedy center.

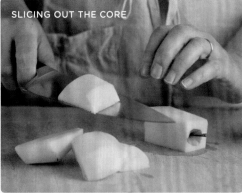

SLICING OUT THE CORE

You can also find hand-cranked apple peelers that strip off the skin of the fruit in a fine ribbon while simultaneously drilling through the center of the apple to remove the seed core. This kind of fun-to-use peeler is often a hit with kids, making it a useful tool not only for getting the job done but also for luring the younger set into doing it. When it's apple season, it's all hands on deck!

REMOVING THE CORE WITH AN APPLE CORER

PEELING & CORING WITH AN APPLE PEELER

DRIED APPLE DICE

2 cups dried fruit from 2 pounds apples

Dried apples are so handy to have around. You can use them in holiday stuffings, trail mixes, and granolas or nibble them for a quick little snack. I have to hide these from my kids or they disappear. They are so addictively chewy that kids will pop them like candy. You can double this recipe if you have the room in your oven.

INGREDIENTS

- **2** cups cold water
- **6** (500 mg) vitamin C tablets, crushed, or 1 teaspoon vitamin C powder
- **2** pounds baking apples (about 6)

PREPARE

1. Preheat the oven to 170°F.

2. Pour the water into a large bowl. Add the vitamin C and stir to dissolve to create an anti-browning bath. Peel, core, and cut the apples into ½-inch dice, adding them to the bath as you work. Soak the diced apples for 10 minutes.

PRESERVE

Dry:

1. Drain the fruit and pat it dry. Arrange the apples in a single layer on two 11- by 17-inch baking sheets lined with parchment paper. Set the baking sheets in the oven, and prop open the oven door with a wooden spoon handle to allow moisture to escape. Dry the apples in the oven for 3 to 4 hours, until leathery. The pieces are fully dry when you can squeeze a handful and they don't stick together.

2. Cool the apple cubes, and then condition them by transferring them to a covered container and letting them sit for 1 day. This allows the dried fruit to redistribute any trapped moisture. If you notice moisture collecting on the sides of the container, repeat the drying process for another hour or so. Fully dried apples will keep in an airtight container for up to 1 year.

USE IT UP!

Homemade Granola

Makes about 1½ quarts

I am picky about my granola. I like mine with gobs of stuff in it — dried fruits, nuts, seeds, you name it. You can substitute your own favorites for the additions I've included here. Feel free to add more, if you like. Coconut shreds or flakes, more dried fruit or nuts, or even chocolate nibs, once the mix has cooled. It's all good.

INGREDIENTS

- **1** teaspoon neutral-flavored vegetable oil, such as organic canola
- **½** cup brown sugar
- **¼** cup cranberry juice
- **¼** cup honey
- **1** teaspoon ground cinnamon
- **1** teaspoon salt
- **3** cups rolled oats
- **1** cup Dried Apple Dice (see page 55)
- **½** cup dried fruit, such as cranberries, raisins, or currants
- **1** cup nuts and seeds, such as walnuts, hazelnuts, almonds, pepitas, or sunflower seeds, or a combination

PREPARE

1. Preheat the oven to 300°F. Grease a rimmed baking sheet with the oil.

2. Combine the sugar, juice, honey, cinnamon, and salt in a small saucepan and bring to a simmer over medium heat, stirring to dissolve the sugar.

3. Put the oats in a medium bowl and pour in the sugar mixture, stirring to coat the oats evenly. Spread the mixture in an even layer on the prepared baking sheet and bake for 20 minutes, stirring once.

4. In the same medium bowl, combine the dried apples, other dried fruit, and nuts and seeds. Add the toasted oats and stir to combine. Return to the baking sheet and bake for another 20 minutes, stirring once. Cool completely and store in an airtight container.

→ Any dried fruit will be delicious in this granola.

PEEL AND PIP PECTIN

Makes about 1 quart

I am often asked, "What did they do before there was pectin in a box?" The answer? They made their own — and so can you. For die-hard DIYers or those who are just curious, it's a neat technique to master. Making pectin doesn't take any special skill, and it's a fascinating example of kitchen science at work. Plus, for those of us with the cooking kink, the satisfaction of making deeply "from scratch" jams makes it worth the extra effort. And the payoff? Jams and jellies made with homemade pectin have simply the best texture — gelled but not tough, very silky and tender. If you have never tried it, you should give it a go at least once. Your preserve-making ancestors would be very impressed.

INGREDIENTS

- **4** pounds underripe crab or tart apples, quartered, but not peeled or cored
- **4** cups water
- **¼** cup bottled lemon juice

PREPARE

1. Combine the apples, water, and lemon juice in a large nonreactive pot and bring to a boil. Reduce the heat and simmer for 1 hour, uncovered, stirring occasionally to prevent scorching.

2. Line a colander with a triple layer of cheesecloth or have ready a jelly bag in its frame, and set either device over a large pot or bowl. Gently pour the apple mixture into your straining setup. Allow the cooked fruit to drain for 3 to 4 hours, until all the juice has been released. (Do not press on the draining fruit; doing so will cloud the liquid.) Use immediately or preserve for later use.

PRESERVE

Refrigerate: Cover and refrigerate for up to 5 days.

Freeze: Pectin can be frozen for up to 6 months. However, freezing will weaken the pectin slightly, so you will have to use about one-third more of it for the same gelling effect as refrigerated or canned pectin.

Can: Use the boiling-water method as described on page 20. Wipe out your pot, return the strained juice to it, and bring it to a boil. Ladle the pectin into clean, hot half-pint canning jars, leaving ¼ inch of headspace between the top of the pectin and the lid. Run a bubble tool along the inside of the glass to release trapped air. Wipe the rims clean; center lids on the jars and screw on jar bands until they are just fingertip-tight. Process the jars by submerging them in boiling water to cover by 2 inches for 10 minutes. Turn off the heat, remove the canner lid, and let the jars rest in the water for 5 minutes. Remove the jars and set aside for 24 hours. Check the seals, and then store in a cool, dark place for up to 1 year.

Fruit Preserves with Peel and Pip Pectin

Makes 2-3 cups, depending on the fruit and amount of pectin you use

Homemade pectin does not act in the same way as the "instant" pectin you buy in a box. You have to give it time to gel. When you use homemade pectin, you cook your jam or jelly as you would a "classic" or "long-cooking" spread. That is, you must simmer your recipe until it reaches the gel stage. (See page 28 for more on reaching the gel stage.)

The strength of your homemade pectin — its ability to gel your spread — will vary depending on the amount of pectin in the apples you used to make it and the amount of pectin in the fruit you are preserving. Check the chart on page 27. For fruits with medium gelling ability, start with ¼ cup homemade pectin. For fruits with lower gelling fortitude, start with ½ cup homemade pectin in the pot. Granted, using homemade pectin can take a little finesse. But even if the results aren't precisely as you intended, they are bound to be delicious. So get in that kitchen and play with your food. Here is a basic formula to get you started.

INGREDIENTS

- **1** pound fruit, peeled, pitted, and prepped as necessary
- **½–1** cup sugar
- **¼–½** cup Peel and Pip Pectin (see page 58)
- **1** tablespoon bottled lemon juice

PREPARE

1. Combine the fruit, sugar, pectin, and lemon juice in a nonreactive pot and slowly bring to a boil, stirring constantly. Reduce the heat and simmer, continuing to stir, until the gel stage is reached (see page 28).

2. Remove from the heat and allow the jam to rest for 5 minutes, giving it an occasional gentle stir to release trapped air; it will thicken slightly. Skim off any foam.

PRESERVE

Refrigerate: Cool, cover, and refrigerate for up to 3 weeks.

Can: Use the boiling-water method as described on page 20. Ladle the preserves into clean, hot 4-ounce or half-pint jars, leaving ¼ inch of headspace between the top of the preserves and the lid. Run a bubble tool along the inside of the glass to release trapped air. Wipe the rims clean; center lids on the jars and screw on jar bands until they are just fingertip-tight. Process the jars by submerging them in boiling water to cover by 2 inches for 10 minutes. Turn off the heat, remove the canner lid, and let the jars rest in the water for 5 minutes. Remove the jars and set aside for 24 hours. Check the seals, and then store in a cool, dark place for up to 1 year.

EARL GREY JELLY

Makes about 4 cups

I have always been a fan of Earl Grey tea. It tastes like fireplace/cat on the lap/rain on the roof in a teacup. Earl Grey tea gets its signature flavor from bergamot, a fragrant orange, which flavors the beverage and this jelly. Not an Earl Grey fan? Then you can substitute any other tea you like, or use herbs alone, as described in the variation below. Whichever kind of leaves you use, it's tea and toast times two.

INGREDIENTS

- **2** cups water
- **½** cup good-quality loose-leaf Earl Grey tea or 8 Earl Grey tea bags
- **4** cups Peel and Pip Pectin (see page 58)
- **¼** cup bottled lemon juice
- **4** cups sugar

PREPARE

1. Bring the water to a boil. Remove from the heat, add the tea, and let steep for 5 minutes to make a strong tea. Strain.

2. Combine the brewed tea, pectin, and lemon juice in a large nonreactive pot and bring to a boil. Add the sugar and stir to dissolve. Continue to cook at a steady boil, stirring frequently to prevent scorching, until the jelly reaches the gel stage (see page 28), about 30 minutes.

3. Remove from the heat. Allow the jelly to rest for 5 minutes, giving it an occasional gentle stir to release trapped air; it will thicken slightly. Skim off any foam.

PRESERVE

⊘ **Refrigerate:** Cool, cover, and refrigerate for up to 3 weeks.

🅱 **Can:** Use the boiling-water method as described on page 20. Ladle the jelly into clean, hot 4-ounce or half-pint jars, leaving ¼ inch of headspace between the top of the jelly and the lid. Run a bubble tool along the inside of the glass to release trapped air. Wipe the rims clean; center lids on the jars and screw on jar bands until they are just fingertip-tight. Process the jars by submerging them in boiling water to cover by 2 inches for 10 minutes. Turn off the heat, remove the canner lid, and let the jars rest in the water for 5 minutes. Remove the jars and set aside for 24 hours. Check the seals, and then store in a cool, dark place for up to 1 year.

VARIATION:

Herb Jelly

This is perhaps one of the best tricks in the book. Everyone who tasted this jelly wanted more. Use the recipe for Earl Grey Jelly, substituting herbs for the tea and white wine for the water. You needn't strain out the herbs after they have steeped; they look great in the jar. You can use either dried or fresh herbs in this recipe. This makes an elegant jelly that tastes great on savory scones or as a glaze for roast chicken.

Some terrific flavorings include:

- **2** tablespoons fresh woody herbs such as thyme, rosemary, or oregano, chopped
- **¼** cup fresh tender herbs such as lemon verbena, dill, or sage, chopped
- **1** tablespoon dried herb (including any of the above) or a blend such as herbes d' Provence

USE IT UP!

Farmstead Cheese Wrap with Herb Jelly

Serves 2

My vegetarian in-laws turned me on to this idea — a salad in a wrap as a fun and fabulous meatless meal. It's a quick solution when you don't know what to make for lunch or are looking for something light to order off a heavily carnivorous menu. Any salad can be treated this way. I've tarted mine up with cheese and Herb Jelly, but vegans can leave out the cheese and still have a great bite.

INGREDIENTS

- **2** tablespoons Herb Jelly (see page 61)
- **2** large flour tortillas
- **3** cups assorted salad greens such as chopped romaine, mâche, baby spinach, or mesclun
- **2** tablespoons vinaigrette (the Classic Vinaigrette on page 147 would be divine, or you could use 1½ tablespoons olive oil and 2 teaspoons vinegar whisked together with a little salt and pepper)
- **2** ounces cheese, any variety, preferably local, crumbled or cut into slices
  Extras such as a handful of chopped nuts, a slice of roasted red pepper or avocado, or ¼ cup cooked beans (optional, but great)

PREPARE

1. Divide the jelly between the tortillas and spread in a band across the middle of each wrap, leaving a 1-inch margin on each side.

2. Toss the greens with vinaigrette and divide between the tortillas, spreading the greens out on top of the jelly. Top the greens with the cheese and any extras you care to add.

3. Working with one tortilla at a time, fold 1 inch of each side of the wrap toward the middle. Fold the bottom of the wrap up over the filling, and then roll the filled wrap away from you. Place seam side down on a plate and slice in half.

→ These wraps are also delicious with Wine Jelly (page 148).

Apricots

Apricots are responsible, at least in part, for the writing of this book. Just a few short days after the publication of my first preserving book, *Put 'em Up!*, I received an e-mail. The sender said she liked the book and was looking forward to cooking from it. She had just returned from the farmers' market with a basket full of apricots, however, and was chagrined to find that the sweet little fruit was not featured in the book's recipe list. "No apricots?" she wanted to know. When it came time to select fruits for this book, "apricots" was the first word I typed. What can I say? When Deborah Madison makes a request, it's wise to listen.

Apricots are not as prized in the United States as they are in some countries, such as Turkey, and that's a shame. These attractive fruits, often with a lipstick kiss of pink blush across their orange cheek, are as alluring as they are delicious. Their subtle flavor supports sweet as well as savory treatments. Unlike peaches, which require peeling and, in the case of the clingstone varieties, a little work to excavate the pit, apricots are easy to prep. There's no need to skin them. Just remove the stem, insert your knife through to the pit, and cut all the way through longitudinally. Separate the two halves and pop out the pit. Now you're ready to go.

CLASSIC APRICOT JAM

Makes about 4 cups

Apricots are precious things. Their early spring bloom means that they are dangerously vulnerable to frost, which can rob tree owners of their prized crop for the entire season. So when apricots are in your market, it's a good idea to take advantage. Stock up and make gobs of this classic jam while you can. Apricots don't have a lot of pectin, so this jam can be a bit softer than most, a texture that I find pleasing with this delicate fruit. If you want a stiffer gel, Quick Apricot Jam (page 68), which contains added pectin, is the one for you.

INGREDIENTS

- ½ cup water
- ¼ cup bottled lemon juice
- **2** pounds apricots
- **3** cups sugar

PREPARE

1. Combine the water and lemon juice in a large nonreactive pot. Pit the apricots, adding them directly to the lemon water as you go. Add the sugar and slowly bring to a boil, stirring constantly to prevent scorching. Reduce the heat and simmer until the gel stage is reached (see page 28), about 25 minutes.

2. Remove from the heat. Allow the jam to rest for 5 minutes, giving it an occasional gentle stir to release trapped air; it will thicken slightly. Skim off any foam.

PRESERVE

Refrigerate: Cool, cover, and refrigerate for up to 3 weeks.

Can: Use the boiling-water method as described on page 20. Ladle the jam into clean, hot 4-ounce or half-pint jars, leaving ¼ inch of headspace between the top of the jam and the lid. Run a bubble tool along the inside of the glass to release trapped air. Wipe the rims clean; center lids on the jars and screw on jar bands until they are just fingertip-tight. Process the jars by submerging them in boiling water to cover by 2 inches for 10 minutes. Turn off the heat, remove the canner lid, and let the jars rest in the water for 5 minutes. Remove the jars and set aside for 24 hours. Check the seals, then store in a cool, dark place for up to 1 year.

VARIATION:
Brandied Apricot Jam

Add ½ cup brandy to the jam as it nears the gel stage to bring a savory edge to this sweet treat.

Recipes

66

Spring Rolls with Asian Dipping Sauce

Makes 15 rolls

Spring rolls are a great way to use up leftovers or odd bits from the crisper drawer. Anything tastes great in them, particularly when they are served with this dipping sauce made with your very own apricot jam! You can make up a big batch and freeze them. Then just cook them up — no defrosting necessary — and you will win the clever hostess prize at your next cocktail party.

SPRING ROLL INGREDIENTS

- **1** cup diced leftover meat or seafood, such as chicken, pork, salmon, or shrimp
- **1** cup shredded cabbage or leftover sautéed greens
- **½** cup diced water chestnuts, radishes, or kohlrabi
- **½** cup shredded carrot, zucchini, or squash
- **2** tablespoons diced green onion or shallot
- **2** tablespoons soy sauce
- **1** teaspoon sesame oil
- **12** spring roll wrappers (available in the refrigerated section of your local grocery store and at Asian markets)
- **1** cup neutral-flavored vegetable oil, such as organic canola

DIPPING SAUCE INGREDIENTS

- **¼** cup Classic Apricot Jam (see page 65)
- **1** tablespoon soy sauce
- **1** teaspoon freshly grated ginger
- **1** teaspoon rice vinegar
  Pinch of red pepper flakes (optional)

PREPARE

1. To make the spring rolls, combine the meat, cabbage, water chestnuts, carrots, and green onion with the soy sauce and sesame oil in a large bowl, and mix well.

2. To prepare the rolls, lay out a wrapper in front of you so that it looks like a diamond. Brush the seams of the top triangle of the wrapper with water. Spoon 2 tablespoons of the filling into a log shape, 2 inches above the bottom of the wrapper. Starting with the point closest to you, roll the wrapper over the filling until you've reached the midpoint of the wrapper. Fold the far left and right points toward the middle and continue to roll into shape. Smooth the dampened seam with a finger to seal it, and place the roll on a baking sheet, seam side down. Repeat with the remaining rolls. (You can freeze them at this point by arranging on a baking sheet and freezing until solid, at least 4 hours and up to two days. Transfer frozen rolls to an airtight container until ready to use. Do not defrost before proceeding.)

3. Heat the vegetable oil in a large skillet over medium-high heat. Gently place the rolls in the hot oil, working in batches if necessary to avoid crowding the pan, and fry until browned on both sides, 3 to 4 minutes per side. Remove to paper towels or a flattened brown paper bag to drain.

4. Meanwhile, make the sauce by combining the jam, soy sauce, ginger, rice vinegar, and red pepper flakes, if using, in a small bowl and whisking together. Serve the rolls with the sauce.

→ The dipping sauce is also delicious when prepared with Quick Apricot Jam (page 68), Classic Peach Jam (page 183), or Quick Peach Jam (page 180) in place of Classic Apricot Jam.

QUICK APRICOT JAM

Makes about 5 cups

With even less sugar than Classic Apricot Jam (page 65), this recipe spotlights the sunny brightness of the fruit. The ease of prep and short time in the pot make for a fast turnaround in the kitchen — welcome news if you have a lot of fruit or little time.

INGREDIENTS

- **2** cups sugar
- **1** tablespoon Pomona's Universal Pectin
- ½ cup water
- ¼ cup bottled lemon juice
- **2** pounds apricots
- **1** tablespoon calcium water (from the Pomona's Universal Pectin kit)

PREPARE

1. Combine the sugar and pectin in a small bowl and set aside.

2. Combine the water and lemon juice in a large, nonreactive pot. Halve, pit, and roughly chop the apricots, adding them to the pot as you go to prevent browning.

3. Bring the pot with the fruit to a boil, reduce the heat, and simmer for 5 minutes, until softened, crushing the fruit with a potato masher. Add the calcium water and stir. Slowly add the pectin mixture, stirring constantly to avoid clumping. Bring to a boil, reduce the heat, and simmer for 1 to 2 minutes, continuing to stir constantly, until the sugar is completely dissolved.

4. Remove from the heat. Allow the jam to rest for 5 minutes, giving it an occasional gentle stir to release trapped air; it will thicken slightly. Skim off any foam.

PRESERVE

Refrigerate: Cool, cover, and refrigerate for up to 3 weeks.

Can: Use the boiling-water method as described on page 20. Ladle the jam into clean, hot 4-ounce or half-pint jars, leaving ¼ inch of headspace between the top of the jam and the lid. Run a bubble tool along the inside of the glass to release trapped air. Wipe the rims clean; center lids on the jars and screw on jar bands until they are just fingertip-tight. Process the jars by submerging them in boiling water to cover by 2 inches for 10 minutes. Turn off the heat, remove the canner lid, and let the jars rest in the water for 5 minutes. Remove the jars and set aside for 24 hours. Check the seals, then store in a cool, dark place for up to 1 year.

USE IT UP!

Sticky Chicken Legs

Serves 4

This is a great entertaining recipe and can be doubled or even tripled to serve a crowd. The chicken legs are fabulous even at room temperature, so make them ahead of time and bring them to your next potluck or picnic. Leave out the pepper flakes and they become perfect, finger-licking-good fare for the younger set, too.

INGREDIENTS

- **½** cup Quick Apricot Jam (see page 68)
- **¼** cup soy sauce
- **2** garlic cloves, minced
- **1** tablespoon freshly grated ginger
- **¼** teaspoon red pepper flakes (optional)
- **8–10** chicken legs

PREPARE

1. Preheat the oven to 425°F.

2. Combine the jam, soy sauce, garlic, ginger, and red pepper flakes, if using, in a small bowl, and whisk together.

3. Put the chicken legs in a large baking pan, pour the sauce over them, and toss to coat. Bake, basting occasionally and turning once, for 30 to 40 minutes, until the chicken is browned and the skin begins to retract from the foot end of the legs. Serve hot or at room temperature.

→ You can easily substitute Classic Apricot Jam (page 65), Classic Peach Jam (page 183), or Quick Peach Jam (page 180) for Quick Apricot Jam in the glaze for the chicken legs; all are delicious.

APRISAUCE

Makes about 6 cups

Friend and editor Gabrielle Langholtz turned me on to the idea of Aprisauce, a sophisticated turn on applesauce. Babies love it — at least they do when I consent to share. It's really versatile — sweet enough for desserts but also handy in savory recipes, where it takes on spicy heat like a champ. You can whisk it together with a little hot sauce for a quick dip for grilled shrimp or use it as a glaze, as in the pork chop recipe that follows. Or just enjoy it straight or spooned over yogurt or ice cream.

INGREDIENTS

4 pounds apricots, pitted

½ cup water

¼ cup bottled lemon juice

1½ cups sugar

PREPARE

1. Combine the apricots, water, and lemon juice in a large nonreactive pot and slowly bring to a boil, stirring frequently to avoid scorching the fruit. Reduce the heat and simmer until the fruit breaks down, about 10 minutes.

2. Remove from the heat and purée with an immersion blender for a smooth texture.

3. Return to medium heat, add the sugar, and simmer until thickened, about 20 minutes. Aprisauce is fully cooked when a dollop on a plate does not weep.

PRESERVE

Refrigerate: Cool, cover, and refrigerate for up to 3 weeks.

Can: Use the boiling-water method as described on page 20. Ladle the sauce into clean, hot half-pint jars, leaving ½ inch of headspace between the top of the jam and the lid. Run a bubble tool along the inside of the glass to release trapped air. Wipe the rims clean; center lids on the jars and screw on jar bands until they are just fingertip-tight. Process the jars by submerging them in boiling water to cover by 2 inches for 10 minutes. Turn off the heat, remove the canner lid, and let the jars rest in the water for 5 minutes. Remove the jars and set aside for 24 hours. Check the seals, and then store in a cool, dark place for up to 1 year.

USE IT UP!

Broiled Pork Chops with Apricot Glaze

Serves 4

Who knew that adding a little glaze could make such a difference? The glaze adds flavor and protects the pork during cooking, keeping it moist and flavorful. The cooking curbs the fruitiness of the glaze and gives the chops a deep brown color. So not only does it taste great, it's "eating with your eyes" at its best.

INGREDIENTS

- **½** cup Aprisauce (see page 70)
- **4** garlic cloves, minced
- **2** tablespoons honey
- **2** tablespoons red wine vinegar, bottled or the homemade version on page 146 or apple cider vinegar, bottled or the homemade version on page 52
- **1** teaspoon salt
  Freshly ground black pepper
- **4** bone-in pork chops, about 1 inch thick

PREPARE

1. Preheat the broiler.

2. Combine the Aprisauce, garlic, honey, vinegar, salt, and pepper to taste in a small bowl and whisk until smooth. Dip each chop in the glaze and set on a grated broiler pan.

3. Set the pan in the oven, so that the chops are 4 to 5 inches from the heating element. Broil, turning once and brushing with the glaze, until browned and cooked through, with an internal temperature of 160°F, about 10 minutes per side.

4. Allow the chops to rest for 5 minutes before serving.

APRICOT HABANERO SALSA

Makes about 5 cups

Come summertime, I am all about salsas. Not just for chip dipping — although that's tasty, too — but as toppings for grilled foods and more. A few spoonfuls can make a simple meal of rice and beans taste like a feast. And salsas are great in slaws and salads, where they pick up the flavor of the dish and add color and contrast as well. Salsas aren't just about tomatoes. I make them with lots of different fruits. Stone fruits such as apricots, peaches, and plums are a particular treat. Their sweetness rubs up against the fruitiness of the chile, balancing the pepper's heat and accentuating its flavor.

INGREDIENTS

- **1** cup apple cider vinegar
- **1** cup water
- **½** cup dark brown sugar
- **½** cup granulated sugar
- **1** onion, finely diced
- **1** garlic clove, minced
- **½–1** habanero chile, seeds and membranes removed, and finely minced (see box)
- **1** tablespoon freshly grated ginger
- **1** teaspoon salt
- **½** teaspoon ground cinnamon
- **2** pounds apricots

PREPARE

1. Combine the vinegar, water, brown sugar, granulated sugar, onion, garlic, habanero, ginger, salt, and cinnamon in a large, nonreactive pot. Bring to a boil, reduce the heat, and simmer for 10 minutes. Remove from the heat.

2. Peel, pit, and dice the apricots, adding them directly to the vinegar mixture as you work. Return the mixture to a boil, and then reduce the heat and simmer until thickened, about 15 minutes, stirring frequently to avoid scorching the salsa.

Why do you . . .
use habanero chiles?

Why, indeed. I love their fruity flavor, but these little firebombs can really pack some heat. You can substitute less-fiery chiles in this and any canning recipe as long as you keep the proportions the same. You can even swap in sweet peppers if spice is not your thing, as long as you don't change the total pepper quantity called for. So feel free to replace the habanero with a jalapeno or a small piece of a poblano. Or dial it up to "11" and get supremely hot with ghost pepper, if that's how you roll.

⊘ **Refrigerate:** Cool, cover, and refrigerate for up to 3 weeks.

ⓒ **Can:** Use the boiling-water method as described on page 20. Ladle the salsa into clean, hot half-pint or pint jars, leaving ½ inch of headspace between the top of the salsa and the lid. Run a bubble tool along the inside of the glass to release trapped air. Wipe the rims clean; center lids on the jars and screw on jar bands until they are just fingertip-tight. Process the jars by submerging them in boiling water to cover by 2 inches for 15 minutes. Turn off the heat, remove the canner lid, and let the jars rest in the water for 5 minutes. Remove the jars and set aside for 24 hours. Check the seals, then store in a cool, dark place for up to 1 year.

→ Use gloves when working with chiles to avoid irritating your hands. And feel free to substitute any stone fruit for the apricots in this recipe.

Why do you ...
rinse onion?

Rinsing onions or shallots before you add them to salads washes away the sulfur compounds that alliums release when they are cut. That means you can keep the salad for a few days in the fridge without it taking on the sulfur smell caused by these compounds.

USE IT UP!

Spiced Chicken Salad

Serves 6-8

Chicken salad doesn't have to be a mayo-heavy creamy thing. This spiced-up version has clean, lively flavors and is super versatile. You can make it any time of the year, using whatever kind of vegetables are in season near you. You can vary the amount of salsa that you use, depending on how spicy you like your food. It's terrific as it is, served on a bed of greens, or rolled up in a wrap. A new lunchtime favorite.

INGREDIENTS

2–4 tablespoons Apricot Habanero Salsa (see page 72)

2 tablespoons neutral-flavored vegetable oil, such as organic canola

2 tablespoons rice wine or white wine vinegar

1 tablespoon soy sauce

1 teaspoon dark sesame oil

3 cups assorted seasonal vegetables, such as diced cucumber, peppers cut into strips, blanched snow peas, green beans or sugar snap peas, sliced radishes, spinach or other tender lettuces, hardy greens such as kale cut into chiffonade, shredded cabbage, or roasted sweet potatoes or other root vegetables

1 cup cooked chicken or white beans

1 small red onion or large shallot, minced and rinsed in cold water

1 tablespoon sesame seeds

PREPARE

1. To make the dressing, combine the salsa, vegetable oil, vinegar, soy sauce, and sesame oil in a small bowl, and whisk together.

2. Combine the vegetables, chicken, and onion in a large bowl and toss with the dressing. Garnish with the sesame seeds. Serve immediately or refrigerate for up to 2 days.

DRIED APRICOTS

2 cups dried fruit from 2 pounds apricots

I don't dry enough fruit to merit buying a dehydrator. And I really don't have the space for gadgets. So I use this oven-drying method to put up amounts of fruit too small to can but a bit too big to eat fresh. Because I don't treat them with sulfur, these apricots will not retain the bright orange hue that commercially produced fruit exhibits. Fine with me — they still taste great!

INGREDIENTS

12 (500 mg) vitamin C tablets, crushed, or 2 teaspoons vitamin C powder

4 cups water

2 pounds apricots

PREPARE

1. Preheat the oven to 170°F.

2. Combine the vitamin C and water in a large bowl and stir to dissolve. Halve and pit the apricots, adding them to the water as you go.

3. You can dry apricots in halves or slices. To prepare halves for drying, push your thumb against the skin side of each apricot half to flip it inside out. To dry slices, cut the pitted and halved apricots into ½-inch wedges. Either way, return the apricots to the acidulated water as you prep them to prevent browning. After you have added the last of the fruit, let it soak for 5 minutes.

PRESERVE

Dry:

1. Drain the fruit and pat it dry. Arrange the fruit on wire racks, such as cake cooling racks, set over baking sheets to capture any drips. Two pounds of fruit will fill two 11- by 17-inch racks with plenty of room for air circulation. Do not crowd the fruit onto one rack; crowded fruit won't dry properly. Place the racks in the oven and prop the door open with a wooden spoon to allow steam to escape. Drying times will vary depending on the size of your apricots. Slices can take up to 7 hours, and halves up to 10. The fruit is completely dry when you can squeeze it in your hand and it doesn't stick together, yet it remains pliable.

2. Cool the apricots to room temperature, and then condition them by transferring them to a covered container and letting them sit for 1 day. This allows the dried fruit to redistribute any trapped moisture. If you notice moisture collecting on the sides of the container, repeat the drying process for another hour or so. Fully dried apricots will keep in an airtight container for up to 1 year.

USE IT UP!

Wild Rice Salad

Serves 8–12 as a side dish

This salad always gets raves. The deep jewel tones of the fruit against the black rice make it a beauty. Don't skimp on the seasonings — the rice drinks up the vinaigrette, and a little extra mustard and vinegar can make the difference between dull and delightful. You can change up the dried fruit to use whatever you may have on hand. The fact that you can serve it at room temperature makes this a wonderful side dish for the holidays; you can make it ahead and then get on with the festivities.

INGREDIENTS

- **1** cup long-grain brown rice
- **1** cup wild rice
- **1** shallot, minced
- **¼** cup balsamic vinegar
- **2** tablespoons Dijon mustard
- **1** teaspoon salt
  Freshly ground black pepper
- **½** cup olive oil
- **1** cup assorted dried fruit, such as sliced Dried Apricots (see page 76), dates, prunes, currants, Dried Cranberries (see page 125), and cherries
- **¼** cup flat-leaf parsley, chopped
- **¼** cup toasted hazelnuts (optional)

PREPARE

1. In separate pots, boil the brown rice and wild rice in 8 cups salted water each until tender, about 45 minutes. Brown rice is ready when a grain, bitten in half, no longer reveals a white dot in its center. Wild rice is done when about half of the grains have begun to split, and the remainder are tender but intact. Drain both rices thoroughly.

2. While the rice is cooking, make the dressing. Rinse the minced shallot in cold water, drain, pat dry with a paper towel, and add to a large bowl. Add the vinegar, mustard, salt, and pepper to taste, and whisk to blend. Slowly whisk in the oil.

3. Add the hot rice to the dressing and toss to coat the grains. Add the dried fruit and parsley and toss to combine. Garnish with hazelnuts, if using, and serve within 2 hours or refrigerate for up to 2 days (bring to room temperature before serving).

APRICOTS IN HONEY SYRUP

Makes about 6 pints

If you've ever closed your eyes and imagined your shelves full of neatly arranged canned loveliness, the very essence of summer in a jar, you may not know it, but you are envisioning canned apricots. Iconic in their beauty, apricots' blushing skins flirt temptingly in the jar, and the syrup takes on the golden hue of the fruit for a truly picture-perfect preserve. They're almost too pretty to eat. Almost.

INGREDIENTS

7 cups water

12 (500 mg) vitamin C tablets, crushed,
or 2 teaspoons vitamin C powder

6 pounds very firm apricots

¾ cup sugar

¾ cup honey

PREPARE

1. Combine 4 cups of the water with the vitamin C in a large bowl, and stir to dissolve. Halve and pit the apricots, adding them to the acidulated water as you go. Allow them to soak for at least 5 minutes.

2. Drain the apricots and pack them into clean, hot pint jars, cut side up, leaving approximately ¾ inch of space between the top of the apricots and the top of the jar.

3. Combine the remaining 3 cups water and the sugar and honey in a small saucepan and bring to a boil. Ladle the syrup over the apricots to cover by ¼ inch, leaving ½ inch of headspace at the top of the jar.

PRESERVE

Can: Use the boiling-water method as described on page 20. Run a bubble tool along the inside of the glass to release trapped air. Wipe the rims clean; center lids on the jars and screw on jar bands until they are just fingertip-tight. Process the jars by submerging them in boiling water to cover by 2 inches for 25 minutes. Turn off the heat, remove the canner lid, and let the jars rest in the water for 5 minutes. Remove the jars and set aside for 24 hours. Check the seals, then store in a cool, dark place for up to 1 year.

→   This recipe can be halved.

USE IT UP!

Apricots in Phyllo Nests

Serves 4

I love to eat foods made with phyllo, those delicate Middle Eastern pastry sheets that are used to wrap spanikopita (spinach pie) and are layered between walnuts and honey for baklava. But getting the leaf-thin sheets to do as you wish can be a challenge. That's why I love to make phyllo "nests" — you get all the flavor of the pastry and it's perfectly fine to make a mess of the sheets in the process. In fact, they'll look better for it.

INGREDIENTS

- **4** sheets phyllo dough, thawed and covered with a damp tea towel
- **¼** cup unsalted butter, melted
- **2** teaspoons sugar
- **12** Apricots in Honey Syrup halves (see page 78)
- **½** cup whipped cream

PREPARE

1. Preheat the oven to 400°F. Line an 11- by 17-inch baking sheet with parchment paper.

2. Lay one sheet of phyllo in front of you (keep the remaining sheets covered with the damp tea towel, as they dry out quickly). Gently brush the sheet with some of the melted butter. Scrunch up the sheet by pushing the short sides toward each other, and then bending the ends together to form a roughly shaped wreath. Dab on a bit more melted butter and sprinkle with ½ teaspoon of the sugar. Repeat with the remaining three sheets, arranging them on the baking sheet as you go.

3. Bake for 10 to 12 minutes, until the dough is just starting to color on the edges. Remove from the oven and let cool. (You can make this part of the recipe up to 1 hour ahead, or more if the day is not humid.)

4. Arrange a nest on each of four serving plates. Nestle three apricot halves inside each nest, and top with whipped cream. Serve immediately.

→ This recipe is also delicious with home-canned peaches or plums in place of the Apricots in Honey Syrup.

Blackberries & Raspberries

*B*ramble. Don't you love that word? It calls to mind long-lingering summer days, with lemonade and hammocks. I am not lucky enough to have my own berry bramble, but there are some wild ones in my neighborhood that gift me some fruit. And the farmers in the market keep me flush with the little jewels, too. You can use wild or cultivated berries in these recipes — whatever is fresh and available in your area.

Blackberries and raspberries are really clusters of fruit held together by a common fibrous structure called a "receptacle." When picked, raspberries leave their receptacle behind, coming off the cane as a cone-shaped, hollow cluster of berries. Blackberries, on the other hand, retain their receptacle. This anatomical distinction influences how you handle the berries. Both are quite delicate, so take care to be gentle when picking or handling them or you can easily crush them. Without an attached receptacle, raspberries are especially fragile. Their hollow shape also means that they can easily pick up a lot of water when being rinsed. For this reason, some cooks forego washing their berries before use.

MIXED BERRY JAM

Makes about 5 cups

This is a good solution for those turn-of-the-season times when one berry is coming into season and one is going out, or simply when you find yourself with a bit of this and that. I like to combine berries of similar hues to give a visual cue as to what's in the jar, but you needn't stick to this script — a berry jumble is equally as sweet.

INGREDIENTS

- **4** cups sugar
- **1** tablespoon Pomona's Universal Pectin
- **2** quarts assorted berries (about 3 pounds), such as blackberries and blueberries, or raspberries and strawberries
- **¼** cup water
- **¼** cup bottled lemon juice
- **1** tablespoon calcium water (from the Pomona's Universal Pectin kit)

PREPARE

1. Combine the sugar and pectin in a small bowl.

2. Combine the berries and water in a medium nonreactive pot and slowly bring to a boil over low heat. Reduce the heat and simmer for 5 to 10 minutes, until the berries completely break down. Add the lemon juice and calcium water, stirring to combine. Slowly add the pectin mixture, stirring constantly to avoid clumping. Bring to a boil, reduce the heat, and simmer for 1 to 2 minutes, continuing to stir constantly, until the sugar is completely dissolved.

3. Remove from the heat. Allow the jam to rest for 5 minutes, giving it an occasional gentle stir to release trapped air; it will thicken slightly. Skim off any foam.

PRESERVE

Refrigerate: Cool, cover, and refrigerate for up to 3 weeks.

Can: Use the boiling-water method as described on page 20. Ladle the jam into clean, hot 4-ounce or half-pint jars, leaving ¼ inch of headspace between the top of the jam and the lid. Run a bubble tool along the inside of the glass to release trapped air. Wipe the rims clean; center lids on the jars and screw on jar bands until they are just fingertip-tight. Process the jars by submerging them in boiling water to cover by 2 inches for 10 minutes. Turn off the heat, remove the canner lid, and let the jars rest in the water for 5 minutes. Remove the jars and set aside for 24 hours. Check the seals, then store in a cool, dark place for up to 1 year.

VARIATION:

Berry and Herb Jam

Add 1 teaspoon dried herbs such as sage, thyme, or rosemary to the simmering berries to make a savory jam to serve with roasts or as a great addition to a cheese plate.

USE IT UP!

Linzer Tart Cookies

Makes 24 cookies

Linzer tarts are pretty little things, aren't they? But it's hard to find a good linzer. So often they are made with shortening or filled with run-of-the-mill commercial jelly. Now you can make your own, pretty as a picture and full of good things. You can make these with the traditional almonds and raspberry jam or substitute other nuts and jams, as I do here. They are ready to eat as soon as you assemble them, but I find they are even better the next day, after the jam and cookie have gotten to know each other a bit.

INGREDIENTS

- **1** cup unsalted butter, softened
- ½ cup sugar
- **1** egg
- **2** cups all-purpose flour
- **1** cup ground nuts, such as almonds, walnuts, or hazelnuts
- ¼ teaspoon salt
- ⅛ teaspoon ground cinnamon
- ⅓ cup confectioners' sugar
- ½ cup Mixed Berry Jam (see page 81)

PREPARE

1. Combine the butter and sugar in a large bowl and use an electric hand mixer to cream them together. Add the egg and beat to combine. In a separate bowl, combine the flour, nuts, salt, and cinnamon, and mix well. Blend the dry ingredients into the butter mixture 1 cup at a time, until all combined. Divide the dough in half, pat into disks, wrap tightly in plastic, and refrigerate for 1 hour.

→ Nuts, particularly nut pieces, go rancid quickly. For a fresher, nuttier taste, buy whole nuts and grind them yourself by giving them a few pulses in a food processor or by putting them in a plastic bag and mashing them with a meat mallet.

2. Preheat the oven to 350°F. Line two baking sheets with parchment paper.

3. Remove one disk of dough from the refrigerator. On a lightly floured surface, roll it out to ⅛-inch thickness. Using a 2½-inch cookie cutter or a glass, cut out circles. Arrange the circles on the prepared baking sheets. Gather up the scraps, reroll, and repeat. You should have 24 circles. Bake for 18 to 20 minutes, until golden. Let cool for 5 minutes, and then remove to a cooling rack.

4. Meanwhile, line two additional baking sheets with parchment paper. Roll out the second disk of dough in the same manner as the first. Cut out circles, using the same cookie cutter or glass as you did with the first batch. Cut a 1-inch hole in the middle of each circle before putting it on the baking sheet (an apple corer is perfect for this). A pastry scraper is a useful tool for transferring the delicate rings to the baking sheet. Bake and cool as above.

5. When all the cookies are completely cool, spread a teaspoon of jam on each of the cookies without a hole. Dust those with a hole with confectioners' sugar, and then set each one atop one of the jammed cookies.

FROZEN BERRIES

White-shouldered, flavorless, out-of-season berries? You deserve better than that. Use this method to stock up on the summer jewels when they're summer-ripe and delicious, and you can throw them in a smoothie or blend them into your muffins and pancake batters for a burst of fresh-from-the-farm berry goodness all year round. Freezing berries is also a smart strategy for delayed jam making. You can transfer berries out of the deep freeze and into the jam pot at any time of year.

INGREDIENTS

Any quantity berries, stemmed

PREPARE

Spread out the berries on a rimmed baking sheet. (Make sure they're not touching one another.) Transfer the sheet to the freezer and freeze until the berries are solid, at least 4 hours and up to 2 days.

PRESERVE

Freeze: Transfer the frozen berries to airtight containers or bags. Press out as much air as possible, then return to the freezer. The berries will keep frozen for up to 6 months.

USE IT UP!

Double Berry Pie

Makes 1 (9-inch) pie

With frozen berries, you can serve berry pie anytime of year and still not be accused of stepping out on your local foodshed. I like to use a combination, if for no other reason than, hey, I can, but also because all those flavors working together taste great. This kind of pie is sometimes called a bumbleberry, but that refers to the mix of fruit, not a new heirloom variety of berry-bearing bramble.

CRUST INGREDIENTS

- 1¼ cups all-purpose flour
- ½ cup (1 stick) unsalted butter
- ¼ teaspoon salt
- 3 tablespoons ice water

FILLING INGREDIENTS

- 6 cups assorted Frozen Berries (see page 84)
- ½ cup plus 1 tablespoon sugar
- 1 tablespoon lemon juice
- ¼ cup cornstarch

PREPARE

1. To make the crust, combine the flour, butter, and salt in a food processor and pulse until the mixture resembles coarse cornmeal. Drizzle in the water, pulsing until a dough forms. Shape the dough into a disk, wrap in waxed paper or plastic, and refrigerate for at least 1 hour.

2. Preheat the oven to 375°F. Butter a 9-inch pie plate.

3. To make the filling, combine the berries, the ½ cup sugar, and the lemon juice in a large bowl. Sift the cornstarch over the mixture and stir to combine.

4. On a lightly floured surface, roll out the dough to a circle of ¼-inch thickness. Carefully transfer it to the pie plate, pressing it into the corners of the dish. Trim as necessary, making sure that the dough overlaps the sides of the pan by an inch. Pour the berry filling into the crust, and sprinkle with the 1 tablespoon sugar. Bake for about 1 hour and 15 minutes, until the crust is brown and the filling is bubbling (the filling will thicken as it cools). Let cool before serving.

KITCHEN HOW-TO

Cleaning Berries

I give my berries a gentle shower in a wire-mesh strainer and then softly tap the strainer with my hand to release trapped water. You can also lay your rinsed berries out on a cloth to "drip dry." Whichever method you use, be careful to dry them thoroughly before proceeding with your recipe.

BERRY JELLY

Makes about 3 cups

Crystal-clear jelly, made from just a fruit's juice, is a delight on the shelf and even more so on the plate. Because all the pulp and pips are removed in the jelly-making process, jelly is an ideal solution for those of us who love the taste of bramble fruit, such as blackberries and raspberries, but don't enjoy having the seeds catch in our teeth. For the most sparkling jelly, don't boil the fruit or press on the jelly bag, which will cloud your juice.

INGREDIENTS

- **2** quarts berries (about 3 pounds)
- ¼ cup water
- **2** cups sugar
- **3** teaspoons Pomona's Universal Pectin
- ¼ cup bottled lemon juice
- **3** teaspoons calcium water (from the Pomona's Universal Pectin kit)

PREPARE

1. Combine the berries and water in a medium nonreactive saucepan and slowly bring to a simmer. Reduce the heat to low and gently simmer for 5 minutes to release the fruit's juices, being careful not to crush or press the fruit, which will cloud your jelly.

2. Line a colander with a triple layer of cheesecloth or have ready a jelly bag in its frame, and set either device over a bowl. Remove the fruit from the heat and gently pour into your straining setup. Allow the cooked fruit to drain for at least 2 hours, until all the juice has been released. Do not press on the draining fruit.

3. Combine the sugar and pectin in a small bowl.

4. Measure 2 cups of the strained juice into a medium, nonreactive saucepan. Bring to a boil, and stir in the lemon juice and calcium water. Sprinkle in the pectin mixture, stirring constantly to disperse evenly. Return to a boil and simmer for 1 to 2 minutes, stirring constantly, to dissolve the mixture.

5. Remove from the heat. Allow the jam to rest for 5 minutes, giving it an occasional gentle stir to release trapped air; it will thicken slightly. Skim off any foam.

JELLY BAG SETUP

When using a jelly bag, insert it into the frame seam side out for easier cleaning.

PRESERVE

🌀 **Refrigerate:** Cool, cover, and refrigerate for up to 3 weeks.

🇺 **Can:** Use the boiling-water method as described on page 20. Ladle the jam into clean, hot 4-ounce or half-pint jars, leaving ¼ inch of headspace between the top of the jam and the lid. Run a bubble tool along the inside of the glass to release trapped air. Wipe the rims clean; center lids on the jars and screw on jar bands until they are just fingertip-tight. Process the jars by submerging them in boiling water to cover by 2 inches for 10 minutes. Turn off the heat, remove the canner lid, and let the jars rest in the water for 5 minutes. Remove the jars and set aside for 24 hours. Check the seals, then store in a cool, dark place for up to 1 year.

BERRY JELLY

USE IT UP!

Berry Vinaigrette

Makes ⅔ cup

Adding a dollop of Berry Jelly to the vinaigrette gives it a nice whiff of fruit, of course, but it also adds a lovely viscosity that helps the dressing better cling to the leaves of your salad. It's particularly good with a salad of bitter greens, where the sweetness plays off the tongue tingle of the vegetables.

INGREDIENTS

- **2** tablespoons Berry Jelly (see page 86)
- **2** tablespoons red wine vinegar
- **2** teaspoons Dijon mustard
  Salt and freshly ground black pepper
- **½** cup olive oil

PREPARE

Combine the jelly, vinegar, mustard, and a pinch each of salt and pepper in a medium bowl and whisk together. Slowly drizzle in the olive oil, whisking all the while to emulsify. This vinaigrette will keep in the refrigerator for up to 1 week.

→ The vinaigrette is also delicious when prepared with Wine Jelly (page 148) or Blackberry Gastrique (page 90) in place of the Berry Jelly.

BERRY APPLE LEATHER

Makes about 16 fruit leather strips

Unless you have your own berry patch, these fruits can seem a bit precious to turn into a quickly devoured kids' snack (my brood and their friends can go through the equivalent of pounds of fruit in minutes). To stretch the berries (and your effort), I've mixed them with apples. The apples act as a neutral flavor base, so in the end all you'll taste are the luscious berries.

INGREDIENTS

- 1½ pounds apples (about 3–4 large), chopped
- 1 quart berries (about 1½ pounds)
- ½ cup water
- ¼ cup sugar

PREPARE

1. Preheat the oven to 170°F. Line two 11- by 17-inch rimmed baking sheets with parchment paper.

2. Combine the apples and berries with the water in a large nonreactive pot and bring to a boil. Simmer until the fruit breaks down, about 15 minutes. Run the cooked fruit through a food mill to purée and remove peels and pips.

3. Return the fruit purée to the pot, add the sugar, and simmer over low heat, stirring frequently, until the mixture thickens to the consistency of baby food.

PRESERVE

Dry:

1. Divide the purée between the baking sheets. Spread the purée over the sheets, tilting them back and forth to create an even layer about ⅛ inch thick. Dry in the oven for about 2 hours, until tacky to the touch. Be careful not to overdry, or the leather will become brittle.

2. Let cool to room temperature. Slide the parchment paper onto a cutting board and roll the leather into a tube. Slice the dried fruit into 2-inch strips. Store in a covered jar for up to 1 month.

USE IT UP!

Stained Glass Cookies

Makes about 6 dozen cookies

The fruit leather pieces on these cookies give them a modernist look — sort of the Mondrian of pastries. The graphic look is a nice contrast to all of the ribbon and frou-frou of the holidays. And a great introduction to modern art paintings for the kids.

INGREDIENTS

- ½ cup (1 stick) unsalted butter, softened
- ¾ cup plus 1 tablespoon sugar
- ½ cup milk
- 1 egg
- 1½ teaspoons vanilla extract
- ¼ teaspoon salt
- 2½ cups all-purpose flour
- 4 (2-inch) strips Berry Apple Leather (see page 88), cut into "confetti"

PREPARE

1. Combine the butter and the ¾ cup sugar in a large bowl, and use an electric hand mixer to cream them together, until fluffy. Add ¼ cup of the milk, the egg, and the vanilla, and beat until combined. Add the salt, then beat in the flour, ½ cup at a time, until just combined. Divide the dough in half, pat into disks, wrap tightly in plastic, and refrigerate for 1 hour.

2. Preheat the oven to 375°F. Line two baking sheets with parchment paper.

   Remove one dough disk from the refrigerator. On a lightly floured surface, knead it once or twice, then roll it out to ⅛-inch thickness. Using a paring knife, cut the dough diagonally into 2-inch strips and then in the opposite direction to make 2-inch diamonds. Arrange on a baking sheet, 1 inch apart.

3. Brush each cookie with some of the remaining ¼ cup milk. Top each cookie with two or three bits of fruit leather. Sprinkle with the remaining tablespoon sugar. Bake for 12 to 14 minutes, until just beginning to color around the edges.

4. Let cool for 5 minutes, and then remove to a cooling rack. Repeat with the remaining dough.

→   Any kind of fruit leather will work well in this recipe.

BLACKBERRY GASTRIQUE

Makes about 1 cup

Oh, gastrique. My new favorite thing. Just a drizzle of this lively, deeply flavored sauce will turn an everyday meal into something special. Swipe a tablespoon across the plate and then fan a few slices of grilled steak, game, or vegetables on top for a little "wow" factor. For more on making gastriques, see page 157.

INGREDIENTS

- **1** cup sugar
- ¼ cup water
- **1** cup red wine vinegar
- **1** cup blackberries
  Pinch of salt

PREPARE

1. Combine the sugar and water in a medium nonreactive saucepan and bring to a light boil over medium-low heat. Do not stir. Cook until the sugar melts and begins to color slightly, 5 to 7 minutes, washing down the sides of the pan with a pastry brush dipped in water as necessary.

2. When the sugar begins to color, pour the vinegar into the pan, but be careful — the vinegar will hiss and spit a good bit. The caramel will harden when the liquid hits it but will dissolve again as it simmers. Simmer until reduced by about half, about 5 minutes.

3. Add the berries and continue to simmer until the sauce takes on the color and fragrance of the fruit and thickens slightly, about 10 minutes. Strain through a fine-mesh strainer. Finish with a sprinkle of salt.

PRESERVE

Refrigerate: Cool, cover, and refrigerate for up to 3 weeks.

Freeze: Divide among compartments in an ice cube tray or small containers, cover, and freeze for up to 6 months.

Can: Use the boiling-water method as described on page 20. Ladle the gastrique into clean, hot 4-ounce jars, leaving ¼ inch of headspace between the top of the gastrique and the lid. Run a bubble tool along the inside of the glass to release trapped air. Wipe the rims clean; center lids on the jars and screw on jar bands until they are just fingertip-tight. Process the jars by submerging them in boiling water to cover by 2 inches for 10 minutes. Turn off the heat, remove the canner lid, and let the jars rest in the water for 5 minutes. Remove the jars and set aside for 24 hours. Check the seals, then store in a cool, dark place for up to 1 year.

→ The pectin in the fruit can cause the gastrique to set up a bit over time. Thin the sauce, if necessary, by warming it slightly.

Why don't you...
stir the sugar and water when making caramel?

The sugar syrup that you make by combining just a little bit of water with a much greater volume of sugar is called a "super-saturated solution." Essentially, the heat of the pan has allowed you to jam much more sugar into the water than you could at room temperature. It's a highly unstable liquid that is ready to crystallize at any moment (if you hung a string in it and let it cool, the sugar would indeed cling to the fibers of the cord and you would get rock candy). Disturbing the syrup by stirring or shaking the pan too vigorously could be all the encouragement the solution needs to recrystallize, giving you a gritty caramel rather than a smooth, liquid one. Handle the pan as little as possible, and gently wash down the sides with a pastry brush dipped in water to keep any drying caramel on the sides of the hot pan from introducing grit-making sugar crystals and wrecking your work.

BLACKBERRY GASTRIQUE

USE IT UP!

Scottadito with Berry Gastrique

Serves 4

Scottadito is Italian for "finger burning." This dish got the name because the chops are so tempting that diners usually cannot wait for them to cool before picking them up and having a taste, even if it means singeing their fingers on the still-hot chops. The gastrique makes them even more inviting. Dig in!

INGREDIENTS

- ¼ cup freshly squeezed lemon juice
- 2 garlic cloves, sliced
- 1 teaspoon fresh rosemary, chopped
- ½ teaspoon salt
    Freshly ground black pepper
- ¼ cup olive oil
- 2 pounds baby lamb chops
- 2 tablespoons Blackberry Gastrique (see page 90)

PREPARE

1. Combine the lemon juice, garlic, rosemary, salt, and pepper to taste in a small bowl and whisk together until the salt dissolves. Add the oil in a steady stream, whisking steadily to emulsify.

2. Arrange the chops in a small baking dish and pour the marinade over them. Turn the chops to coat them with the marinade on both sides. Cover with plastic wrap and refrigerate for at least 2 hours, and up to 12 hours.

Recipe continues on next page →

Scottadito with Berry Gastrique, continued

3. Preheat the grill or broiler. Remove the chops from the marinade and scrape off any excess. Grill the chops over hot coals or 3 to 4 inches from the heating element of the broiler, until browned on both sides but still rare in the middle, 3 to 4 minutes per side.

4. Arrange the chops on a serving platter and drizzle with gastrique. Serve immediately.

Blueberries

I love to go blueberry picking with my kids. And sometimes they like to go with me. But on the days when I am in a load-up-the-trug-mamma's-making-jam kind of mood and they are not, it's equally nice to have them nearby, reading under the shade of the bushes as I settle into the Zen of the job. Sort of like *Blueberries for Sal*, except for the bears.

Blueberries are native to North America and grow abundantly here. Lowbush, wild varieties grow low to the ground, as their name suggests, and have small, tart berries. The highbush varieties are taller specimens that are easier to harvest and therefore more commonly cultivated. Their larger, sweeter berries are more available commercially.

BLUEBERRY SYRUP

Makes about 3 cups

When I was a little girl, breakfast on summer vacation would mean a trip to the pancake house. I loved silver-dollar cakes because their small size would allow me to douse each one with a different flavor of syrup — maple, raspberry, vanilla, chocolate, or blueberry. I doubt there was much fruit in those brightly hued liquid sugars, but they were great fun for a kid. I make this berry-based syrup to bring that fruit-flavored joy to the table in an honest-to-goodness way.

INGREDIENTS

- **1** quart blueberries (about 1½ pounds)
- **1** cup sugar
- **¼** cup bottled lemon juice
- **¼** cup water

PREPARE

Combine the blueberries, sugar, lemon juice, and water in a medium nonreactive pot. Slowly bring to a boil, and then reduce the heat and simmer until the berries fall apart, 5 to 10 minutes. Strain through a fine-mesh sieve, pressing on and then discarding the solids.

KITCHEN HOW-TO
Prepping Blueberries

Once the picking is done, blueberries are a snap to prep. Both lowbush and highbush varieties are coated with a dusty-looking "bloom" that protects the berry. A quick rinse removes it. Then just give the berries a quick sort for any leaves or stems that may have made it into the bucket, and you're ready to go.

PRESERVE

Refrigerate: Cool, cover, and refrigerate for up to 3 weeks.

Can: Use the boiling-water method as described on page 20. Ladle the syrup into clean, hot half-pint jars, leaving ¼ inch of headspace between the top of the syrup and the lid. Run a bubble tool along the inside of the glass to release trapped air. Wipe the rims clean; center lids on the jars and screw on jar bands until they are just fingertip-tight. Process the jars by submerging them in boiling water to cover by 2 inches for 10 minutes. Turn off the heat, remove the canner lid, and let the jars rest in the water for 5 minutes. Remove the jars and set aside for 24 hours. Check the seals, then store in a cool, dark place for up to 1 year.

→ I've had the occasional batch of Blueberry Syrup try to set up on me. If your syrup has started to gel, just heat it up for a few seconds over low heat or in the microwave to liquefy it before using it in a recipe or pouring it on your pancakes.

BLUEBERRY SYRUP

USE IT UP!

Blueberry Lemonade

Makes 5 cups

I always serve a "mocktail" when I entertain — a special booze-free beverage. It gives kids a chance to enjoy a libation that's a treat and gives the grown-ups an alternative to the bar if they would like one. This lemonade, refreshing to both young and old, is a welcome addition at any gathering.

INGREDIENTS

- **½** cup Blueberry Syrup (see page 94)
  Juice of 4 lemons (about ½ cup)
- **¼** cup sugar
- **4** cups water or seltzer
  Ice

PREPARE

Combine the syrup, lemon juice, and sugar in a large pitcher and stir until the sugar dissolves. Add the water or seltzer and stir to combine. Serve over ice.

BLUEBERRY KETCHUP

Makes about 3 cups

Yes, ketchup made out of blueberries. Tomatoes are a fruit, too, after all. Try this condiment and you'll be surprised at how well the berries clear the savory line. I love it on burgers. It's not too sweet, and it's laced with the same spices found in the classic version, making this ketchup both fresh and familiar.

INGREDIENTS

- **2** shallots, unpeeled
- **1** teaspoon olive oil
- **1** quart blueberries (about 1½ pounds)
- **1** cup firmly packed brown sugar
- **½** cup red wine vinegar
- **1** tablespoon freshly grated ginger
- **1** garlic clove, minced
- **1** teaspoon ground allspice
- **½** teaspoon ground cinnamon

PREPARE

1. Preheat the oven to 375°F.

2. Coat the shallots with the oil and bundle in a double thickness of aluminum foil. Place the bundle on a baking sheet and roast in the oven for about 1 hour, until the shallots are tender when pierced with a knife. When they're cool enough to handle, peel and dice them.

Bottle suitable for refrigerator storage; not approved for canning

3. Combine the roasted shallots with the blueberries, sugar, vinegar, ginger, garlic, allspice, and cinnamon in a large nonreactive pot and slowly bring to a boil, stirring frequently to prevent scorching. Reduce the heat and simmer until thickened, about 30 minutes. Purée with an immersion blender.

PRESERVE

⊘ **Refrigerate:** Cool, cover, and refrigerate for up to 3 weeks.

Ⓒ **Can:** Use the boiling-water method as described on page 20. Ladle the ketchup into clean, hot 4-ounce or half-pint jars, leaving ¼ inch of headspace between the top of the ketchup and the lid. Run a bubble tool along the inside of the glass to release trapped air. Wipe the rims clean; center lids on the jars and screw on jar bands until they are just fingertip-tight. Process the jars by submerging them in boiling water to cover by 2 inches for 15 minutes. Turn off the heat, remove the canner lid, and let the jars rest in the water for 5 minutes. Remove the jars and set aside for 24 hours. Check the seals, then store in a cool, dark place for up to 1 year.

USE IT UP!

Sweet Potato Oven Fries

Serves 4

Sweet potato fries are a great alternative to your regular spud side. Roasted in the oven, they take on a wonderful caramelized exterior but stay sweet and creamy inside. Serve them with Blueberry Ketchup for an extra-delicious, extra-colorful BBQ addition.

INGREDIENTS

2 pounds sweet potatoes, peeled and cut into 2-inch pieces

1 tablespoon olive oil

1 teaspoon chili powder

1 teaspoon dried thyme leaves

Salt and freshly ground black pepper

Blueberry Ketchup (see page 96), for serving

PREPARE

1. Preheat the oven to 425°F.

2. Toss the sweet potatoes with the oil, chili powder, thyme, and a pinch of salt and pepper. Arrange on a rimmed baking sheet in a single layer. Roast for about 20 minutes, until dark brown in spots and tender throughout. Serve with Blueberry Ketchup.

BLUEBERRY VINEGAR

Makes about 1 quart

You'll be surprised at the versatility of this vinegar. You can use it in vinaigrettes, sure, but it's so good you'll want to drink it. And you can, in Blueberry Shrub. Raspberries, strawberries, and blackberries are well served by this treatment, too. A well-stocked pantry can never have too many flavored vinegars.

INGREDIENTS

- **1** pint blueberries
- **2** cups distilled white vinegar
- **1** cup sugar

PREPARE

1. Sterilize a 1-quart canning jar by submerging it in boiling water for 10 minutes. Add the berries to the hot jar.

2. Bring the vinegar and sugar just to the boil, stirring to dissolve the sugar, and then pour over the berries. Top the jar with a square of wax or parchment paper larger than the opening to prevent the lid from corroding. Screw on the lid and shake the jar. Set aside in a cool, dark place for about 1 week, shaking the jar daily. Strain out the solids, sterilize the jar again, and decant the vinegar back into the resterilized jar or some other decorative food-grade jar that has been sterilized.

PRESERVE

Keeps at room temperature for about 3 months.

Refrigerate: Will keep in the refrigerator for about 6 months.

USE IT UP!

Blueberry Shrub

Serves 1

What's old is new again. Blueberry Shrub is one of those oldies but goodies that is seeing a revival of interest. And why not? Popular in colonial times, it's a great quencher with a dash of history on the side.

INGREDIENTS

- Ice
- **2** tablespoons Blueberry Vinegar
- Seltzer or water

PREPARE

Fill a tall glass with ice. Add the vinegar and top with seltzer or water.

→ This recipe is equally delicious with any berry vinegar.

CLASSIC BLUEBERRY JAM

Makes 5 cups

Blueberry jam is perhaps one of the easiest jams to make; if you're new to the preserving craft this is a great place to start. And, well, let's face it, even if you're an old pro you can never have too much blueberry jam. Scrumptious and not nearly as common as strawberry and grape in the grocery-store aisle, blueberry jam on the shelf is the telltale sign that a canner is in the house (or at least has left behind a very thoughtful hostess gift).

INGREDIENTS

- **2** quarts blueberries (about 2½ pounds)
- ¼ cup water
- **4** cups sugar
- ¼ cup bottled lemon juice

PREPARE

1. Combine the berries and water in a large nonreactive pot and slowly bring to a boil, stirring and crushing the berries to release their juice. Add the sugar and lemon juice, stirring to dissolve the sugar. Reduce the heat and continue to cook at a vigorous simmer, stirring frequently, until the jam reaches the gel stage (see page 28).

2. Remove from the heat. Allow the jam to rest for 5 minutes, giving it an occasional gentle stir to release trapped air; it will thicken slightly. Skim off any foam.

PRESERVE

Refrigerate: Cool, cover, and refrigerate for up to 3 weeks.

Can: Use the boiling-water method as described on page 20. Ladle the jam into clean, hot 4-ounce or half-pint jars, leaving ¼ inch of headspace between the top of the jam and the lid. Run a bubble tool along the inside of the glass to release trapped air. Wipe the rims clean; center lids on the jars and screw on jar bands until they are just fingertip-tight. Process the jars by submerging them in boiling water to cover by 2 inches for 10 minutes. Turn off the heat, remove the canner lid, and let the jars rest in the water for 5 minutes. Remove the jars and set aside for 24 hours. Check the seals, then store in a cool, dark place for up to 1 year.

VARIATION:

Blueberry Bourbon Jam

Add ¼ cup bourbon to the nearly gelled jam for a luscious twist on this classic recipe.

USE IT UP!

Pan-Roasted Chicken with Blueberry Reduction

Serves 4–6

I know that some of the recipes in this book might sound weird, and this blueberry and chicken combo is probably one of them. But the flavors really work together. The roasting, of course, renders the skin a rich, mahogany brown that looks terrific and tastes even better. And the sweet and sour flavors of the reduction are a perfect match — the candy flavor of the fruit marries with the sweetness of the caramelized skin, and the tang of the fruit brings an acidic counterpoint.

INGREDIENTS

1   chicken, cut into 10 pieces (breasts halved, and wings and back reserved for stock)

2   teaspoons kosher salt

1   tablespoon unsalted butter

1   tablespoon extra-virgin olive oil

1   shallot, finely diced

1   tablespoon all-purpose flour

1   cup dry white wine

1   cup chicken stock, preferably homemade

1   pinch dried thyme
    Freshly ground black pepper

2   tablespoons Classic Blueberry Jam (see page 99) or Blueberry Bourbon Jam (see page 99)

PREPARE

1. Preheat the oven to 375°F.

2. Using paper towels, dry the chicken pieces thoroughly. Sprinkle with the salt.

    Heat the butter and oil in a large oven-safe skillet over medium-high heat. Add the chicken, putting the thickest pieces in the center of the pan, and cook until the skin has darkened to a deep golden brown and the pieces easily release from the pan. Using tongs, turn the chicken pieces over and slide the pan onto the center rack of the oven. Roast for about 20 minutes, until the internal temperature reaches 165°F. Remove the chicken to a platter and set aside in a warm oven (do not cover the chicken or the skin will lose its crispness).

3. Slip an oven mitt over the handle of your pan or you will certainly reach for the hot handle during the next step (and we can compare scars). Drain off all but 2 tablespoons of the fat in the pan. Return the pan to the heat, add the shallot, and sauté until it is translucent, about 2 minutes. Whisk in the flour and then the wine. Simmer until thickened, about 5 minutes. Add the stock, thyme, and pepper to taste, and simmer until reduced and slightly thickened, 2 to 3 minutes. Add the jam and whisk to dissolve.

    Ladle the sauce onto a high-sided serving platter and top with the chicken pieces (ladling sauce over chicken would cover up and soften the gorgeous brown skin). Serve immediately.

→ This recipe is also delicious with raspberry jam or Blackberry Gastrique (page 90) used in place of the blueberry jam.

Cherries

*C*herries are a fabulous fruit to preserve. While you can preserve both sweet and sour varieties, I find that sour cherries are much harder to find, even in farmers' markets. So I use sweet, dark cherries in my recipes. Their color is so alluring, deeper than ruby, almost black, their texture is nothing but seductive, and somehow they manage to be all at once plump, firm, and yielding. Mercy.

Cherries are often the first of the stone fruits — a produce family that includes peaches, plums, nectarines, and apricots — to appear in the market. The pit, or stone, of all of these fruits contains a low level of cyanide. Did your mind instantly flash on a calculation of all of the cherry pits you've swallowed in your lifetime? Don't worry; swallowing the pits from a few cherries isn't going to have any impact on your health. Some recipes even include specially processed pits for their almond-like flavor. While eating a few raw pits won't hurt you, I pit all of my stone fruit when I use them in recipes.

While I am not a fan of gadgets, in my view a cherry pitter is an essential tool for any recipe that calls for more than two cherries. There are a wide variety of them on the market, from very low-tech varieties to more complicated designs. I use the simplest kind. It looks like a pair of pliers but the ends have a little cup with a hole in it on one side and a small metal plunger on the other that pushes the pit out when you squeeze them together. It's quick, efficient, and great for martini olives, too!

CHERRY MOSTARDA

Makes about 4 cups

Mostarda has ancient roots, dating back to medieval times when sweet fruits were bathed in a purée of mustard and sugar to preserve them for the upper classes who could afford the luxury of such exotic ingredients. This is not quite a mustard but has enough mustardy tang to make it your new favorite sandwich topper. The yellow mustard seeds give it an interesting texture and look great in the jar, too. Make multiple batches because once word gets out, everyone is going to be vying for space on your gift list for this one. A treat fit for the royal court to be sure.

INGREDIENTS

- **2** tablespoons dry mustard
- **2** cups fruity red wine
- **2** quarts cherries (about 3 pounds), stemmed, pitted, and halved
- **3** cups sugar
- **½** cup apple cider vinegar
- **¼** cup mustard seeds
- **¼** cup bottled lemon juice
- **1** teaspoon freshly ground black pepper
- **½** teaspoon salt

PREPARE

1. In a small bowl, whisk the dry mustard with 1 tablespoon of the wine to make a slurry. Combine the slurry, the remaining wine, and the cherries, sugar, vinegar, mustard seeds, lemon juice, pepper, and salt in a large nonreactive pot and bring to a boil. Reduce the heat and simmer vigorously until the liquid is reduced by half and the cherries become soft and begin to lose their shape, 15 to 20 minutes.

2. Remove from the heat. Allow the mostarda to rest for 5 minutes, giving it an occasional gentle stir to release trapped air; it will thicken slightly. Skim off any foam.

PRESERVE

Refrigerate: Cool, cover, and refrigerate for up to 3 weeks.

Can: Use the boiling-water method as described on page 20. Ladle the mostarda into clean, hot 4-ounce or half-pint jars, leaving ¼ inch of headspace between the top of the mostarda and the lid. Run a bubble tool along the inside of the glass to release trapped air. Wipe the rims clean; center lids on the jars and screw on jar bands until they are just fingertip-tight. Process the jars by submerging them in boiling water to cover by 2 inches for 10 minutes. Turn off the heat, remove the canner lid, and let the jars rest in the water for 5 minutes. Remove the jars and set aside for 24 hours. Check the seals, then store in a cool, dark place for up to 1 year.

USE IT UP!

Nut-Crusted Goat Cheese with Cherry Mostarda

Makes one log

Okay, when I was growing up, I could tell that the party was a big, fancy affair when they rolled out the nut-crusted port wine cheese ball. My taste buds have led me toward more hand-crafted fromages, but I am still a sucker for some nut-crusted cheese. Here is an updated version of my childhood treat, suitable for the swankiest soiree.

INGREDIENTS

- ½ cup pecans, finely chopped
- **2** teaspoons olive oil
- ½ teaspoon dried thyme
  Salt and freshly ground black pepper
- **1** (7-ounce) log fresh goat cheese, preferably locally produced
- ½ cup Cherry Mostarda (see page 103), for serving
  Water crackers

PREPARE

1. Preheat the oven to 325°F.

2. In a small bowl, combine the pecans with the oil, thyme, and a pinch of salt and pepper, and stir to combine. Spread the mixture on a baking sheet and roast for 5 to 7 minutes, until fragrant, keeping a close eye on the nuts so that they don't burn. Let cool completely.

3. Roll the goat cheese log in the nut mixture, pressing gently to encourage the nuts to coat the cheese. Serve immediately, accompanied by Cherry Mostarda and water crackers, or wrap the cheese tightly in wax paper and refrigerate for up to 2 days.

→ Classic Cherry Jam (page 112) is also a delicious accompaniment to this cheese dish.

CHERRY ALMOND RELISH

Makes about 5 cups

Cherries are one of those fruits that can teeter on the edge between sweet and savory so elegantly. This relish takes advantage of that balancing act in a spread that tempers its candy-ness with an assertive vinegar tang. Use it in place of mayonnaise on a sandwich, where the almonds will add a pleasing little crunch.

INGREDIENTS

- **3** cups sugar
- **1** cup apple cider vinegar
- **½** cup water
- **2** quarts cherries (about 3 pounds), stemmed, pitted, and halved
- **¼** cup bottled lemon juice
- **1** onion, finely diced
- **1** garlic clove, minced
- **1** teaspoon ground allspice
- **½** cup slivered almonds

PREPARE

1. Combine the sugar, vinegar, and water in a large nonreactive pot and slowly bring to a boil, stirring to dissolve the sugar. Add the cherries, lemon juice, onion, garlic, and allspice, and simmer vigorously until thickened, 25 to 30 minutes. Add the almonds and simmer for another 5 minutes.

2. Remove from the heat. Allow the jam to rest for 5 minutes, giving it an occasional gentle stir to release trapped air; it will thicken slightly. Skim off any foam.

PRESERVE

Refrigerate: Cool, cover, and refrigerate for up to 3 weeks.

Can: Use the boiling-water method as described on page 20. Ladle the relish into clean, hot half-pint jars, leaving ½ inch of headspace between the top of the relish and the lid. Run a bubble tool along the inside of the glass to release trapped air. Wipe the rims clean; center lids on the jars and screw on jar bands until they are just fingertip-tight. Process the jars by submerging them in boiling water to cover by 2 inches for 10 minutes. Turn off the heat, remove the canner lid, and let the jars rest in the water for 5 minutes. Remove the jars and set aside for 24 hours. Check the seals, then store in a cool, dark place for up to 1 year.

USE IT UP!

Turkey Wrap with Cherry Almond Relish

Makes 1 wrap sandwich

Thanksgiving leftovers? You might want to roast a bigger bird just so you can be sure to get yourself one of these. I'm crazy about Cherry Almond Relish, and it makes this wrap really special. You can substitute any kind of meat you like or leave it out for a veggie nosh.

INGREDIENTS

- **1** burrito-size tortilla wrap
- **1** tablespoon Cherry Almond Relish (see page 106)
- **½** cup fresh lettuce, such as arugula, spinach, mâche, or a mix
- **¼** pound cooked, sliced turkey
- **1** ounce mild cheese, such as domestic Camembert, sliced

PREPARE

Lay the wrap flat. Smear the relish in a 2-inch band across the middle of the wrap, leaving about a 1-inch margin on either side. Layer the lettuce, turkey, and cheese on the bottom third of wrap, maintaining that 1-inch margin. Fold in the left and right sides of the tortilla and then, starting with the edge closest to you, roll up the wrap away from you and over the ingredients. Secure with a toothpick if desired.

→ Another good relish to try with this wrap is Savory Cranberry Relish (page 116).

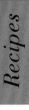
MARASCHINO CHERRIES

Makes 1 quart

Traditional maraschino cherries are made with maraschino liqueur, a lovely but somewhat pricey and elusive tipple to stock in the home bar. A decent-quality vodka and a bit of almond extract make for great cherries and a lovely infused liqueur with much less hassle and expense. We can't make enough of this one — its vibrant cherry taste and eye-catching red color make it a real crowd-pleaser. Don't leave out the sugar; it adds flavor and helps maintain the texture of the fruit so the cherries don't turn to mush.

INGREDIENTS

- **2** cups cherries, stemmed and pitted
- **2** cups vodka
- **1** cup sugar
- **1** teaspoon almond extract

PREPARE

Sterilize a 1-quart glass jar by submerging it in boiling water for 10 minutes. Combine the cherries, vodka, sugar, and almond extract in the jar and shake to dissolve the sugar. Set aside in a cool, dark place for 5 days to allow the flavors to develop, shaking daily.

PRESERVE

Refrigerate: Store in the refrigerator for up to 4 months.

USE IT UP!

Momma's Manhattan

Serves 1

My mom, Nancé, loves everything about NYC, including its namesake cocktail. We have gone on crawls through town looking for the best and found some great sips. (Sometimes my work research is extra fun.) She always takes hers "on the sweet side," so I've come up with this recipe that's very cherry, just for her.

INGREDIENTS

- **2** ounces rye whiskey or bourbon
- **1** ounce sweet vermouth
- **½** ounce infusing liquid from Maraschino Cherries
  Ice
- **2** Maraschino Cherries

PREPARE

Combine the whiskey, sweet vermouth, and cherry infusing liquid in a cocktail shaker filled with ice. Cap and shake vigorously for at least 1 minute. Strain into a chilled martini glass. Serve, garnished with the cherries.

CHERRY ANCHO CHILE JAM

Makes about 5½ cups

Ancho chiles are the dried version of poblano peppers, rich in flavor and relatively light in heat. You can find ancho chiles pre-ground or buy them whole and give them a whir in your coffee grinder. Add enough chile to suit your taste — a little gives a light smoky flavor and a bit of a tongue tingle, while a bit more yields a distinctly sweet and spicy jam.

INGREDIENTS

- **2** cups sugar
- **2** teaspoons Pomona's Universal Pectin
- **2** quarts cherries (about 3 pounds), stemmed, pitted, and chopped
- **1** cup water
- **1-2** tablespoons ancho chile powder
- **2** teaspoons calcium water (from the Pomona's Universal Pectin kit)
- **¼** cup bottled lemon juice

PREPARE

1. Combine the sugar and pectin in a small bowl and set aside.

2. Place the cherries, water, and chile powder in a large nonreactive pot and slowly bring to a boil, stirring frequently to prevent scorching. Simmer until fruit has softened and released its juices, about 10 minutes. Stir in the calcium water and lemon juice. Slowly add the pectin mixture, stirring constantly to avoid clumping. Bring to a boil, reduce the heat, and simmer for 1 to 2 minutes, continuing to stir constantly, until the sugar is completely dissolved.

3. Remove from the heat. Allow the jam to rest for 5 minutes, giving it an occasional gentle stir to release trapped air; it will thicken slightly. Skim off any foam.

PRESERVE

Refrigerate: Cool, cover, and refrigerate for up to 3 weeks.

Can: Use the boiling-water method as described on page 20. Ladle the jam into clean, hot 4-ounce or half-pint jars, leaving ¼ inch of headspace between the top of the jam and the lid. Run a bubble tool along the inside of the glass to release trapped air. Wipe the rims clean; center lids on the jars and screw on jar bands until they are just fingertip-tight. Process the jars by submerging them in boiling water to cover by 2 inches for 10 minutes. Turn off the heat, remove the canner lid, and let the jars rest in the water for 5 minutes. Remove the jars and set aside for 24 hours. Check the seals, then store in a cool, dark place for up to 1 year.

USE IT UP!

Pulled-Pork Tacos with Cherry Ancho Chile Jam

Serves 6–8, with leftovers

I do my pulled pork in a slow cooker. I know, I know, not so authentic — but it's still the makings of a great meal. This is a great one for Friday night when you want something a little special but might not have extra time after a busy day to turn it out. Put it together in the morning and it will be ready for family movie night or a fun, easy dinner party.

INGREDIENTS

- **1** (3- to 4-pound) pork butt roast, preferably bone-in
- **1** cup red wine
- **1** cup whole tomatoes, preferably home-canned
- **4** garlic cloves, peeled
- **1** onion, halved and peeled
- **1** tablespoon chili powder
- **1** teaspoon dried thyme
- **1** bay leaf
  Salt and freshly ground black pepper
- **12–16** corn or flour tortillas
  About ¼ cup Cherry Ancho Chile Jam (see page 110)
  Accompaniments of choice, such as sour cream, chopped cilantro, bell pepper strips, diced jalapeno, and pickled chiles

PREPARE

1. Heat a large skillet over medium-high heat. Place the roast in the pan and sear on all sides, 2 to 3 minutes per side.

2. Place the roast in a slow cooker. Deglaze the pan with the wine, scraping up the browned bits with a whisk or spatula as you simmer the wine for a minute or two.

3. Add this wine sauce to the slow cooker, along with the tomatoes, garlic, onion, chili powder, thyme, and bay leaf. Season generously with salt and pepper. Cover and set the heat to low. Allow the slow cooker to do its magic for 8 to 10 hours, until the pork is fork-tender (which means that a fork inserted into the meat slides back out again easily).

4. Remove the roast to a cutting board. Strain the liquid from the slow cooker through a fine-mesh sieve into a glass measuring cup or gravy separator, and allow it to settle for 10 to 15 minutes. Skim off the top layer of fat and pour the rest of the drippings into a small saucepan. Bring to a boil and simmer until reduced by half, 15 to 20 minutes.

5. Meanwhile, use two forks to pull the pork into shreds, discarding bone and excess fat. Transfer to a serving platter and moisten with the reduced pan drippings.

6. Lightly grill the tortillas over the open flame of your gas stove burners or in a dry skillet. Paint the inside of each tortilla with 1 to 2 teaspoons of Cherry Ancho Chile Jam, and fill with the pulled pork and accompaniments of your choice.

→ These tacos are also delicious served with Apricot Habanero Salsa (page 72).

CLASSIC CHERRY JAM

Makes 5 cups

When I am asked to name a favorite jam, this is the one. The color is a deep, sexy red and the texture is soft and inviting — thick, but syrupy enough to coat your tongue with sweet, sharp cherry flavor, and studded with chunks of fruit. It's great on toast, but I think the best way to have it is with fresh chèvre and a little cracked black pepper. Serve it that way on some crostini for a cocktail nibble. (Or, honestly, it makes a great topping for a spoon. Just dip and lick.)

INGREDIENTS

- **2** quarts cherries (about 3 pounds), stemmed, pitted, and halved
- **¼** cup water
- **4** cups sugar
- **¼** cup bottled lemon juice

PREPARE

1. Combine the cherries and water in a medium nonreactive pot. Bring to a boil, stirring and crushing the fruit to release the juice. Add the sugar and stir to dissolve. Stir in the lemon juice. Continue to cook, stirring frequently, until the preserves reach the gel stage (see page 28), about 20 minutes.

2. Remove from the heat. Allow the jam to rest for 5 minutes, giving it an occasional gentle stir to release trapped air; it will thicken slightly. Skim off any foam.

PRESERVE

Refrigerate: Cool, cover, and refrigerate for up to 3 weeks.

Can: Use the boiling-water method as described on page 20. Ladle the jam into clean, hot 4-ounce or half-pint jars, leaving ¼ inch of headspace between the top of the jam and the lid. Run a bubble tool along the inside of the glass to release trapped air. Wipe the rims clean; center lids on the jars and screw on jar bands until they are just fingertip-tight. Process the jars by submerging them in boiling water to cover by 2 inches for 10 minutes. Turn off the heat, remove the canner lid, and let the jars rest in the water for 5 minutes. Remove the jars and set aside for 24 hours. Check the seals, then store in a cool, dark place for up to 1 year.

USE IT UP!

Sautéed Duck Breast with Cherry Reduction

Serves 4–6

This dish is good. Cancel-the-reservations, we're-staying-home-for-dinner good. I often make this for special occasions, when I really want to treat my guests — and myself — to a scrumptious meal. If you are looking for something special for Valentine's Day or a star showing for a birthday celebration, this is the one. Puréed sweet potatoes or pumpkin risotto and sautéed bitter greens round out the meal.

INGREDIENTS

3–4 duck breasts (about 2 pounds total)
  Salt
1 shallot, minced
1 cup fruity red wine
½ cup chicken stock, preferably homemade
1 teaspoon cornstarch
2 tablespoons Classic Cherry Jam (see page 112)
  Freshly ground black pepper

PREPARE

1. Preheat the oven to 400°F (if you want the duck cooked to more than rare).

2. Heat a large skillet over medium-high heat. Score the fat on the duck breasts by lightly grazing over it with a very sharp knife in a ½-inch crosshatch pattern, being careful not to cut through to the meat. Sprinkle generously with salt and place fat side down in the pan. Reduce the heat to medium-low and cook until the breasts are browned and the majority of the fat has rendered out, 10 to 12 minutes. Turn and cook another 3 to 5 minutes, until browned, and then remove from the pan. At this point, the meat will be quite rare. If this is to your taste, you can stop here; just set the duck aside while you make the sauce. Otherwise, transfer the breasts to a rimmed baking sheet and pop them in the oven for 3 to 5 minutes for medium doneness (be careful not to overcook or the duck will take on a liverish flavor).

3. Pour out all but 2 tablespoons of drippings from the pan (reserve the drippings for another use; duck fat is marvelous). Add the shallots to the pan and sauté until translucent, 1 to 2 minutes. Add the wine, increase the heat to medium-high, and simmer until the mixture is reduced to a syrup, 3 to 5 minutes.

4. Stir the cornstarch into the chicken stock to create a slurry and add it to the pan, whisking until it reaches a boil and thickens. Whisk in the cherry jam, simmer for 1 to 2 minutes to thicken, and season with salt and pepper.

5. To serve, slice the duck on the bias and arrange on a platter or individual plates. Spoon the sauce over the top.

→ The sauce for this dish is also delicious with Cranberry Jelly (page 118) in place of the cherry jam.

Keeping Cooking Wine on Hand

A little wine in the pot heightens the flavor of many dishes. Of course, wine brings its own delicious taste, but more than that, it helps open up the flavor of the food. Why? Because some flavor compounds are not water soluble. You need the alcohol to break them down and make them accessible to your taste buds. Without the alcohol in the dish, you would miss a whole level of palate pleasers.

It's an odd day when I don't have an open bottle on the counter, but to make sure that I always have some cooking wine at the ready, I keep a little secret stash — in my freezer! The freezing doesn't greatly affect the taste (though I wouldn't freeze wine destined for the glass). I simply keep two pint-size canning jars on the door of my freezer (one for white and one for red) and pour in any leftover dregs of bottles (or even glasses!) that haven't been finished. Because of the alcohol content of the wine, it never freezes beyond the slush stage, so I can just scoop out whatever I need when I need it without having to pop a cork.

Cranberries

Cranberries. So Pilgrimmy delicious. They are probably forever married in the American psyche to the holidays — you would be hard-pressed to find a Thanksgiving table without them represented. And the juice — particularly since Carrie Bradshaw got us all quaffing cosmopolitans — has its fans. Yet few of us cook with the fresh, raw berries. Until now, I hope.

Though their tart, slightly bitter taste keeps them from the "berries to eat out of hand" category, these crimson beauties are a delight in the kitchen. Their naturally high pectin level means that they gel easily into jams and jellies. And their flavor, while not as sweet as that of other berries, plays well with savory dishes. You can add the berries, fresh or frozen, directly to baked goods, or you can process them into juice, jam, or sauce to mellow their pucker power.

Cranberries grow in many cool, temperate parts of the world, ripening in the falling temperatures of autumn, and they can be found fresh in the market from then through the end of the year. They last quite a long time under refrigeration; you can keep them in your crisper for up to 2 months. Give them a rinse before using and pick through to remove any shriveled berries before proceeding with your recipe. If you want to keep them for longer, freeze as you would other berries (see page 84). They make for fantastic eating during the holidays or anytime.

SAVORY CRANBERRY RELISH

Makes 6 cups

Ah, cranberries, they're not just for Thanksgiving anymore. At least not if you're using them this way. Don't be put off by the long list of ingredients; the prep is a snap. The warm spices of this relish pair perfectly with the smoke of grilled foods, so add some to your summer spread and make every day a holiday.

INGREDIENTS

- **1** cup lightly packed dark brown sugar
- **1** cup honey, preferably wild and local
- **1** cup water
- **½** cup red wine vinegar
  Zest and juice of 1 orange
- **1** shallot, minced
- **1** tablespoon minced fresh ginger
- **1** bay leaf
- **1** cinnamon stick
- **1** teaspoon ground coriander
- **1** teaspoon mustard seeds
- **½** teaspoon ground cloves
- **½** teaspoon salt
- **¼** teaspoon freshly ground black pepper
- **2** pounds cranberries

PREPARE

1. Combine the sugar, honey, water, vinegar, orange zest and juice, shallot, ginger, bay leaf, cinnamon stick, coriander, mustard seeds, cloves, salt, and pepper in a large nonreactive pot and bring to a boil. Reduce the heat and simmer for 5 minutes. Add the cranberries and continue to simmer until the berries burst and the sauce thickens, 15 to 20 minutes.

2. Remove from the heat. Allow the jam to rest for 5 minutes, giving it an occasional gentle stir to release trapped air; it will thicken slightly. Skim off any foam.

PRESERVE

Refrigerate: Cool, cover, and refrigerate for up to 3 weeks.

Can: Use the boiling-water method as described on page 20. Ladle the relish into clean, hot half-pint jars, leaving ½ inch of headspace between the top of the relish and the lid. Run a bubble tool along the inside of the glass to release trapped air. Wipe the rims clean; center lids on the jars and screw on jar bands until they are just fingertip-tight. Process the jars by submerging them in boiling water to cover by 2 inches for 10 minutes. Turn off the heat, remove the canner lid, and let the jars rest in the water for 5 minutes. Remove the jars and set aside for 24 hours. Check the seals, then store in a cool, dark place for up to 1 year.

USE IT UP!

Blue Cheese Biscuits with Savory Cranberry Relish

Makes about 16

Biscuits should be their own food group. Breakfast, lunch, or dinner, it is better on a biscuit. One of my favorite childhood memories is my Southern-born, Southern-bred great-grandmother, in a cloud of flour, rolling out her biscuits for our breakfast meal. I am sure that she would scoff at me for filling them with blue cheese, but hey, I guess that's what I get for being a Yankee.

INGREDIENTS

- **2** cups all-purpose flour
- **1** teaspoon salt
- **½** teaspoon baking powder
- **½** cup (1 stick) cold unsalted butter, cubed
- **½** cup plus 2 tablespoons milk
- **2** ounces blue cheese, crumbled
  Savory Cranberry Relish (see page 116), for serving

PREPARE

1. Preheat the oven to 425°F.

2. Combine the flour, salt, and baking powder in a food processor and pulse once or twice to blend. Add the butter and pulse until the mixture resembles coarse crumbs. Add the ½ cup milk and the cheese and process just until a dough forms.

3. Transfer the dough to a lightly floured work surface. Use a few strokes with a rolling pin to flatten the dough to a ½-inch-thick disk. Do not overwork the dough. Cut into 2-inch triangles. Brush with the 2 tablespoons milk. Bake for 18 to 20 minutes, until lightly browned. Serve with Savory Cranberry Relish.

→ Cherry Almond Relish (page 106) is another delicious accompaniment to these biscuits.

CRANBERRY JELLY

Makes 5 cups

Designed to more closely replicate the jelly-tube-in-a-can that is often demanded by at least a few at the Thanksgiving table, this thick, sweet gel is a crowd-pleaser for lovers of the (gasp!) commercial version. But its fruit-forward flavor will suit the homemade-sauce lovers, too. Since it's not made exclusively from fruit juice, it's not technically a jelly, but your guests will be too busy swooning over its taste to argue about semantics.

INGREDIENTS

- **2** pounds cranberries
- **2** cups water
- **1** cinnamon stick
- **1** teaspoon coriander seeds
- **½** teaspoon ground allspice
- **½** teaspoon black peppercorns
- **½** teaspoon salt
- **4** cups sugar

PREPARE

1. Combine the cranberries, water, cinnamon stick, coriander seeds, allspice, peppercorns, and salt in a large nonreactive pot and bring to a boil. Reduce the heat and simmer until the fruit has burst and the sauce has thickened, 15 to 20 minutes.

2. Remove from the heat, pluck out the cinnamon stick, and run the mixture through a food mill. Return the purée to the pot, add the sugar, and bring to a boil. Simmer until the gel stage is reached (see page 28), 10 to 15 minutes, stirring constantly. (Because of the high pectin content of cranberries, this jelly can overcook in a heartbeat. Keep a close watch on the pot.)

3. Remove from the heat. Allow the jelly to rest for 5 minutes, giving it an occasional gentle stir to release trapped air; it will thicken slightly. Skim off any foam.

PRESERVE

Refrigerate: Cool, cover, and refrigerate for up to 3 weeks.

Can: Use the boiling-water method as described on page 20. Ladle the jelly into clean, hot 4-ounce or half-pint jars, leaving ¼ inch of headspace between the top of the jelly and the lid. Run a bubble tool along the inside of the glass to release trapped air. Wipe the rims clean; center lids on the jars and screw on jar bands until they are just fingertip-tight. Process the jars by submerging them in boiling water to cover by 2 inches for 10 minutes. Turn off the heat, remove the canner lid, and let the jars rest in the water for 5 minutes. Remove the jars and set aside for 24 hours. Check the seals, then store in a cool, dark place for up to 1 year.

USE IT UP!

Cranberry Mayonnaise

Makes about ¾ cup

Make your own mayonnaise? That's right. If you have never given this little trick of kitchen witchery a try, you will be shocked at the huge difference between this authentic creation and the stuff you get in a jar. It's like cashmere versus polyester. I use straight-from-the-nest farm eggs because they taste heavenly, and also because they are fresher than those in the store — a definite bonus anytime, but particularly when dealing with raw eggs. This mayo is a showstopper on a turkey sandwich, or any sandwich or wrap, for that matter.

INGREDIENTS

- **1** impeccably farm-fresh egg yolk (egg white reserved for another use)
- **2** teaspoons freshly squeezed lemon juice
- **1** teaspoon Dijon mustard
  Pinch of salt
- **½** cup olive oil or neutral-flavored vegetable oil, such as organic canola
- **3** tablespoons Cranberry Jelly (see page 118)
  Freshly ground black pepper

PREPARE

1. Whisk the egg yolk in a medium bowl until lightened in texture and color, 1 to 2 minutes.

2. Whisk in the lemon juice, mustard, and salt. Slowly whisk in the oil, starting with just a few drops at a time, and adding more oil only after each addition has been fully incorporated.

3. Whisk in the jelly and season with a few grinds of pepper. This mayonnaise will keep, covered and refrigerated, for up to 5 days.

CRANBERRY MOLASSES

Makes 2 cups

I love the pomegranate molasses that is often used in Persian food; its sweet/tart flavor can really jazz up a dish. This cranberry molasses works the same way and is easy to make with just a small amount of berries you might have left over from the holidays. Drizzle a little over a salad or a bowl of rice for an unexpected blast of flavor.

INGREDIENTS

4 cups water

½ pound cranberries

2 cups dark brown sugar

PREPARE

1. Combine the water and cranberries in a medium nonreactive pot and bring to a boil. Reduce the heat and simmer until the berries pop and soften, 15 to 20 minutes. Remove from the heat and press through a fine-mesh sieve.

2. Combine the strained cranberry juice and sugar in a small skillet or saucier and bring to a boil. Reduce the heat and simmer until thick enough to coat the back of a spoon, 10 to 15 minutes (the molasses will continue to thicken as it cools).

PRESERVE

Refrigerate: Cool, cover, and refrigerate for up to 3 weeks.

Can: Use the boiling-water method as described on page 20. Ladle the molasses into clean, hot 4-ounce jars, leaving ¼ inch of headspace between the top of the molasses and the lid. Run a bubble tool along the inside of the glass to release trapped air. Wipe the rims clean; center lids on the jars and screw on jar bands until they are just fingertip-tight. Process the jars by submerging them in boiling water to cover by 2 inches for 10 minutes. Turn off the heat, remove the canner lid, and let the jars rest in the water for 5 minutes. Remove the jars and set aside for 24 hours. Check the seals, then store in a cool, dark place for up to 1 year.

USE IT UP!

Duck Confit Salad with Cranberry Molasses

Serves 2

I don't know what it is about duck, but the moment the air turns chill, it's what I want. I become obsessed. I'll take it any way it's prepared — roasted, pan-seared, in soups, or like this, in a gorgeous confit. The rich flavors really hit the spot. The bitter greens, dressed in the tart pan sauce, cut the decadence of the duck just enough, and the sweet-and-sour molasses makes it a standout dish, good enough for a smart little lunch for friends.

INGREDIENTS

- **1** tablespoon extra-virgin olive oil
- **4** slices from a baguette
- **1** garlic clove, smashed and peeled
- **2** confit duck legs
- **1** small sweet potato, peeled and cut into ½-inch dice
- **1** shallot, sliced
- **½** cup white wine
- **1** tablespoon red wine vinegar
- **1** head frisée or other bitter lettuce, torn into pieces
- **1** cup arugula or other spicy greens
  Salt and freshly ground black pepper
- **2** tablespoons Cranberry Molasses (see page 120)

PREPARE

1. Heat the oil in a medium skillet over medium-high heat. Add the baguette slices and toast until golden, about 3 minutes per side. Remove from the pan and rub one side of each toast lightly with the garlic clove. Set aside.

→ This dish is also good with Blackberry Gastrique (page 90) in place of the Cranberry Molasses.

2. Add the duck legs to the skillet and weight down with another heavy pan to maximize their contact with the hot cooking surface. Reduce the heat to medium-low and cook until the skin is brown and crisp and most of the fat has been rendered, 10 to 12 minutes per side. Remove from the pan and set aside.

3. Raise the heat to medium, add the sweet potato to the pan, season with salt, and sauté until cooked through and beginning to brown, 8 to 10 minutes. Remove with a slotted spoon and set aside.

4. Add the shallot to the pan and sauté until translucent, 1 to 2 minutes. Deglaze the pan with the white wine, scraping up the browned bits, and simmer until reduced to a syrup, 2 to 3 minutes. Whisk in the red wine vinegar and salt and pepper to taste, and then remove from the heat. Toss the frisée and arugula in the hot pan until the greens just begin to wilt.

5. Divide the greens and their sauce between two plates. Top with sweet potato cubes and then a duck leg. Drizzle molasses over the salad, adjust seasoning, and serve with the garlicky toasts.

CRANBERRY QUINCE PRESERVES

Makes about 9 cups

This is probably one of the prettiest preserves in the book. Adding the sugar early on in the cooking ensures that the quince pieces hold their shape and the sugar syrup remains clear. The late addition of the cranberries tinges the syrup and brings a tart edge to the sweet, tender pieces of quince. It's a fun one to make and a real star on the shelf.

INGREDIENTS

- **2** cups water
- **¼** cup bottled lemon juice
- **3** pounds quince
- **4** cups sugar
- **1** pound cranberries

PREPARE

1. Combine the water and lemon juice in a large nonreactive pot. Core and chop the quince into 1-inch pieces, adding them to the lemon water as you go to prevent browning. Add the sugar and bring to a boil over medium-high heat, stirring to dissolve the sugar and prevent scorching. Reduce the heat and simmer, stirring occasionally, until the quince is tender and translucent, 20 to 40 minutes, depending on the ripeness of the fruit.

2. Add the cranberries and continue to simmer until the cranberries burst and the preserves are thick, about 15 minutes.

3. Remove from the heat. Allow the preserves to rest for 5 minutes, giving the mixture an occasional gentle stir to release trapped air; it will thicken slightly. Skim off any foam.

PRESERVE

Refrigerate: Cool, cover, and refrigerate for up to 3 weeks.

Can: Use the boiling-water method as described on page 20. Ladle the preserves into clean, hot half-pint jars, leaving ¼ inch of headspace between the top of the preserves and the lid. Run a bubble tool along the inside of the glass to release trapped air. Wipe the rims clean; center lids on the jars and screw on jar bands until they are just fingertip-tight. Process the jars by submerging them in boiling water to cover by 2 inches for 10 minutes. Turn off the heat, remove the canner lid, and let the jars rest in the water for 5 minutes. Remove the jars and set aside for 24 hours. Check the seals, then store in a cool, dark place for up to 1 year.

FILLED CRÊPES, *recipe on following page* →

USE IT UP!

Filled Crêpes

Makes 16–18 (6-inch) crêpes

Crêpes, thin French pancakes, are one of those dishes that sound really fancy and complicated but are truly easy to make. Just remember that, as Jacques Pépin says, the first crêpe is for the pan. Meaning that the first crêpe will invariably stick or burn. Just feed it to your dog (or pigs, chickens, or compost bin) and keep going. Clarified butter is the key — it makes the crêpes glide over your pan and, because it lacks butter solids, has a high smoking point so it won't burn like whole butter. Use it and, once the pan gets "primed" by that first crêpe, you will be turning them out like a regular crêperie. And remember, flipping a crêpe without a spatula is just a confidence game — if you think you can do it, you can.

INGREDIENTS

6 tablespoons unsalted butter

2 eggs

1¼ cups milk

1 cup flour

Pinch of salt

Cranberry Quince Preserves
  (see page 122)

Confectioners' sugar, for dusting

PREPARE

1. Melt 2 tablespoons of the butter. Combine it with the eggs, milk, flour, and salt in a blender and purée. The mixture should have the consistency of thick cream. Alternatively, you can whisk the batter up in a large bowl until thoroughly blended. Refrigerate for at least 2 hours and up to 1 day.

2. To make clarified butter, heat the remaining 4 tablespoons butter in a small saucepan over low heat until melted. Skim off the foam. Carefully pour the golden butter into a small, heatproof bowl, leaving the white milk solids at the bottom of the pot behind. Discard the foam and solids. (Clarified butter can be made up to a week in advance, covered, and refrigerated. Reheat it before proceeding.)

3. Heat a small skillet over medium heat. Use a pastry brush to paint the pan with clarified butter. Stir the batter and pour 2 to 3 tablespoons into the pan, swirling it around to spread the batter thinly over the bottom of the pan. Cook until the edges appear dry and the crêpe begins to brown on the bottom, 1 to 2 minutes. Use tongs to lift and flip the crêpe, and let brown on the other side, about another minute. (With a little practice, you will be able to shake the pan to free the crêpe and then jerk it toward you to flip the crêpe over.) Set the cooked crêpe aside on a wire rack to cool and repeat with remaining batter.

4. Once cool, crêpes can be stacked on top of each other. To serve, spread a tablespoon or two of the preserves across the middle of each crêpe, roll up like a tube, and dust with confectioners' sugar.

DRIED CRANBERRIES

3 cups fresh cranberries will give you a generous ½ cup dried cranberries

Have some extra berries left over from the holidays? This recipe is a great way to use up as few or as many as you have on hand. The sugar helps protect the fruit during drying, keeping the skin soft and pliable. Don't skip it or the berries will dry up to papery little husks.

INGREDIENTS

- **4** cups water
- **2** cups sugar
- Up to 3 cups cranberries

PREPARE

1. Preheat the oven to 170°F. Line two 11- by 17-inch baking sheets with parchment paper.

2. Bring the water to a boil in a medium nonreactive pot. Add the sugar and stir to dissolve. Add the berries and simmer until they pop (unpopped berries will not dry properly), about 5 minutes. Remove the berries with a slotted spoon or spider and spread in a single layer on the prepared baking sheets, being careful to tease apart any clumps of berries. (You can process more berries in the same manner, using the sugar solution a second time, or refrigerate it and use it to sweeten cocktails, lemonade, or iced tea.)

PRESERVE

◉ Dry:

1. Set the baking sheets in the oven, and prop open the oven door with a wooden spoon handle to allow moisture to escape. Dry the berries in the oven for 4 to 5 hours, until most of them have dried. The berries are fully dried when you can squeeze a couple between your fingers and don't find any pulpy middles. Turn off the oven heat and allow the berries to cool in the closed oven overnight.

2. To condition the berries, transfer them to a covered container and let them sit for 1 day. This allows the dried fruit to redistribute any trapped moisture. If you notice moisture collecting on the sides of the container, repeat the drying process for another hour or so. Fully dried cranberries will keep in an airtight container for up to 1 year.

Recipes

126

USE IT UP!

Cranberries in Port

Makes about 3 cups

This is sort of a riff on the raisin sauce that is often served with ham. It's very good with pork, but don't limit yourself. The deep flavors of the port will stand up to the wildest of beasts — venison, elk, duck, and pheasant would all be lovely with it. Not feeling meaty? Try it drizzled over some halloumi (pan-fried Greek cheese).

INGREDIENTS

- ½ cup Dried Cranberries (see page 125)
- ½ cup port
- 1 cup sugar
- 1 cup water
- ¼ teaspoon ground allspice
  Freshly ground black pepper
  Salt

PREPARE

1. Combine the cranberries and port in a small bowl and let soak for at least 4 hours, and up to overnight.

2. Bring the sugar and water to a boil in a small saucepan, stirring to dissolve the sugar. Continue to boil until the syrup begins to take on a pale golden color, about 5 minutes. Remove from the heat and cool slightly. Whisk in the cranberry mixture, including the soaking liquid. Return to the heat, add the allspice and a few grinds of black pepper, and simmer gently for 5 minutes, until slightly thickened. Season with salt and serve alongside your favorite roast.

Grapefruit

*G*rapefruit is a fairly sophisticated citrus, don't you think? Too tart for the playground set. The sum total breakfast order of the "off-to-tennis" crowd. Deserving of its own specialized serrated spoon for excising sections with grace and tact. Yes, grapefruit holds its head high.

Grapefruit is a perfect ingredient, then, for elevating your preserves to new heights. In marmalades and jams, it offers a delightful and surprising veer away from the expected orange and lemon, with the cutting bite of its tang providing a bright, bracing note on the breakfast table.

You can use any variety of grapefruit in these recipes — traditional white, pink, or red. Grapefruit is harvested in the United States in the cooler months — sometimes as early as October and as late as June — and is always abundantly available during the holidays, making it a fine winter preserving project. Fresh grapefruit can last up to 2 months under refrigeration, so do stock up and, when the blizzard hits, get to making one of these recipes.

BROILED GRAPEFRUIT MARMALADE

Makes about 5 cups

Broiled grapefruit makes an elegant breakfast or dessert dish. The caramelized sugar turns it a deep amber color and tempers the tartness of the fruit. This marmalade is a spin-off of that classic treat, turning it into a deep golden spread with bright citrus flavor balanced by the warm flavors of caramel and vanilla.

INGREDIENTS

- **4** grapefruit (about 1 pound each)
- **2** cups brown sugar
- **1½** cups water
- **4** cups granulated sugar
- **½** vanilla bean
- **¼** cup bottled lemon juice

PREPARE

1. Preheat the broiler. Using a vegetable brush, scrub the fruit with a nontoxic, odorless dish soap and hot water.

2. Prep two of the grapefruit: Cut off the tops and bottoms of the grapefruit deeply enough to remove the solid disks of pith and reveal the flesh of the fruit. Cut each grapefruit in half, equatorially. Using an apple corer, remove the pithy core from the fruits, and then feel around the open segments and pinch out any seeds.

3. Pack the grapefruit halves snugly into a 2-quart baking dish. Top each half with ¼ cup brown sugar, pressing it in to fill the core cavity and cover each fruit. Broil 3 to 4 inches from the heating element for 2 to 3 minutes, until dark brown and bubbly. Keep a close watch, as the sugar can go from caramel to ash very quickly. Remove and set aside to cool.

4. Meanwhile, prep the remaining two grapefruit: Using a vegetable peeler, remove the zest from the fruits and then supreme them (see page 130), reserving the flesh and juice and discarding the membranes and pith. Combine the zest with ½ cup of the water in a food processor and purée. Add the reserved flesh and juice and purée again. Remove the purée to a large nonreactive pot.

5. Purée the broiled fruit, pith and all, two halves at a time, and add to the pot. Use a little liquid from the puréed fruit to "rinse out" any caramelized drippings left in the baking dish, and add these to the pot. Add the remaining 1 cup water to the mixture, bring to a boil, and then remove from the heat. Let sit for at least 4 hours and up to 8 hours to soften the rinds.

6. Measure the volume of the cooled grapefruit mixture (you should have about 4 cups), and return to the pot with an equal amount of granulated sugar, the remaining 1 cup brown sugar, the vanilla bean half, and the lemon juice. Slowly bring to a boil, stirring constantly to prevent the sugar from scorching. Simmer until the gel stage is reached (see page 28), 10 to 15 minutes.

7. Remove from the heat. Allow the marmalade to rest for 5 minutes, giving it an occasional gentle stir to release trapped air; it will thicken slightly. Skim off any foam.

PRESERVE

🄑 **Can:** Use the boiling-water method as described on page 20. Ladle the marmalade into clean, hot half-pint jars, leaving ¼ inch of headspace between the top of the marmalade and the lid. Run a bubble tool along the inside of the glass to release trapped air. Wipe the rims clean; center lids on the jars and screw on jar bands until they are just fingertip-tight. Process the jars by submerging them in boiling water to cover by 2 inches for 10 minutes. Turn off the heat, remove the canner lid, and let the jars rest in the water for 5 minutes. Remove the jars and set aside for 24 hours. Check the seals, then store in a cool, dark place for up to 1 year.

→ This marmalade, even more than others, benefits from a few weeks on the shelf to allow its flavors to blend and mellow, so I don't recommend it as a refrigerator jam. Canning it will yield the best results.

USE IT UP!

Grapefruit-Glazed Grapefruit

Serves 4

So nice, we named it twice. This lovely dessert uses Broiled Grapefruit Marmalade to glaze broiled grapefruit. Double happiness!

INGREDIENTS

2 grapefruit
Just over ¼ cup Broiled Grapefruit Marmalade (see page 128)
4 teaspoons sugar

PREPARE

1. Preheat the broiler.

2. Slice the grapefruit in half equatorially and arrange cut side up in a glass baking dish. Top each half with a heaping tablespoon of marmalade, smoothing out the marmalade to coat the fruit. Sprinkle a teaspoon of sugar over the top of each.

3. Place the grapefruit 4 inches under the broiler's heating element, and broil until bubbling and just starting to brown on top, 5 to 7 minutes. Serve warm.

KITCHEN HOW-TO
Supreming a Fruit

This is a nifty technique for turning a simple citrus fruit into elegant, pith-free sections.

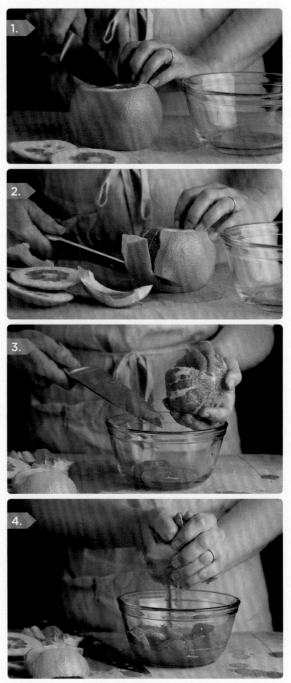

1. To do it, use a very sharp knife to slice off the buttons from both ends of the fruit. Set the fruit, flat side down, on a cutting board and perch your fingers on top to steady it.

2. Slice the peel and pith from the fruit by sawing down in narrow latitudinal strips, just below the pith. Be mindful not to cut too deeply or you will sacrifice too much flesh — run the blade as close to the pith as possible and continue working around the fruit until it is bare.

3. Next, to remove the sections from the membranes, hold the skinned fruit in your non-dominant hand over a small bowl. Slice just to the side of the membrane on one side of a section and then the other, freeing it and removing it to the bowl. You can flick out any seeds as they become exposed.

4. Continue until all of the sections have been freed from the membranes. I usually squeeze the membranes and core in my fist, letting any juice clinging to them join the bowl of fully supremed sections.

GRAPEFRUIT AND SULTANA CONSERVE

Makes about 9 cups

The gold color of the sultanas is pretty in the thick set of this grapefruit conserve, and they provide a little flavor bomb of sweetness in each bite. Don't substitute regular brown raisins, as they can look shockingly similar to those prehistoric bugs trapped in amber that you see at natural history museums or crafted into jewelry. A nice exhibit, maybe even cute earrings. Not a good look in a jam.

INGREDIENTS

- **4** grapefruit (about 1 pound each)
- **8** cups sugar
- **1** cup sultanas (golden raisins)
- **¼** cup bottled lemon juice

PREPARE

1. Using a vegetable brush, scrub the fruit with a nontoxic, odorless dish soap and hot water.

2. Peel the grapefruit, reserving the peels from two of them (you can use the peels from the other two grapefruit in another recipe, such as the Candied Grapefruit Rinds on page 136). Julienne the reserved peels, and cut the julienned strips into 1-inch lengths. Put the cut peels in a medium nonreactive pot, add enough water to cover, and bring to a boil. Reduce the heat and simmer for 5 minutes. Drain and then repeat to soften the peel and remove some of its bitterness.

3. Meanwhile, remove any large pieces of the pithy white membrane from the four grapefruit and separate them into sections. Cut the sections into thirds and pick out and discard the seeds.

4. Combine the cooked and drained peels and cut sections in a large pot. Add the sugar, sultanas, and lemon juice. Bring to a boil, then reduce the heat and simmer until the gel stage is reached (see page 28), about 30 minutes.

5. Remove from the heat. Allow the conserve to rest for 5 minutes, giving it an occasional gentle stir to release trapped air; it will thicken slightly. Skim off any foam.

PRESERVE

Can: Use the boiling-water method as described on page 20. Ladle the conserve into clean, hot half-pint jars, leaving ¼ inch of headspace between the top of the conserve and the lid. Run a bubble tool along the inside of the glass to release trapped air. Wipe the rims clean; center lids on the jars and screw on jar bands until they are just fingertip-tight. Process the jars by submerging them in boiling water to cover by 2 inches for 10 minutes. Turn off the heat, remove the canner lid, and let the jars rest in the water for 5 minutes. Remove the jars and set aside for 24 hours. Check the seals, then store in a cool, dark place for up to 1 year.

→ The sharp flavor of the citrus peel in this recipe will benefit from a few weeks on the shelf to allow its flavors to blend and mellow, so I don't recommend it as a refrigerator jam. Canning will yield the best results.

USE IT UP!

Sautéed Greens with Grapefruit Dressing

Serves 4 as a side dish

Earthy, herbaceous greens meet sprightly grapefruit in this side dish mash-up that will change the way you look at greens. You can serve this dish warm or at room temperature, so it's great for company or a potluck.

INGREDIENTS

- **1** tablespoon Grapefruit and Sultana Conserve (see page 131)
- **2** teaspoons red wine vinegar
- **2** tablespoons extra-virgin olive oil
- **1** onion, diced
- **½** pound greens, such as mature spinach, kale, or chard, center ribs removed and leaves chopped
- **½** cup water or stock
   Salt and freshly ground black pepper

PREPARE

1. Combine the conserve and vinegar in a small bowl, and whisk together.

2. Heat the oil in a large skillet over medium-high heat. Add the onion and sauté until translucent, 5 to 7 minutes. Add the greens, cover the pan, and cook until wilted, about 3 minutes, lifting the lid and tossing with tongs occasionally to prevent burning.

3. Add the conserve mixture, water, and salt and pepper to taste. Simmer until the greens are tender and the sauce is reduced, 2 to 3 minutes. Serve warm or at room temperature.

→ This recipe is also delicious with Lemon Ginger Marmalade (page 153) in place of the Grapefruit and Sultana Conserve.

GRAPEFRUIT SECTIONS IN LAVENDER SYRUP

Makes 4 pints

The lavender blossoms found in sachets have often been doused with additional scented oils to boost their "lavenderness." Such buds might smell great, but they are not suitable for eating. Look for "culinary" lavender for kitchen use. I call for dried lavender here, which is easier to store, but you can substitute fresh, unsprayed blossoms, using ¼ cup fresh for one tablespoon dried. And save the leftover peels from this recipe; you can use them in making Candied Grapefruit Rinds (page 136).

INGREDIENTS

- **2½** cups water
- **2** cups sugar
- **1** tablespoon dried culinary lavender
- **6** pounds grapefruit (5–6)

PREPARE

1. Combine the water and sugar in a medium saucepan and bring to a boil. Remove from the heat and add the lavender. Allow to steep for 10 to 15 minutes.

2. Meanwhile, peel the grapefruit and separate into sections. Arrange the sections in a single layer in a large nonreactive pot. Pour the hot syrup over them and gently poach for 5 minutes, keeping them just under a simmer.

3. Divide the grapefruit sections among clean, hot pint jars, setting the sections in flat, slightly overlapping layers to get the best pack. Leave approximately ¾ inch between the top of the fruit and the top of the jar.

4. Return the sugar syrup to a boil. Carefully ladle the syrup over the fruit, covering it by ¼ inch. If you plan to can the grapefruit, be sure to leave ½ inch of headspace between the top of the liquid and the lid.

PRESERVE

Refrigerate: Cool, cover, and refrigerate for up to 3 weeks.

Can: Use the boiling-water method as described on page 20. Run a bubble tool along the inside of the glass to release trapped air. Wipe the rims clean; center lids on the jars and screw on jar bands until they are just fingertip-tight. Process the jars by submerging them in boiling water to cover by 2 inches for 10 minutes. Turn off the heat, remove the canner lid, and let the jars rest in the water for 5 minutes. Remove the jars and set aside for 24 hours. Check the seals, then store in a cool, dark place for up to 1 year.

USE IT UP!

Lavender Grapefruit with Vanilla Custard

Serves 6

This vanilla custard recipe is a great one to have up your sleeve. The only trick to it is taking it off the heat right when it comes to temperature, or you can get lumps. Don't worry if you have a few; just press the custard through a fine-mesh strainer for a smooth sauce. It thickens as it chills and leaves you with a creamy pudding. I flavor this one with butter and vanilla, but a shot of amaretto or almond extract would be lovely, too.

INGREDIENTS

- **3** cups milk
- **6** egg yolks
- ½ cup sugar
- ¼ cup cornstarch
- ½ teaspoon salt
- **1** tablespoon unsalted butter
- **2** teaspoons vanilla extract
- **1** pint Grapefruit Sections in Lavender Syrup (see page 134)

PREPARE

1. Heat the milk in a large saucepan over medium heat; do not boil.

2. Combine the egg yolks, sugar, cornstarch, and salt in a large heatproof bowl and whisk until well blended. Add one-third of the hot milk to the egg mixture and whisk immediately, until combined, to temper the eggs.

Add the blended egg mixture to the remaining hot milk in the saucepan and reduce the heat to low. Cook, whisking constantly, until the mixture has thickened and the temperature reaches 170°F on a candy thermometer. Remove from the heat, and whisk in the butter and vanilla.

3. Transfer the custard to a bowl. Set a sheet of plastic wrap over it, so the plastic sits right on the surface of the custard, to keep a skin from forming. Cool for at least 4 hours and up to 2 days.

4. To serve, spoon ½ cup custard into a bowl and garnish with three or four of the preserved grapefruit sections, drizzling a teaspoon of the lavender syrup over the custard if desired.

→ This custard is also delicious topped with Apricots in Honey Syrup (page 78) or Poached Quince (page 217).

CANDIED GRAPEFRUIT RINDS

Makes about 4 cups

Master this easy recipe and you will never throw out a citrus rind again. The candying process yields chewy, sweet treats, and a final dusting with sugar makes them sparkle on the plate. You can substitute any thick-skinned citrus such as navel oranges or lemons, but stay away from thin-skinned fruits such as tangerines that don't provide enough pith to offer a toothsome result. Whichever kind of fruit you use, don't throw out the sugar syrup left over at the end of the process — it's a great sweetener in hot or cold beverages.

INGREDIENTS

Peels, including pith, from 2 well-scrubbed grapefruit
1 cup water
5 cups sugar
1 vanilla bean

PREPARE

1. Cut the peels into ¼-inch strips. Cover the peels with cold water in a large nonreactive saucepan and bring to a boil, stirring to ensure that all of the peels are heated through. Strain and repeat two more times to remove the bitter flavor from the pith and to soften the peels. After the third round, set aside the peels to drain while you make the syrup.

2. Bring the water to a boil and gradually add 4 cups of the sugar, stirring to dissolve. Add the peels and the vanilla bean, return to a boil, and then reduce the heat and simmer gently until the peels are translucent and tender, about 1 hour.

PRESERVE

Dry: Using tongs, remove the peels to a drying rack placed over a baking sheet and separate them so they don't touch. Let dry for 4 to 5 hours. When quite dry but still tacky, roll the peels in the remaining 1 cup sugar to coat. The candied peels will keep, stored in an airtight container, for up to 1 month.

USE IT UP!

Chocolate-Dipped Rinds

Makes about 4 cups of candied rinds

This is a great dessert for kids to make — if you can get them to save any chocolate for the fruit. They are terrific on a dessert tray, poking out between cookies or other small bites, or served solo with coffee at the end of the meal — a dessert for the dessert. Pack a dozen or so in a fancy little box for an easy, inexpensive, but super-elegant handmade gift.

INGREDIENTS

- **1½** cups chocolate morsels (any type of chocolate)
- **4** cups Candied Grapefruit Rinds (see page 136)

PREPARE

1. Line two 11- by 17-inch baking sheets with parchment paper.

2. Melt the chocolate in a double boiler (or a small heatproof bowl set over a pot of simmering water).

3. Carefully dip the rinds, one at time, into the melted chocolate, covering half to three-quarters of the rind with chocolate. Lay on the parchment-lined baking sheets to dry. These chocolate-dipped rinds will keep in an airtight container for 1 week.

KITCHEN HOW-TO
How Much Can You Do with Six Grapefruit?

In the course of my recipe testing I was pleasantly surprised to see just how far six grapefruit can go. From just a half-dozen fruit you can make the Grapefruit Sections in Lavender Syrup (page 134) and use some of the peels to make Candied Grapefruit Rinds (page 136), plus you get a pint of grapefruit and vanilla syrup from making the candied rinds. That's a lot of treats from a little fruit!

GRAPEFRUIT LIQUEUR

Makes about 1 quart

Citrus liqueur is a necessary ingredient in a number of cocktails — margaritas and sangria being two that benefit from a splash of it. This version brings a fruit-forward flavor to the party that is so good, you'll want to sip it straight up.

INGREDIENTS

- **1** grapefruit
- **2** cups vodka
- **1** cup sugar

PREPARE AND PRESERVE

1. Sterilize a 1-quart glass jar by submerging it in boiling water for 10 minutes.

2. Using a vegetable brush, scrub the fruit with a nontoxic, odorless dish soap and hot water. Remove the zest from the grapefruit with a vegetable peeler.

3. Supreme the fruit (see page 130), removing and discarding all white pith, membranes, and seeds. Combine the grapefruit zest and flesh with the vodka and sugar in the jar. Shake to dissolve the sugar. Set aside in a cool, dark place for about 2 weeks, shaking every day or so.

4. After 2 weeks, taste the infusion. If you'd like a stronger fruit flavor, let set for another week or so. When the flavor is to your liking, sterilize a 1-quart jar by submerging it in boiling water for 10 minutes. Let cool, then strain the infusion into the jar and let rest for 1 week to allow any tiny fruit particulates to settle out of the liquid. Carefully decant the liquid into a fresh sterilized jar or bottle.

GRAPEFRUIT LIQUEUR

USE IT UP!

Ultimate Margarita

Makes 1 perfect cocktail

I am picky about my margaritas. None of that cloying Lemon-X mix for me. If I am going to take a trip to tequila land, I want good hooch and fresh juice. Homemade Grapefruit Liqueur gets me there, first class.

INGREDIENTS

- **1** jigger (1½ ounces) high-quality white tequila such as Don Julio
- **1** shot (1 ounce) Grapefruit Liqueur
- **1** ounce freshly squeezed lime juice
- **1** tablespoon orange juice (trust me)
  Ice

PREPARE

Combine the tequila, liqueur, lime juice, and orange juice in a cocktail shaker filled with ice, cover, and shake for at least 1 minute. Confidently pour* the contents of the shaker into a rocks glass or strain into a chilled martini glass and serve.

→ Slow pouring is actually sloppy pouring — the contents of your shaker will dribble down its side rather than flow into your glass. As my dad, former owner of Caesar's Cellar Lounge in Baltimore, Maryland, used to tell me, "Pour with confidence and you'll never spill a drop."

Grapes

There is nothing more picturesque than grapes growing on the vine. I have had the very good fortune to travel to the California wine country as the grapes are maturing and at harvesting season. The vines twist in such well-articulated gestures, it's like the plants are growing in their own graceful, expressive modern dance. The light filters through the leaves, showing all of their veiny insides. And the fruit shrinks and swells with the flow of the rain. Grape vines have such personality that it is no wonder they are often tended with such care and dedication — for the life they have of their own and the liveliness that, under the proper circumstances, they can give us.

Whether the life of your grape is destined to be honored in the bottle or one of these recipes, I do hope that you will find yourself in a vineyard at some point. Or at least take the chance to linger over the many different varieties of grapes available at farmers' markets. As I learned from a table grape grower in California, the grapes that are picked for the grocery store are picked unripe for ease of transport and extended shelf life (and, as he tells me, so that they are more likely to stay on the vine and not drop onto the store floor, where they are more slippery than a banana peel — a ripe bunch of grapes is a grocery-store lawyer's nightmare). On the other hand, grapes found at farmers' markets are much more likely to have been harvested ripe — full of sunshine and flavor — and it is remarkable to taste the different varieties. Concord grapes, of course, have the characteristic "grape" flavor that has been contorted into everything from lollipops to kids' toothpaste. Muscat grapes are just as sweet but with the delicate, slightly musky flavor that tastes of the wine that bears the grapes' name. Tiny little champagne grapes are tasty and look like something out of a Vermeer painting. There are so many more options than just green or red.

FROZEN GRAPES

Too many grapes, too little time? Stash them in the freezer and you'll have an instant treat (pop-able popsicles), the makings of your next batch of jam, or fun, fruity "ice cubes" that will chill but not dilute your chardonnay. Think this is too easy to be any good? Try it! They are a delight.

INGREDIENTS

Any quantity grapes (1 quart fills a standard baking sheet nicely)

PREPARE

Wash and dry the grapes thoroughly. Line an 11-by 17-inch baking sheet with parchment paper and arrange the grapes on it in a single layer. Set the sheet flat in your freezer. Let freeze overnight, and up to 24 hours, to allow the grapes to freeze solid, but no longer or you risk freezer burn or the taint of "freezer taste" on your fruit. (This method of freezing grapes individually prevents the fruit from freezing together into one big grape-berg, so you can remove just a few grapes at a time.)

PRESERVE

Freeze: Transfer the frozen grapes to a sealable freezer bag, pressing out as much air as possible. They'll keep in the freezer for up to 6 months.

USE IT UP!

Elderflower Sparkler

Serves 1

"And your mother smells of elderberries!" Remember that line from Monty Python and the Holy Grail? *Well, if elderberries smell anything like the lively elixir used in this sparkler, it was a compliment indeed. St-Germain elderflower liqueur is sustainably sourced and produced, and this flowery cordial brings a whiff of the French countryside to your glass. And I mean that in a good way.*

INGREDIENTS

1 ounce St-Germain elderflower liqueur
1 teaspoon freshly squeezed lemon juice
½ cup ice
4 ounces Prosecco or sparkling wine
2 Frozen Grapes

PREPARE

Combine the liqueur, lemon juice, and ice in a cocktail shaker and shake to chill. Pour into a champagne flute. Top with Prosecco. Garnish with grapes and serve.

CLASSIC CONCORD GRAPE JAM

Makes about 4 cups

This jam is a classic. Its rich, grapey tang is miles distant from the bland sweetness of store-bought versions. This grape jam has a depth of flavor that is almost winelike and gives it a running start toward adding some oomph to savory dishes.

INGREDIENTS

- **8** cups Concord grapes (about 2 pounds), stems removed
- **½** cup water
- **4** cups sugar
- **¼** cup bottled lemon juice

PREPARE

1. Pinch the grapes to separate the skins from the flesh. As you work, put the skins in a large nonreactive pot and the flesh in a medium pan. Add the water to the pot of skins and bring to a boil. Reduce the heat and simmer for 15 to 20 minutes.

2. Meanwhile, bring the grape flesh to a simmer and cook until it loses shape, 5 to 10 minutes. Cool slightly and run through a food mill to remove the seeds.

3. Add the milled grape pulp to the pot with the skins. Add the sugar, stirring until it dissolves. Stir in the lemon juice. Bring to a boil and simmer, stirring, until you reach the gel stage (see page 28), about 10 minutes.

4. Remove from the heat. Allow the jam to rest for 5 minutes, giving it an occasional gentle stir to release trapped air; it will thicken slightly. Skim off any foam.

PRESERVE

Refrigerate: Cool, cover, and refrigerate for up to 3 weeks.

Can: Use the boiling-water method as described on page 20. Ladle the jam into clean, hot 4-ounce or half-pint jars, leaving ¼ inch of headspace between the top of the jam and the lid. Run a bubble tool along the inside of the glass to release trapped air. Wipe the rims clean; center lids on the jars and screw on jar bands until they are just fingertip-tight. Process the jars by submerging them in boiling water to cover by 2 inches for 10 minutes. Turn off the heat, remove the canner lid, and let the jars rest in the water for 5 minutes. Remove the jars and set aside for 24 hours. Check the seals, then store in a cool, dark place for up to 1 year.

Recipes

Butter-Basted Steak with Grape Reduction

142

Serves 2

You could use any cut of steak in this recipe. I love porterhouse, but strip steaks, filets, rib eyes, or any steak suitable for pan sautéing will work. Ask your farmer or butcher what they have on hand.

This recipe is based on an Alain Ducasse recipe published in the New York Times *in 2002. Don't be put off by the shocking amount of butter in this recipe. It bastes the steak, but the steak does not soak it up. Save the drippings from the pan and the garlic cloves (you can keep them in the fridge for 3 to 4 days). Slip off the garlic peels if they haven't already shed them during cooking, mash the garlic with the solidified drippings, and smear the mixture on toasted baguettes, broiling if you like, for out-of-this-world garlic bread.*

INGREDIENTS

- **4** tablespoons unsalted butter
- **2** tablespoons extra-virgin olive oil
- **2** (1½-inch-thick) steaks, preferably grass-fed

  Kosher salt
- **6** garlic cloves, whole and unpeeled
- **1** shallot, minced
- ¼ teaspoon dried thyme
- **1** cup red wine
- **1** tablespoon Classic Concord Grape Jam (see page 141)

PREPARE

1. Melt the butter and oil in a skillet over medium-high heat. Season the steaks on both sides with kosher salt, add them to the pan, and strew the garlic cloves around them. Sear the steak to your desired doneness, turning every 2 to 3 minutes to ensure even cooking. (When you press a finger on the steak in the pan, a rare steak feels like the webbing between your thumb and pointer finger when your hand is relaxed, a medium steak feels like the same point when your fingers are spread, and a well-done steak feels like the tip of your nose.) Remove the steaks to a cutting board and allow them to rest. Remove the garlic cloves and set them aside.

2. Pour off all but a tablespoon of butter from the pan. Add the shallot and thyme to the pan and sauté until the shallot is translucent, 2 to 3 minutes. Add the wine to the pan and simmer until it is reduced by half. Whisk in the jam.

3. Plate the steaks and drizzle a little of the grape reduction on each. Serve immediately.

→ The reduction sauce is also delicious when made with Classic Cherry Jam (page 112) or Blackberry Gastrique (page 90).

GREEN GRAPE AND MOSCATO JELLY

Makes about 4 cups

You could call this preserve "Grapes, Two Ways." Bright, tangy green grape pulp is suspended in the lusciously flavored sweet moscato wine, made from muscat grapes. Use small jars for this precious jelly, and if you can find muscat grapes, use them for a double dose of the fruit.

INGREDIENTS

- **1** cup sugar
- **2** teaspoons Pomona's Universal Pectin
- **3** pounds green grapes (Muscat if available), stems removed
- **½** cup water
- **1** cup moscato wine
- **2** tablespoons bottled lemon juice
- **2** teaspoons calcium water (from the Pomona's Universal Pectin kit)

PREPARE

1. Combine the sugar and pectin in a small bowl and set aside.

2. Combine the grapes and water in a large nonreactive pot and slowly bring to a boil, stirring frequently to prevent scorching. Reduce the heat and simmer until the fruit is softened, about 15 minutes. Remove from the heat and let cool slightly.

3. Run the grapes through a food mill to remove the skins. Return the pulp to the pot, and add the wine, lemon juice, and calcium water. Slowly add the pectin mixture, stirring constantly to avoid clumping. Bring to a boil, reduce the heat, and simmer for 1 to 2 minutes, continuing to stir constantly, until the sugar is completely dissolved.

4. Remove from the heat. Allow the jelly to rest for 5 minutes, giving it an occasional gentle stir to release trapped air; it will thicken slightly. Skim off any foam.

PRESERVE

Refrigerate: Cool, cover, and refrigerate for up to 3 weeks.

Can: Use the boiling-water method as described on page 20. Ladle the jelly into clean, hot 4-ounce jars, leaving ¼ inch of headspace between the top of the jelly and the lid. Wipe the rims clean. Center lids on the jars and screw on jar bands until they are just fingertip-tight. Process the jars by submerging them in boiling water to cover by 2 inches for 10 minutes. Turn off the heat, remove the canner lid, and let the jars rest in the water for 5 minutes. Remove the jars and set aside for 24 hours. Check the seals, then store in a cool, dark place for up to 1 year.

USE IT UP!

Parmesan Frico

Makes 16 nibbles

Frico are fun to make and a striking hors d'oeuvre or garnish for soup or salad. I like to lay the cooked frico on a rolling pin so that they cool into crisp, curved shapes, ideal for holding a bit of garnish, such as a pinch of microgreens or a dollop of moscato jelly. Use the best cheese you can find to make tasty frico.

INGREDIENTS

- **4** ounces Parmigiano Reggiano, coarsely grated
- **1** tablespoon all-purpose flour
  Green Grape and Moscato Jelly (see page 144), for serving

PREPARE

1. Combine the cheese and flour in a small bowl.

2. Heat a medium nonstick or well-seasoned cast-iron skillet over medium heat. Working 1 tablespoon at a time, sprinkle the cheese in 2-inch circles on the pan (leaving just enough space between the shreds to see little glimpses of the pan will give you lacey frico). Be sure to give each cheese mound a good amount of space around it, as they will spread out a bit as they heat and melt — you should have no more than three in the pan at a time.

3. Cook the cheese rounds until they have melted and begun to crisp on the bottom. Use a spatula to gently lift and flip the frico (a short back-and-forth sawing motion with the spatula makes it easier to get it underneath the cheese). Cook for 1 minute more.

4. Transfer the frico to a sheet of parchment and allow to cool — the cheese will crisp as it does so. (Alternatively, you can transfer cooked frico to a rolling pin, where they will take on the rounded shape as they cool.)

5. Repeat to cook the remaining cheese. Serve the cooled frico alongside a small dish of Green Grape and Moscato Jelly that can be dolloped on as desired.

→ Pear Jelly (page 194) or Herb Jelly (page 61) would also make a delicious accompaniment to frico.

HOMEMADE VINEGAR

Makes about 1 quart

Not many people think of making their own vinegar, yet it's easy enough to do. Vinegar actually is a winemaking "mistake"; it's essentially vino that has been exposed to air, converting its sugars to acetic acid. Who knew that messing up could be so delicious?

I have tried a number of different vinegar-making methods. Theoretically, you should just be able to expose your wine to air and let nature take its course, but it's easy to wind up with moldy wine instead of vinegar. I find that I get more consistent results if I inoculate the wine with a bit of "mother," the good bacteria that digests the wine's sugars and converts them to acid, to get the process going before the contaminating molds can take hold.

You can speed the conversion process by purchasing a vinegar "mother" (from a homebrew supplier) and adding it to the wine. But the simpler method is just to jump-start your wine with a little organic, raw vinegar. Because it hasn't been pasteurized, such vinegar will by definition have a bit of mother in it, which makes it a fine catalyst for the vinegar-making process.

This recipe makes about a quart. Once it gets going and you have a healthy culture (also called the "mother") established, you can add bits of wine to the jar and the mother will convert them to vinegar. The older the mother, the more character and nuance it takes on — mommas are like that.

INGREDIENTS

- **1** (750 ml) bottle wine, low sulfite or organic wines work best
- **1** cup unpasteurized, organic vinegar

PREPARE AND PRESERVE

1. Sterilize a large, wide-mouthed glass container, such as a straight-sided jar, by submerging it in boiling water for 10 minutes. Remove the jar from the water and add the wine. Stir in the vinegar. Cover with a double layer of cheesecloth, secured with a rubber band, to prevent contamination by dust and pests. Let the liquid sit in a lonely corner in your kitchen where it won't be disturbed but will benefit from the warmth of the room.

2. After about a month or so, you will begin to see what looks like an oil slick developing on the top of your wine/vinegar. This is the mother forming, and it's a good sign. After about 3 to 4 months, give your vinegar a taste. It should have a nice sharp bite. If it's still soft, let it sit for a few more weeks, until it reaches your desired strength.

3. If you want to stabilize your vinegar, you can strain it and refrigerate it so that it doesn't get any stronger. Some home vinegar makers go an extra step and pasteurize their vinegar by heating it in a saucepan to 160°F. This will certainly stabilize the product, but it will also kill off the probiotics that make homemade vinegar such a healthful product.

USE IT UP!

Classic Vinaigrette

Makes 1 cup

Vinaigrette is so easy to make, I don't know why anyone would want to buy the bottled stuff. Whip up a large batch and it will give you a week's worth of salad dressing.

INGREDIENTS

- ¼ cup Homemade Vinegar (see page 146) or bottled red or white vinegar
- 2 tablespoons Dijon mustard
  Salt and freshly ground black pepper
- ¾ cup extra-virgin olive oil

PREPARE

Combine the vinegar with the mustard and a pinch each of salt and pepper in a medium bowl, and whisk together. Slowly drizzle in the oil, a few drops at a time at first, whisking all the while. Cover and store in the refrigerator until ready to use. If the oil separates out, whisk or shake before use.

> VARIATION:
> ### *Fruity Vinaigrette*
> ---
> Whisk in a bit of jelly (as shown in the photographs) to give your vinaigrette a sweet, tangy flavor and a lovely, glossy sheen.

WINE JELLY

Makes 7 (4-ounce) jars

From the lightest Sauvignon Blanc to a rich, red Cabernet, wine makes a surprisingly delightful jelly. Starting with wine gives you the clear "fruit juice" that you need as your jelly base, so any bottle of vino puts you ahead of the game by at least that step. Herbs bring flavor and visual interest to the jar.

INGREDIENTS

- **2** cups sugar
- **2** teaspoons Pomona's Universal Pectin
- **1** (750 ml) bottle any variety wine
- **1** tablespoon fresh or 1 teaspoon dried herbs (see note)
- **2** teaspoons calcium water (from the Pomona's Universal Pectin kit)

PREPARE

1. Combine the sugar and pectin in a small bowl and set aside.

2. Bring the wine to a boil in a medium nonreactive pot, then reduce the heat, add the herbs, and let simmer for 5 minutes. Stir in the calcium water. Slowly add the pectin mixture, stirring constantly to avoid clumping. Bring to a boil, reduce the heat, and simmer for 1 to 2 minutes, continuing to stir constantly, until the sugar is completely dissolved.

3. Remove from the heat. Allow the jelly to rest for 5 minutes, giving it an occasional gentle stir to release trapped air; it will thicken slightly. Skim off any foam.

→ Floral herbs such as lemon verbena and lavender are good with white wines, while hardier herbs such as sage or thyme pair well with red wines.

PRESERVE

Refrigerate: Cool, cover, and refrigerate for up to 3 weeks.

Can: Use the boiling-water method as described on page 20. Ladle the jelly into clean, hot 4-ounce jars, leaving ¼ inch of headspace between the top of the jelly and the lid. Run a bubble tool along the inside of the glass to release trapped air. Wipe the rims clean; center lids on the jars and screw on jar bands until they are just fingertip-tight. Process the jars by submerging them in boiling water to cover by 2 inches for 10 minutes. Turn off the heat, remove the canner lid, and let the jars rest in the water for 5 minutes. Remove the jars and set aside for 24 hours. Check the seals, then store in a cool, dark place for up to 1 year.

VARIATION:

Mulled Wine Jelly

You can add mulling spices instead of the herbs for a warmly flavored jelly that cozies up beautifully to cold-weather treats. Tie half of a cinnamon stick, 6 peppercorns, 6 cloves, and 1 star anise in a piece of cheesecloth and add to the pot instead of the herbs. Simmer gently for about 15 minutes, remove the spice bag, and then proceed with the recipe.

USE IT UP!

Roasted Lilies with Wine Jelly Drizzle

Serves 4

Onions, shallots, garlic, chives, and leeks have something in common — they are all members of the lily family. Yes, lilies. They may be pungent and spicy when they're raw, but they turn sweet and tender when roasted low and slow, as they are in this recipe. The jelly acts a little bit like a wine reduction, making a sauce out of all the lovely browned bits in the pan, and it brings a sweetness that heightens the caramelized flavors of the lilies. You can use this dish as a garnish for steaks or serve it with a platter of grilled or steamed vegetables. Fabulous!

INGREDIENTS

- **2** onions, peeled and quartered, or 6 cippolini onions, peeled but left whole
- **4** shallots, peeled and halved
- **4** garlic cloves, peeled
- **1** tablespoon extra-virgin olive oil
  Salt and freshly ground black pepper
- **2** tablespoons Wine Jelly (see page 148)

PREPARE

1. Preheat the oven to 400°F.

2. Combine the onions, shallots, and garlic in a 2-quart baking dish, toss with the oil, season with salt and pepper, and cover tightly with aluminum foil. Roast for about 30 minutes, until tender. Uncover, stir in the wine jelly, and roast for another 15 minutes, until beginning to brown in spots. Serve warm.

→ This dish is also delicious with Herb Jelly (page 61) in place of the Wine Jelly.

PICKLED GRAPE LEAVES

Makes 36 leaves

If you have access to grape vines, you can use the leaves in this fun and scrumptious way. The leaves of green grapes are preferable, as they are more tender than those of red grapes. Harvest your leaves in the spring when they are small and haven't yet developed thick stems through their middles.

INGREDIENTS

2 cups water

2 tablespoons kosher salt

3 dozen grape leaves

PREPARE

1. Combine the water and salt in a quart-size, widemouthed canning jar and stir or shake to dissolve the salt.

2. Divide the leaves into three stacks of twelve leaves each. Roll the leaf stacks up into loose bundles and submerge in the brine vertically. Put a lid on the jar and shake to make sure all the leaves are immersed in the brine. Remove the lid.

3. Fill a 4-ounce canning jar with water to make a weight and gently place it on top of the leaf stacks to keep them submerged under the brine. Drape all with a loose-fitting, air-permeable cover, such as cheesecloth or an inverted jelly bag, and secure with a rubber band, being careful not to push the small canning jar weight down into the brine.

4. Set the jar aside for about 1 week, checking daily. Small bubbles will form in the jar and rise to the top, signaling that fermentation is under way. If you notice a white bloom forming on the top of the brine, remove the 4-ounce jar and wash it, scoop off any bloom floating on the ferment, and replace the jar and cover. It's important that the leaves stay submerged; if the leaves become exposed, whether through evaporation or because you have been scooping off brine as you remove bloom, top off the brine with a solution of 1 tablespoon kosher salt mixed with 1 cup water.

5. When the leaves have turned from bright green to olive green and bubbles have stopped forming in the ferment, remove the cover and weight. Scoop off any bloom, put the lid on the jar, and refrigerate.

PRESERVE

Refrigerate: The pickled grape leaves will keep in the refrigerator for 3 to 4 months.

USE IT UP!

Yaprak Dolmas (Stuffed Grape Leaves)

Makes 36 dolmas

This recipe holds a special place in my heart. I learned it from Sündüs Cosar, the mother of my dear friend Adnan, when she was visiting from Turkey. We spent the day rolling these tasty morsels, skewering kebabs, and pinching manta (Turkish dumplings). Not a word of English passed between us, but our shared passion for good food and love of gathering friends and family around the table spoke volumes.

INGREDIENTS

- **36** small Pickled Grape Leaves (see page 150)
- **1** pound ground beef, preferably grass-fed
- **1** small onion, finely diced
- **½** cup fine bulgur
- **¼** cup finely chopped flat-leaf parsley
- **2** tablespoons tomato paste
- **2** teaspoons salt

PREPARE

1. Remove the grape leaves from their pickling liquid, rinse, and soak in a large bowl of cold water for 15 minutes. Drain.

2. Meanwhile, combine the beef, onion, bulgur, parsley, tomato paste, and salt in a small bowl, and use your fingers to combine them.

3. To stuff the leaves, lay a leaf out in front of you, stem end toward you. Using moist fingers, pinch off about 1 teaspoon of filling from the bowl and form it into a thin stick, about 2 inches long, across the bottom of the leaf. Fold the bottom of the leaf up over the filling. Fold in the sides of the leaf, from the outermost point of filling toward the middle of the leaf. Continue to roll the leaf away from you, pinching it firmly to tightly encapsulate the filling. As you roll the dolmas, arrange them in a medium saucepan, packing them in tightly, seam side down, layering them if necessary.

4. Cover the dolmas with cold water and weight down with a plate to keep them from bobbing up during cooking. Gently bring to a simmer and cook until the bulgur is tender, about 45 minutes, adding more water if necessary. Drain and serve hot, at room temperature, or cold.

Lemons

My dedication to local/seasonal eating hits a serious road bump when it comes to lemons. I always have them in my refrigerator. Why? Because, although they are not in my foodshed, lemons are the answer, every time. Sore throat? Tea with lemon. Soup is bland? Add a few drops of lemon juice. Need a marinade, dessert-in-a-pinch, or quick cocktail? Start with lemon. You get the idea.

Lemons are used throughout this book, not only in recipes that feature their flavor, but also for their acid content, which can be used in a number of ways. Lemons contain both ascorbic and citric acid. Their ascorbic acid content makes lemons a very effective anti-browning agent. Submerging fruits, such as cut apples, in a solution of lemon juice and water will keep them from oxidizing. Lemon juice also contains citric acid, which is used to lower the pH of preserving recipes, so that canned foods are safe on the shelf, and to activate pectin, so that spreads reach the desired gel stage.

Besides being useful, lemons are lovely. Their pleasantly puckering taste soothes us when we are ill, refreshes us on hot summer days, and is the key ingredient in many sweet and savory dishes. I have no idea why a hopeless car is called a lemon. What's not to love?

LEMON GINGER MARMALADE

Makes 5 cups

Lemon and ginger, a classic combo of sunny and warm together in one great spread. The rind from the lemon give this marmalade some bite so it's not all frills. This is a great topper for some hearty rustic bread that can stand up to a jam with attitude.

INGREDIENTS

- **2** pounds lemons (8–10)
- **2** cups water
- **4** cups sugar
- **1** (4-inch) knob fresh ginger, minced, (see box on page 154)

PREPARE

1. Using a vegetable brush, scrub the fruit with a nontoxic, odorless dish soap and hot water.

2. Cut off the tops and bottoms of the lemons deeply enough to remove the solid disks of pith and reveal the flesh of the fruit. Quarter the fruits and cut away the center rib. Flick out the seeds with the tip of your knife. Thinly slice the quartered lemons crosswise. Combine the lemon slices with the water in a large nonreactive pot and bring to a boil. Remove from the heat and set aside overnight to soften the rinds.

3. The next day, measure the volume of the lemon mixture (you should have about 4 cups). Return the lemon mixture to the pot and add an equal amount of sugar, along with the ginger. Slowly bring to a hard boil, stirring frequently to avoid burning the sugar. Continue cooking until gel stage is reached (see page 28), about 15 minutes.

4. Remove from the heat. Allow the marmalade to rest for 5 minutes, giving it an occasional gentle stir to release trapped air; it will thicken slightly. Skim off any foam.

PRESERVE

🏺 **Can:** Use the boiling-water method as described on page 20. Ladle the marmalade into clean, hot 4-ounce or half-pint jars, leaving ¼ inch of headspace between the top of the marmalade and the lid. Run a bubble tool along the inside of the glass to release trapped air. Wipe the rims clean; center lids on the jars and screw on jar bands until they are just fingertip-tight. Process the jars by submerging them in boiling water to cover by 2 inches for 10 minutes. Turn off the heat, remove the canner lid, and let the jars rest in the water for 5 minutes. Remove the jars and set aside for 24 hours. Check the seals, then store in a cool, dark place for up to 1 year.

→ Marmalades are really best after they "cure" for a few weeks in the jar, so they're not the best candidates for a refrigerator jam. Canning will yield the best results.

USE IT UP!

Vegetable Stir-Fry with Lemon Ginger Sauce

Serves 4

Instant flavor, minimal prep — this stir-fry is a great middle-of-the-week/don't-know-what-to-make-for-dinner dish. You can use just about any kind of vegetables here; just grab whatever is at its peak in the market (or is lurking around the crisper drawer). Having Lemon Ginger Marmalade on hand means it's done in a jiff.

INGREDIENTS

- **2** tablespoons soy sauce
- **1** tablespoon Lemon Ginger Marmalade (see page 153)
- **1** tablespoon rice wine vinegar or white wine vinegar
- **2** tablespoons neutral-flavored vegetable oil, such as organic canola
- **1** onion, diced
- **1** pound seasonal vegetables, such as sugar snap peas, carrots, asparagus, bok choy, red peppers, broccoli, or a combination, cut into bite-size pieces
- **2** garlic cloves, minced

PREPARE

1. Combine the soy sauce, marmalade, and vinegar in a small bowl and whisk together.

2. Heat the oil in a large skillet over medium-high heat until hot but not smoking. Add the onions and sauté until they are just starting to brown around the edges, about 3 minutes. Add the vegetables and sauté until the colors brighten and the vegetables just begin to soften, about 5 minutes. Add the garlic and sauté another minute. Add the marmalade mixture, and stir to coat the vegetables. Serve immediately.

KITCHEN HOW-TO
Prepping Ginger

When prepping ginger, put down your vegetable peeler. The right tool for the job is a spoon. Why? Because the most flavorful part of the ginger root lies just beneath the skin, and if you're using a vegetable peeler, you're not just cutting away the thin skin, you're cutting down on the root's flavor. Use the blunt edge of the bowl of a spoon to scrape off the thin skin from the ginger and you'll get more flavor from the root. You can then grate the peeled root on a box grater or rasp, or you can mince it by cutting it into coins and smashing them with the heel of your hand against your flattened knife blade, just as you would a garlic clove. (See page 36 for more on mincing.)

MEYER LEMON GASTRIQUE

Makes about 1 pint

This gastrique is one of the neatest tricks to have up your sleeve. It adds a tangy, light note to dessert dishes: drizzle it over a piece of pound cake for an easy and elegant end to the meal. It's also equally terrific in savory territory: use it to cut the richness of dishes such as broiled salmon or the Tasty Thai Chicken (page 158). You can substitute any variety of lemon you like, but the uniquely sweet flavor of Meyer lemons is highlighted in this preparation.

INGREDIENTS

2 lemons, preferably Meyer
1½ cups sugar
¼ cup water
1½ cups white wine vinegar
     Pinch of salt

PREPARE

1. Using a vegetable brush, scrub the fruit with a nontoxic, odorless dish soap and hot water.

2. Using a microplane, remove the zest from the lemons and set aside. Juice the lemons into a small bowl (you should get about ¼ cup juice); discard the peels and pith.

3. Combine the sugar and water in a medium nonreactive saucepan and bring to a light boil over medium-low heat. Do not stir. Cook until the sugar melts and begins to color slightly, 5 to 7 minutes, washing down the sides of the pan with a pastry brush dipped in water as necessary.

4. When the sugar begins to color, pour the vinegar into the pan, but be careful — the vinegar will hiss and spit a good bit. The caramel will harden when the liquid hits it but will dissolve again as it simmers. Simmer for 10 minutes to reduce by about half.

5. Add the zest and continue to simmer until the sauce takes on the color and fragrance of the fruit and thickens slightly, 2 to 3 minutes. Add the juice and simmer for an additional minute. Strain through a fine-mesh strainer. Finish with a sprinkle of salt.

PRESERVE

Refrigerate: Cool, cover, and refrigerate for up to about 1 month.

Freeze: Cool, cover, and freeze for up to 6 months.

Can: Use the boiling-water method as described on page 20. Ladle the gastrique into clean, hot 4-ounce jars, leaving ¼ inch of headspace between the top of the gastrique and the lid. Run a bubble tool along the inside of the glass to release trapped air. Wipe the rims clean; center lids on the jars and screw on jar bands until they are just fingertip-tight. Process the jars by submerging them in boiling water to cover by 2 inches for 10 minutes. Turn off the heat, remove the canner lid, and let the jars rest in the water for 5 minutes. Remove the jars and set aside for 24 hours. Check the seals, then store in a cool, dark place for up to 1 year.

Making Gastrique

The trick to making caramel, on which the recipe is based, is patience. As tempting as it is to stir and fuss to make caramel "happen," you must refrain. Cook the sugar and water without stirring and gently wash down the sides of the pan with a pastry brush to prevent sugar crystals from forming. A little time and deep breathing and before you know it, the caramel will take on its gorgeous golden hue.

1. Bring the water and sugar to a boil and cook until the caramel begins to color.

2. Add the vinegar all at once; careful, it will hiss and spit.

3. The hardened caramel dissolves as it simmers.

4. Add the flavoring component and simmer.

5. Strain and season the gastrique.

→ You can flavor gastrique with a variety of fruits such as berries (see page 90) and tomatoes (see page 259).

USE IT UP!

Tasty Thai Chicken with Lemon Gastrique

Serves 4–6

Thai food has great flavor — spicy and exotic but light as well. It makes for great summer picnic eating. Put a little umbrella in your beverage and call it a party.

INGREDIENTS

- **1** (3- to 4-pound) chicken, cut into 8 pieces
- **1** (13.5-ounce) can unsweetened coconut milk, well shaken
- **¼** cup fresh lime juice
- **¼** cup soy sauce
- **2** tablespoons fish sauce (naam pla)
- **1** teaspoon sugar
- **½** teaspoon red pepper flakes (optional)
- **¼** cup Meyer Lemon Gastrique (see page 156)
- **¼** cup minced cilantro (optional)

PREPARE

1. Arrange the chicken in a baking dish just large enough to fit all of the pieces in a single layer. Combine the coconut milk, lime juice, soy sauce, fish sauce, sugar, and red pepper flakes, if using, in a small bowl, and whisk together. Pour the mixture over the chicken, and turn the pieces to coat them evenly. Cover and refrigerate for at least 4 hours and up to 8.

2. Preheat the oven to 375°F.

3. Drain the chicken, discarding the marinade. Arrange the chicken in a single layer in a large baking pan. Roast for about 45 minutes, until the internal temperature reaches 165°F.

4. Arrange the chicken on a serving platter and drizzle with the gastrique. Garnish with cilantro, if you like, and serve hot or at room temperature.

LEMON, RED ONION, AND OREGANO JAM

Makes 5 cups

This recipe is a tad intense to prep. Halfway through julienning the lemon zest I start to curse the fuss of it. But all the fuss is forgotten when the heat hits the pot — the perfume of the lemons and lovely pink hue that the onions bring to the picture dispel all memory of tedium. This is truly a gorgeous jam.

INGREDIENTS

- **2** pounds lemons (8–10)
- **2** cups water
- **4** cups sugar
- **4** teaspoons Pomona's Universal Pectin
- **1** pound red onions (about 1 large or 2 medium), diced
- **½** cup red wine vinegar
- **2** tablespoons dried oregano
- **½** teaspoon salt
- **¼** teaspoon freshly ground black pepper
- **4** teaspoons calcium water (from the Pomona's Universal Pectin kit)

PREPARE

1. Using a vegetable brush, scrub the fruit with a nontoxic, odorless dish soap and hot water.

2. Remove the zest from the lemons with a vegetable peeler, being sure to leave any white pith behind. Julienne the zests. (See page 35 for more on julienne.) Combine the zests and water in a small nonreactive saucepan and bring to a boil. Reduce the heat, cover, and simmer gently for 30 minutes to soften the zests.

Recipe continues on next page →

3. Combine 2 cups of the sugar with the pectin in a small bowl and set aside.

4. Supreme the lemons (see page 130), discarding the white pith and seeds. Combine the lemon flesh with the softened zests and their simmering liquid in a large nonreactive pot. Add the remaining 2 cups sugar, onion, vinegar, oregano, salt, and pepper. Bring to a boil, stirring to dissolve the sugar, and then reduce the heat and simmer, stirring occasionally, until the onions are translucent, about 10 minutes.

5. Stir in the calcium water. Slowly add the pectin mixture, stirring constantly to avoid clumping. Bring to a boil, reduce the heat, and simmer for 1 to 2 minutes, continuing to stir constantly, until the sugar is completely dissolved.

6. Remove from the heat. Allow the jam to rest for 5 minutes, giving it an occasional gentle stir to release trapped air; it will thicken slightly. Skim off any foam.

PRESERVE

Refrigerate: Cool, cover, and refrigerate for up to 3 weeks.

Can: Use the boiling-water method as described on page 20. Ladle the jam into clean, hot half-pint jars, leaving ¼ inch of headspace between the top of the jam and the lid. Run a bubble tool along the inside of the glass to release trapped air. Wipe the rims clean; center lids on the jars and screw on jar bands until they are just fingertip-tight. Process the jars by submerging them in boiling water to cover by 2 inches for 10 minutes. Turn off the heat, remove the canner lid, and let the jars rest in the water for 5 minutes. Remove the jars and set aside for 24 hours. Check the seals, then store in a cool, dark place for up to 1 year.

Freezing Citrus Juice

I am not a fan of frozen juice concentrates. They never live up to the promise of fresh fruit taste. Having frozen juice on hand is another story. If you are the recipient of a citrus box that you just can't seem to get to the bottom of, or you have a tree in your backyard (lucky you!), and you find yourself with too many tart treats to eat, this is a great solution.

Using a rasp or the rectangular holes on a box grater, remove the zest of the fruit, being careful not to take any of the bitter white pith. Juice the fruit into a measuring cup with a spout, for easy pouring. Fill the compartments of an ice cube tray three-quarters full with juice, and divide the zest among the filled compartments. Cover with plastic wrap and freeze solid, at least 8 hours but no more than 1 day. Remove the cubes from the tray and quickly transfer to freezer bags or other freezer containers. They'll keep in the freezer for 3 to 4 months.

To use the frozen juice, defrost the cubes and use them as you would fresh juice, or pop them, still frozen, into iced tea, lemonade, or shrub (page 98) for a tangy, tasty, and pretty presentation.

USE IT UP!

Kefta with Lemony Yogurt Spread

Serves 6–8

Kefta — the "good for company" burger! These lamb patties are studded with spices and herbs that elevate them a step above typical barbecue fare. The yogurt spread is a cinch to make and throws the whole dish over the top — it's also great on grilled chicken so, while you've got the jam jar open, better make extra. You can serve these kefta on a bed of greens or couscous, wrapped in a pita, or in a traditional burger bun, topped with a bit of the sauce. This recipe makes a nice-size batch — they reheat beautifully and can even be wrapped well and frozen.

KEFTA INGREDIENTS

- **2** eggs
- **1** medium onion, grated
- **2** garlic cloves, minced
- **¼** cup parsley, chopped
- **¼** cup red wine
- **2** teaspoons kosher salt
- **1** teaspoon dried oregano
- **1** teaspoon dried thyme
  Freshly ground black pepper
- **2** cups fresh white bread crumbs
- **2** pounds ground lamb
- **¼** cup olive oil (if pan-frying)

YOGURT SAUCE INGREDIENTS

- **½** cup Lemon, Red Onion, and Oregano Jam
  (see page 159)
- **½** cup plain yogurt
  Salt

PREPARE

1. To make the kefta, whisk the eggs in a large bowl. Add the onion, garlic, parsley, wine, salt, oregano, and thyme, season generously with pepper, and whisk to combine. Add the bread crumbs and stir to combine (the bread crumbs will soak up most of the egg mixture). Add the lamb and, using your hands, mix it with the bread mixture. Be sure not to overwork the mix or your kefta will be tough. Divide the mixture into palm-sized portions and form into patties.

2. To grill the kefta, fire up a charcoal grill. Grill the kefta over medium-hot coals until browned on both sides and the center is no longer pink. If you prefer to pan-fry the kefta, preheat the oven to 350°F. Heat the oil in a large skillet over medium-high heat. Sauté patties until browned on both sides, about 3 minutes per side, working in batches as necessary. Remove the browned patties to a rimmed baking sheet and bake 5 to 10 minutes, until cooked through.

3. To make the sauce, combine the jam and yogurt in a small bowl, and whisk together until well combined. Season with salt to taste. Serve as an accompaniment to the kefta.

LEMON CRANBERRY CHUTNEY

Makes 6 cups

Tart and sassy, this chutney has all the flavor punch needed to keep pace with even the most assertive of curries. It is particularly delicious with creamy main dishes.

INGREDIENTS

- **2** pounds lemons (8–10)
- **2** cups water
- **½** pound yellow onion (1 large or 2 medium), diced
- **2** cups lightly packed brown sugar
- **1** cup Dried Cranberries (page 125)
- **1** cup granulated sugar
- **½** cup apple cider vinegar
- **2** tablespoons freshly grated ginger
- **1** tablespoon minced garlic
- **1** tablespoon salt
- **1** tablespoon yellow mustard seeds
- **½** teaspoon ground allspice

PREPARE

1. Using a vegetable brush, scrub the fruit with a nontoxic, odorless dish soap and hot water.

2. Cut off the tops and bottoms of the lemons deeply enough to remove the solid disks of pith and reveal the flesh of the fruit. Quarter the fruit and cut away the center rib. Flick out the seeds with the end of your knife. Using the grater blade of a food processor, shred the lemon quarters. Transfer the shredded lemons to a large nonreactive pot, looking out for any large pieces that made it past the blade. Return these larger pieces to the food processor with 1 cup of the water and purée, using the chopping blade. Add

→ The citrus peels in this chutney, like those in marmalades, will taste best if they are allowed to "cure" for a few weeks in the jar, so they're not the best candidates for refrigeration. Canning will yield the best results.

the purée to the pot with the remaining 1 cup water. (Alternatively, the lemons can be sliced thinly by hand and added to the pot with the 2 cups of water.) Bring to a boil, then cover, reduce the heat, and simmer for 1 hour, uncovered, to soften the rinds.

3. Add the onion, brown sugar, cranberries, granulated sugar, vinegar, ginger, garlic, salt, mustard seeds, and allspice. Simmer until thick, about 30 minutes.

4. Remove from the heat. Allow the chutney to rest for 5 minutes, giving it an occasional gentle stir to release trapped air; it will thicken slightly. Skim off any foam.

PRESERVE

Refrigerate: Cool, cover, and refrigerate for up to 3 weeks.

Can: Use the boiling-water method as described on page 20. Ladle the chutney into clean, hot half-pint jars, leaving ½ inch of headspace between the top of the chutney and the lid. Run a bubble tool along the inside of the glass to release trapped air. Wipe the rims clean; center lids on the jars and screw on jar bands until they are just fingertip-tight. Process the jars by submerging them in boiling water to cover by 2 inches for 10 minutes. Turn off the heat, remove the canner lid, and let the jars rest in the water for 5 minutes. Remove the jars and set aside for 24 hours. Check the seals, then store in a cool, dark place for up to 1 year.

USE IT UP!

Braised Chickpeas with Lemon Cranberry Chutney

Serves 4

I am not a vegetarian, but I eat a lot of vegetarian meals. For lots of reasons, but mainly because I just get bored of the "meat and three" pattern on my plate. I like to mix it up. "Meatless Mondays," a charge led in large part by the fabulous chef Kim O'Donnel, are one way to think about reorienting your dinner plate at least part of the time. It's not hard to do. Pizza can easily be vegetarian, and who doesn't like pizza night? Or try this warmly spiced Indian-inspired dish, and serve it with some of your own Lemon Cranberry Chutney. You'll wish that Meatless Monday came more than once a week.

INGREDIENTS

- **2** tablespoons neutral-flavored vegetable oil, such as organic canola
- **1** onion, diced
- **2** garlic cloves, minced
- **1** (2-inch) knob fresh ginger, minced
- **1** tablespoon chili powder
- **1** tablespoon ground coriander
- **1** tablespoon ground cumin
- **1** teaspoon salt
- **1** quart whole tomatoes, preferably home-canned, puréed
- **1** pound waxy potatoes, cut into 1-inch dice
- **3** cups cooked or canned chickpeas
- **¼** cup raisins
- **¼** cup cilantro, chopped

  Hot cooked rice, for serving

  Lemon Cranberry Chutney (see page 162), for serving

PREPARE

1. Heat the oil over medium-high heat in a large skillet. Add the onion and sauté until translucent, 5 to 7 minutes. Add the garlic and ginger and sauté until fragrant, about 1 minute. Add the chili powder, coriander, cumin, and salt, and sauté for 30 seconds to release their oils. Add the tomatoes, potatoes, chickpeas, and raisins. Cover and simmer until the potatoes are nearly tender, 40 to 50 minutes.

2. Remove the lid and cook, uncovered, until the sauce is thickened, 5 to 10 minutes. Garnish with cilantro and serve with rice and Lemon Cranberry Chutney.

→ This recipe is also delicious with Orange and Cumin Chutney (page 174) or Pear and Prune Compote (page 203).

WHOLE DRIED LEMONS

Makes 6–12 dried lemons

Whole dried limes are called "black lemons" in the Middle East, where they are used in pilafs and stews for their depth of flavor and bit of a citrus spike. I have substituted lemons in this recipe. It's true, all of the lovely color will leave the fruit as it cures, but the gorgeous citrus notes remain and bring along with them a deep, funky flavor that develops as the fruit dries.

INGREDIENTS

- **1** gallon water
- **2** cups kosher salt
- **6–12** lemons

PREPARE

1. Using a vegetable brush, scrub the fruit with a nontoxic, odorless dish soap and hot water.

2. Bring the water to a boil in a large stockpot. Add the salt, stirring a couple times to dissolve it. Add the lemons and boil in the salted water for 10 minutes. Remove the fruit with a slotted spoon and dry thoroughly.

PRESERVE

Dry: Arrange the lemons on a wire rack, like a cake cooling rack, and set aside in a well-ventilated, dry area. Allow to air-dry for 4 to 6 weeks, turning over weekly, until completely desiccated, hard, and leathery. Store in an airtight container for up to 1 year.

USE IT UP!

Herbal Tisane

Serves 2

Tisanes are infusions of dried herbs — like tea without the tea. Dried citrus peel and flowers are game, too. I've even seen whole dried spices, such as peppercorns and juniper berries, in tisane mixtures. You can experiment to create your own blend. Well-stocked tea and spice shops have everything you need for your own custom tisane, and if you know your way around botanicals, you can do your own harvesting and drying.

INGREDIENTS

- **2** cups water
- **1** Whole Dried Lemon (see page 164), cut in half
- **1** teaspoon fresh rosemary or 1 tablespoon dried
- **4** peppercorns
  Honey (optional)

PREPARE

Bring the water to a boil in a small pot. Remove from the heat and add the lemon halves, rosemary, and peppercorns. Steep for 5 minutes. Strain into two mugs and serve, sweetened with honey if you like.

LIMONCELLO

Makes about 2 quarts

Alon Shaya, of Domenica Restaurant in New Orleans, told me about this technique for making limoncello. Unlike the common infusion made by steeping lemon peels in neutral spirits, this method uses alcohol evaporation to gently coax the lemon oil and juice from the fruit. Though the process is a bit more time consuming, the result is complex and nuanced — and thoroughly addictive! You can serve it chilled, over ice, or cut with an equal measure of seltzer — light and lemony but lethal.

INGREDIENTS

- **2** pounds lemons (about 8–10)
- **1** (1.5-liter) bottle grain alcohol, such as Everclear
- **4** cups sugar
- **2** cups water

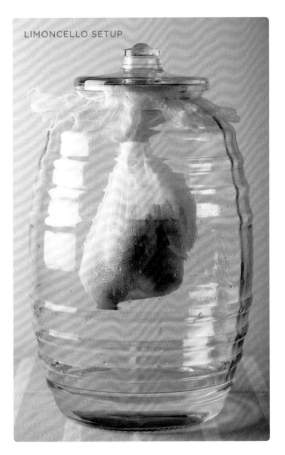

LIMONCELLO SETUP

PREPARE AND PRESERVE

1. Using a vegetable brush, scrub the fruit with a nontoxic, odorless dish soap and hot water.

2. Thoroughly wash a 5-gallon glass jar with a tight-fitting lid. Rinse out the jar with about ¼ cup of the alcohol. Pour the rest of the alcohol in the jar.

3. Place the lemons in the center of a single layer of cheesecloth. Bundle the cloth around the lemons and tie the bundle as close to the fruit as possible with a narrow strip of cheesecloth. Suspend the bundled and tied fruit inside the jar, allowing the loose cloth from the bundle to dangle over the top of the jar. Use a rubber band to secure the loose fabric around the neck of the jar. Cover the jar with the lid, making sure to create an airtight seal. Set the jar aside where it will be undisturbed for 4 to 6 months.

4. The alcohol from the liquor will evaporate and condense on the fruit, releasing the fruit's oils and juices, which will drip down into the liquor at the bottom of the jar. The process is complete when the lemons surrender their color and flavor to the liquor — the fruit will be pale and the liquid will be vibrant.

5. When the lemon liqueur is ready, combine the sugar and water in a small saucepan and bring to a boil, stirring to dissolve the sugar. Let cool to room temperature and then add to the lemon liqueur. Decant into small bottles and allow to cure for at least 2 weeks.

6. The liqueur will keep in the refrigerator for up to 6 months.

USE IT UP!

Lemon Pepper Martini

Serves 2

I am more of a classic cocktail kind of a gal. But back in the day, I knocked back my share of "girly" martinis. One might think of this as a tipple with training wheels, but seeing as it's made with homebrewed hooch, I think it's earned its big girl status.

INGREDIENTS

- **2** tablespoons sugar
- **3** ounces Limoncello (see page 166)
- **1** tablespoon freshly squeezed lemon juice
  Freshly ground black pepper
  Ice
- **1** lemon wedge
- **2** lemon slices (optional)

PREPARE

1. Pour the sugar onto a plate at least as wide as your martini glasses.

2. Combine the Limoncello, lemon juice, and a few grinds of pepper in a cocktail shaker filled with ice. Shake vigorously for about 1 minute.

3. Rub the rims of two chilled martini glasses with the lemon wedge. Invert the glasses and press the rims on the plate to coat with sugar. Carefully strain half of the martini into each glass and serve, garnished with a lemon slice if you like.

Oranges

Oranges always remind me of the holidays. Winter is their peak season, so I am sure that their abundance in the market has helped to form that association. Studding oranges with cloves — that, too, marks oranges as a Christmas fruit for me. Or perhaps it was the vague recollection of an episode of *Little House on the Prairie* in which the orange was featured as a prized and exotic treat to receive as a gift. Oranges truly are a prize. Just as the fields are slowing down, when the last of the apples have dropped in orchards of the Northeast, where I live, I turn to the orange to get my preserving freak on.

I like to see the parade of oranges come into the market, the knobby-ended navels, the slightly bitter juicing Valencias, and my favorite, the blood oranges. Although a ubiquitous item on supermarket shelves, oranges have their season, too, and I want to catch them at their best. I often order directly from some family farmers in Ojai, California, to get oranges and other citrus fruits that are really preserving-worthy.

My first foray into preserving oranges started with marmalades, which are not only very easy to make but perfume your house with their sweet smell for days. I've branched out from there with chutneys, curds, syrups, and other sunny citrusy things. All bring a ray of sunshine to your winter kitchen.

ORANGE CURD

Makes about 2 cups

Citrus curd is tricky. You need to cook it enough so that it is safe on the shelf, but cook it too long and it will curdle. Is it worth the trouble? You bet. Luscious in flavor and texture, curd is easy to love. And it fits so neatly into your kitchen — finding itself at home at the breakfast table, offering to be the helpful hand in a last-minute dessert — that you will find yourself missing the curd when it's not around.

I use only pasture-raised eggs in my curds. Not only are they better for the farmer, the farm, and you, they have a fuller, richer taste than the grain-fed eggs you find at the grocery store, and their saffron yolks tinge the curd a gorgeous color.

INGREDIENTS

- **1** cup sugar
- **4** eggs, preferably from pasture-raised hens
- ¼ cup freshly squeezed lemon juice (from 1 or 2 fruit)
- ¼ cup freshly squeezed orange juice (from 1 or 2 fruit)
  Zest of 1 lemon
  Zest of 1 orange
- ¼ teaspoon kosher salt
- ½ cup (1 stick) unsalted butter, cut into pats

PREPARE

1. Combine the sugar, eggs, lemon juice, orange juice, lemon zest, orange zest, and salt in a medium nonreactive saucepan and whisk together. Set over medium-low heat and cook, whisking constantly, until the mixture warms a bit and begins to thicken (about 120°F on a candy thermometer).

2. Reduce the heat to low, add the butter pats, and continue to cook, whisking constantly, until the curd is as thick as heavy cream and reaches 160°F on a candy thermometer, about 10 minutes (the butter will slowly melt, gradually being incorporated into the egg base). Remove from the heat and strain through a fine-mesh sieve to remove the zest, if you like.

PRESERVE

Refrigerate: Cool, cover, and refrigerate for up to about 3 weeks.

USE IT UP!

Orange Dream Bars with Graham Cracker Crust

Makes 12 bars

This throw-together dessert couldn't be simpler to make. It's a great trick to have up your sleeve when you forget to shop for an after-dinner sweet and need one in a flash. Now that you've made your orange curd, you probably have all the ingredients you need on hand.

INGREDIENTS

- **4** ounces graham crackers (about 19 whole)
- **½** cup packed dark brown sugar
- **¼** teaspoon salt
- **½** cup (1 stick) cold unsalted butter
- **1** cup Orange Curd (see page 169)
- **2** tablespoons confectioners' sugar or zest from 1 orange

PREPARE

1. Preheat the oven to 375°F. Butter a 9-inch square cake pan.

2. Break up the crackers, place them in a food processor fitted with a chopping blade, and process to a meal. Add the sugar and salt and pulse to combine. Add the butter and pulse several times, until a bit of mixture squeezed in your fist holds its shape. Press the crumbs into the prepared pan (a glass is handy for pressing). Bake for 15 minutes. Cool completely.

3. Spread the curd on the crust. Dust with confectioners' sugar or sprinkle with a little orange zest if you like. Slice into bars and serve.

BLOOD ORANGE MARMALADE

Makes about 7 cups

You can use any type of oranges you find at the market, but blood oranges add an alluring pink blush to the finished product. Here we have a classic three-day marmalade. But don't be put off — it really adds up to just about an hour of work in total. Start it on a Friday after work and you will have delicious, handmade stuff to brag about around the water cooler come Monday morning.

INGREDIENTS

3 pounds blood oranges (7–8)
About 3 cups water
6 cups sugar

PREPARE

1. Using a vegetable brush, scrub the fruit with a nontoxic, odorless dish soap and hot water.

2. Cut off the tops and bottoms of the oranges deeply enough to remove the solid disks of pith and reveal the flesh of the fruit. Quarter the fruit and cut away the center rib. Flick out the seeds with the end of your knife. Using the disk blade of a food processor, finely slice the orange quarters. Transfer the sliced oranges to a large nonreactive pot, looking out for any large pieces that made it past the blade. Return these larger pieces to the food processor with 1 cup of the water, and purée using the chopping blade. Add the purée to the pot with enough water to cover, about another 1 cup. (Alternatively, you can slice the oranges thinly by hand and add them to the pot with enough water to cover, about 2 cups.) Bring to a boil. Remove from the heat, cover, and let sit overnight.

3. The next day, bring to a boil and then let sit overnight again.

4. On the third day, measure the volume of the cooled and softened mixture (you should have about 6 cups), and return to the pot with an equal amount of sugar and the remaining 1 cup water. Bring to a boil, stirring constantly to prevent the sugar from burning. Continue cooking until the gel stage is reached (see page 28), 20 to 30 minutes.

5. Remove from the heat. Allow the marmalade to rest for 5 minutes, giving it an occasional gentle stir to release trapped air; it will thicken slightly. Skim off any foam.

PRESERVE

🥫 **Can:** Use the boiling-water method as described on page 20. Ladle the marmalade into clean, hot 4-ounce or half-pint jars, leaving ¼ inch of headspace between the top of the marmalade and the lid. Run a bubble tool along the inside of the glass to release trapped air. Wipe the rims clean; center lids on the jars and screw on jar bands until they are just fingertip-tight. Process the jars by submerging them in boiling water to cover by 2 inches for 10 minutes. Turn off the heat, remove the canner lid, and let the jars rest in the water for 5 minutes. Remove the jars and set aside for 24 hours. Check the seals, then store in a cool, dark place for up to 1 year.

→ Marmalades are really best after they "cure" for a few weeks in the jar, so they're not the best candidates for refrigeration. Canning will yield the best results.

USE IT UP!

Salmon with Orange Glaze

Serves 4

Why wild salmon? Let me count the ways: better for the environment, better for you, protects a time-honored fishing trade, good-quality food . . . and best of all? Better tasting! Wild salmon, caught in season and sold fresh, will convert even the "I don't like fish" into fish eaters. This recipe helps them along the way.

INGREDIENTS

- ½ cup Blood Orange Marmalade (see page 172)
- ½ cup white wine
- 1 tablespoon soy sauce
- 1 (1½-pound piece) wild salmon, about 1 to 1½ inches thick
- 1 scallion, sliced thinly, or 1 tablespoon snipped chives

PREPARE

1. Combine the marmalade, wine, and soy sauce in a food processor or blender and purée. Transfer to a small saucepan, bring to a simmer, and simmer for 2 to 3 minutes to burn off the alcohol in the wine.

2. Preheat the broiler. Arrange the fish, skin side down, on an oiled broiler rack or cake cooling rack set over a baking sheet. Broil the fish, 3 to 4 inches away from the broiler's heating element, for 3 to 5 minutes, until the skin is browned and beginning to bubble.

3. Using a spatula, gently turn the fish over. Drizzle half of the sauce over the fish and broil for about 5 minutes, until brown and nearly cooked through (a knife gently pried into the fish will reveal a raw center).

4. Drizzle the remaining sauce over the fish and broil another minute or two, until fish is cooked through (a knife gently pried into the fish will reveal a bright pink center).

5. Remove from the oven and let rest for 5 minutes to finish cooking. Garnish with scallions or chives and serve.

ORANGE AND CUMIN CHUTNEY

Makes about 4 cups

Chutney may not be a regular item on your grocery list, but it is so useful to have on hand. It can elevate even the simplest snack — a wedge of cheese and a hunk of bread — to a delightful little plowman's lunch. Serve it alongside a roast for a sweet counterpoint to your savory meal. A dollop on the plate can make even plain white rice seem exotic. Make a batch of this chutney and you'll see what a workhorse it can be.

INGREDIENTS

- **2** pounds oranges (about 4)
- **1** tablespoon plus ½ teaspoon kosher salt
- **2** cups brown sugar
- **1** cup dried cherries, cranberries, or a combination of both
- **1** cup apple cider vinegar
- **1** cup water
- **1** yellow onion, diced (about 1½ cups)
- **2** garlic cloves, minced
- **1** tablespoon ground cumin
- **1** tablespoon freshly grated ginger
- **½** teaspoon freshly ground black pepper
- **1** (3- to 4-inch) cinnamon stick

PREPARE

1. Using a vegetable brush, scrub the fruit with a nontoxic, odorless dish soap and hot water.

2. Remove the zest from the oranges with a vegetable peeler and chop finely. Toss the chopped zest with 1 tablespoon of the salt in a small bowl, cover, and set aside overnight to soften. Reserve the zested oranges in a covered bowl in the refrigerator.

3. The next day, rinse the zest in a fine-mesh strainer or tea strainer and put it in a large nonreactive pot. Peel the oranges, separate them into sections, remove any seeds, cut the sections into thirds, and add them to the pot, along with the sugar, cherries, vinegar, water, onion, garlic, cumin, ginger, pepper, cinnamon stick, and the remaining ½ teaspoon salt. Slowly bring to a boil, and then reduce the heat and simmer, uncovered, for 30 minutes. Remove from the heat and remove the cinnamon stick.

4. Allow the chutney to rest for 5 minutes, giving it an occasional gentle stir to release trapped air; it will thicken slightly. Skim off any foam.

PRESERVE

Can: Use the boiling-water method as described on page 20. Ladle the chutney into clean, hot half-pint jars, leaving ½ inch of headspace between the top of the chutney and the lid. Run a bubble tool along the inside of the glass to release trapped air. Wipe the rims clean; center lids on the jars and screw on jar bands until they are just fingertip-tight. Process the jars by submerging them in boiling water to cover by 2 inches for 15 minutes. Turn off the heat, remove the canner lid, and let the jars rest in the water for 5 minutes. Remove the jars and set aside for 24 hours. Check the seals, then store in a cool, dark place for up to 1 year.

→ The citrus peels in this chutney, like those in marmalades, will taste best if they are allowed to "cure" for a few weeks in the jar, so they're not the best candidates for refrigeration. Canning will yield the best results.

USE IT UP!

Cheddar and Chutney Spread

Makes 2 cups

Work with me here. I know that cheddar and chutney can seem an odd combination and even smack of 1950s' pre-fab assembly cooking. But this is no Cheez-Whiz surprise. Put this out at your next cocktail party and it will disappear faster than you can say "processed cheese food." And it takes only 10 minutes to make.

INGREDIENTS

- **8** ounces good-quality cheddar cheese
- **4** ounces cream cheese, softened
- **4** ounces Orange and Cumin Chutney (see page 174)
  Crackers, for serving

PREPARE

1. Shred the cheddar cheese, using a food processor or a box grater.

2. Combine the cream cheese and chutney in a food processer and process until smooth. Add the cheddar cheese and pulse to combine. Pack into a ramekin or crock and refrigerate for at least 4 hours, and up to 2 days. Serve with crackers.

DRIED ORANGE ZEST

This is one of those trash-to-treasure recipes that brings a little delight to your pantry at no additional cost to you. Orange zest — it comes free with any orange and is probably something that gets tossed in the garbage or compost pile more often than not. The next time you are about to dig into a juicy orange, slice off the zest first. A week's worth of oranges will pile up the peels quickly. Then you will have this handy little flavor booster at the ready.

INGREDIENTS

Any quantity oranges

PREPARE

1. Using a vegetable brush, scrub the fruit with a nontoxic, odorless dish soap and hot water.

2. Use a vegetable peeler to remove the zest from the fruit, leaving behind the white pith. Arrange the zest pieces on a wire rack, like a cake cooling rack. Set aside in a well-ventilated, dry place for 3 to 4 days, until leathery. (You can hold the zest at this point for up to 1 week. So you can add zests to the rack as they become available and then proceed to the next step when you have a nice little pile.)

PRESERVE

Dry: Preheat the oven to 170°F. Transfer the zests to a baking sheet, and place on the middle rack of the oven. Bake for 10 to 15 minutes, until brittle. Store as is, or use a spice grinder to whir into a powder. The dried zests will keep in an airtight container for up to 6 months.

USE IT UP!

Winter Lettuce Salad with Orange Dust

Serves 2

You can use this recipe with any lettuce you find at the farmers' market, but I am particularly fond of it with the cold-weather lettuces — those that grow under the cold frame before other plants have even begun to awaken for the season, such as mâche, purslane, and maybe some arugula. Their deep green color looks lovely against the dust, and their slightly bitter flavor tastes great with it, too.

INGREDIENTS

- **2** teaspoons red wine vinegar
- **1** teaspoon Dijon mustard
  Salt and freshly ground black pepper
- **2** tablespoons extra-virgin olive oil
- **4** cups winter greens
- **1** shallot, sliced and rinsed
- **2** tablespoons Dried Cranberries (see page 125)
- **½** teaspoon Dried Orange Zest (see page 176)

PREPARE

1. Combine the vinegar, mustard, and a pinch each of salt and pepper in a small bowl, and whisk together. Slowly add the oil, whisking to emulsify.

2. Toss the greens and shallot with the dressing in a large salad bowl, and then divide between two plates. Garnish with cranberries and zest and serve.

KITCHEN HOW-TO
Cleaning a Coffee Grinder

I love the vibrant flavors and aromas of freshly ground spices, so I usually buy mine whole and give them a whir in the coffee grinder to turn them into powders. Even a whole spice that has been home-ground months before it meets the pan has gobs more flavor than pre-ground powders. To keep my coriander from tasting like my cumin, and to keep delicately flavored things such as orange zest from taking on other flavors, it's important to start with a clean coffee grinder. A quick way to get yours as clean as a whistle is to use it to pulverize a piece of bread or handful of rice. The starch picks up all of the spice dust and oils that the grinding leaves behind. If you use rice, you can save the ground rice powder and use it as a pre-flavored thickener for soups and stews — just add a few teaspoons to the pot in the last 10 minutes of cooking.

ORANGE SYRUP

Makes about 1 cup

Fresh oranges are a delight to eat. Their peels are so fragrant, it's a shame to toss them in the bin. This recipe helps you use up the detritus of snacking oranges in a lovely sweet syrup that is a perfect base for a homemade soda, a great addition to a martini, or a fine substitute for apricot jam when glazing pies and tarts. Give your fruit a scrub before you peel it for eating, and save the peels in an airtight container in your freezer until you have enough. Avid orange eaters, you can double this recipe if you like. You can also substitute grapefruit peels or use a combination of both.

INGREDIENTS

- ½ pound peels from well-scrubbed oranges, chopped
- 2 cups water
- 2 cups sugar

PREPARE

1. Bring a medium nonreactive pot of water to a boil and add the peels. Simmer for 10 minutes, then drain to pull some of the bitter flavor off the peels.

2. Add the water to the pot and bring to a boil. Add the sugar and stir until dissolved. Add the peels, reduce the heat to low, and simmer gently, uncovered, 1 hour to infuse the syrup with citrus flavor. Strain, pressing on the solids. Cool to room temperature.

PRESERVE

Refrigerate: Cover and refrigerate for up to 3 months.

ORANGE SYRUP

USE IT UP!

Citrus Splash

Serves 1

My daughter, Ava, came up with this recipe. It's a sweet treat — sort of like the fancy Italian soda that she sometimes gets when we eat out — and a fine alternative to canned soft drinks.

INGREDIENTS

- 6 ounces seltzer
- 1 ounce Orange Syrup
  Ice
  Orange slice, optional

PREPARE

Combine the seltzer and syrup in a tall glass and gently stir to combine. Add ice. Garnish with an orange slice, if you like, and enjoy.

Peaches

Sorry, Georgia, I know you've got a peach thing, but my people are from South Carolina and their peaches are pretty outstanding. I grew up on them. Every summer one of us "Northerners" (as my South Carolinian relatives called us Baltimoreans) would return from a road trip to the family farm with bushels of perfect peaches. I remember their sweet smell and the little beads of sap that you might find clinging to the odd leaf, something you never find in a supermarket peach — these fruits came straight from the tree to us. And as if that wasn't enough, my Granny Toni had her very own peach tree growing in her backyard. Not to be too dramatic, but if I close my eyes and think about my childhood summers, that's what comes to mind: the smell of peaches.

I grew up eating golden peaches but have since found white peaches and doughnut peaches that have come into the market. White peaches have a more delicate flavor and are not quite as acidic as golden peaches. Doughnut peaches look like peaches that've been run over a bit: they're flattened out and squat. I don't use the doughnuts for preserving, as their odd shape makes them problematic to prep, but if you have them in abundance (and have an abundance of fortitude) you could use them in these recipes. Try them this year and then your summers can smell like peaches, too.

QUICK PEACH JAM

Makes about 8 cups

This jam has a bright taste that is so fresh it's like biting into a peach. The short cooking time and quick gel afforded by the added pectin keep it lovely and lively.

INGREDIENTS

- **2** cups sugar
- **1** tablespoon Pomona's Universal Pectin
- **1** cup water
- **¼** cup bottled lemon juice
- **4** pounds peaches
- **4** teaspoons calcium water (from the Pomona's Universal Pectin kit)

PREPARE

1. Combine the sugar and pectin and set aside.

2. Combine the water and lemon juice in a large nonreactive pot. Peel, pit, and halve the peaches (see page 182), adding them to the lemon water as you go to prevent browning.

3. Bring the pot to a boil, then reduce the heat and simmer for 20 minutes to soften the fruit, mashing with a potato masher occasionally to pulverize the fruit.

4. Add the calcium water and stir to combine. Slowly add the pectin mixture, stirring constantly to avoid clumping. Bring to a boil, reduce the heat, and simmer for 1 to 2 minutes, continuing to stir constantly, until the sugar is completely dissolved.

5. Remove from the heat. Allow the jam to rest for 5 minutes, giving it an occasional gentle stir to release trapped air; it will thicken slightly. Skim off any foam.

PRESERVE

Refrigerate: Cool, cover, and refrigerate for up to 3 weeks.

Can: Use the boiling-water method as described on page 20. Ladle the jam into clean, hot 4-ounce or half-pint jars, leaving ¼ inch of headspace between the top of the jam and the lid. Run a bubble tool along the inside of the glass to release trapped air. Wipe the rims clean; center lids on the jars and screw on jar bands until they are just fingertip-tight. Process the jars by submerging them in boiling water to cover by 2 inches for 10 minutes. Turn off the heat, remove the canner lid, and let the jars rest in the water for 5 minutes. Remove the jars and set aside for 24 hours. Check the seals, then store in a cool, dark place for up to 1 year.

USE IT UP!

Sweet-and-Sour Chicken

Serves 4

This dish is a kid-pleaser. When I make it for the younger set, I leave out the pepper flakes. When I make it for me, I double them.

INGREDIENTS

- ½ cup Quick Peach Jam (see page 180)
- ¼ cup freshly squeezed lemon juice
- ½ cup water
- 1 tablespoon soy sauce
- 2 teaspoons cornstarch
- 2 tablespoons neutral-flavored vegetable oil, such as organic canola
- 1 pound boneless, skinless chicken breast or thigh meat, cut into 1-inch chunks
- 1 teaspoon salt
- 1 onion, cut into large dice
- 1 garlic clove, minced
- 1 tablespoon freshly grated ginger
  Pinch of red pepper flakes (optional)

PREPARE

1. Combine the jam and juice in a small bowl, and whisk together. In a separate bowl, stir together the water, soy sauce, and cornstarch.

2. Heat the oil in a medium skillet over medium-high heat. Season the chicken with salt, add to the hot pan, and sauté until browned but not cooked through, about 2 minutes per side. Use a slotted spoon to remove the chicken from the pan.

3. Add the onion to the pan and sauté until translucent, 5 to 7 minutes. Add the garlic and ginger and sauté until fragrant, 1 to 2 minutes. Stir in the cornstarch mixture and simmer until thickened, 1 to 2 minutes. Stir in the jam mixture and the pepper flakes, if using, and then return the chicken to the pan. Simmer until the chicken is cooked through and the sauce is thickened, about 5 minutes. Serve immediately.

→ This recipe is also delicious with Classic Apricot Jam (page 65), Quick Apricot Jam (page 68), or Classic Peach Jam (page 183) in place of the Quick Peach Jam.

KITCHEN HOW-TO
Prepping Peaches

Peaches fall into two categories — clingstone and freestone. Clingstones, as their name describes, hang on to their pit, and you have to cut the flesh away from the stone to release it. Freestones, on the other hand, give up their pit freely. Blanch both varieties for peeling.

1. To prepare peaches for preserving, fill a large bowl with heavily iced water (about 1 quart of ice cubes for every gallon of water). Bring a large pot of water to a boil. Drop the peaches into the boiling water, no more than six at a time, and return to a boil. Blanch until the skins begin to loosen, 30 to 60 seconds.

2. Scoop the fruit out of the water with a spider or slotted spoon and plunge them into the ice water. Continue blanching the peaches in batches. Remove from the ice bath and drain.

3. The skins will slip off easily for the most part; any clinging bits can be removed with a small paring knife.

4. If you run a knife through a freestone peach, cutting through its circumference from pole to pole all the way down to the pit, you can twist the two halves apart and then pry the pit free of the flesh, leaving two intact, stone-free halves. For clingstone peaches, use a paring knife to trim the flesh away from the stone.

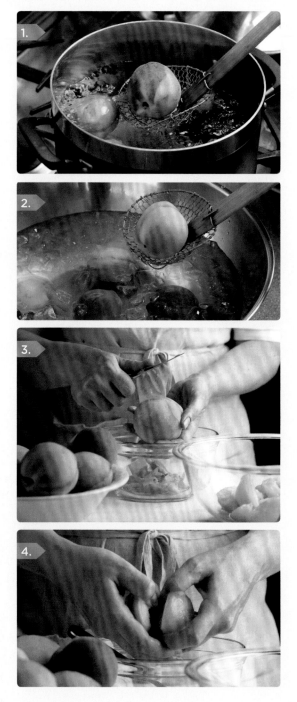

CLASSIC PEACH JAM

Makes about 6 cups

I think all Southerners are born with jars of this in their hands. It's just something everyone south of the Mason Dixon grows up with. And for good reason — it is fabulous. Make a batch and you will never want to be without it either.

INGREDIENTS

- **1** cup water
- **¼** cup bottled lemon juice
- **4** pounds peaches
- **4** cups sugar

PREPARE

1. Combine the water and lemon juice in a large nonreactive pot. Peel, pit, and slice the peaches (see page 182), adding them to the lemon water as you go.

2. Bring the mixture to a boil, then reduce the heat and simmer for 10 minutes to soften the fruit, crushing it with a potato masher if you prefer a smooth-textured jam.

3. Add the sugar and stir to dissolve. Continue to simmer until the gel stage is reached (see page 28), about 30 minutes.

4. Remove from the heat. Allow the jam to rest for 5 minutes, giving it an occasional gentle stir to release trapped air; it will thicken slightly. Skim off any foam.

PRESERVE

Refrigerate: Cool, cover, and refrigerate for up to 3 weeks.

Can: Use the boiling-water method as described on page 20. Ladle the jam into clean, hot 4-ounce or half-pint jars, leaving ¼ inch of headspace between the top of the jam and the lid. Run a bubble tool along the inside of the glass to release trapped air. Wipe the rims clean; center lids on the jars and screw on jar bands until they are just fingertip-tight. Process the jars by submerging them in boiling water to cover by 2 inches for 10 minutes. Turn off the heat, remove the canner lid, and let the jars rest in the water for 5 minutes. Remove the jars and set aside for 24 hours. Check the seals, then store in a cool, dark place for up to 1 year.

USE IT UP!

Marinated Shrimp Skewers

Makes about 12 skewers, serving 4–6

Shrimp are on and off the grill so quickly that I sometimes find it hard to get a nice bit of color on them without overcooking. The sugar in this marinade solves that problem — it caramelizes quickly over the fire, so your shrimp have gorgeous color in an instant. For this same reason, I wouldn't use this marinade on longer-cooking foods — too much time on the heat and it will burn.

INGREDIENTS

- **12** wooden skewers
- **½** cup Classic Peach Jam (see page 183)
- **½** cup freshly squeezed lime juice
- **2** garlic cloves, minced
- **2** teaspoons chili powder
- **1** teaspoon salt
- **2** pounds large domestic Gulf shrimp (16–20 count), peeled and deveined
- **1** onion, cut in half equatorially and then into sixths
- **1** green pepper, cut into chunks (optional)
- **¼** cup neutral-flavored vegetable oil, such as organic canola

PREPARE

1. To keep them from burning during cooking, soak the skewers in a shallow dish of water while the shrimp marinate.

2. Combine the jam, lime juice, garlic, chili powder, and salt in a medium bowl, and whisk together. Add the shrimp and toss to coat. Refrigerate, covered, for at least 1 hour but no more than 2 hours. (Extended stays in acidic marinades "cook" the shrimp. A good idea for ceviche, but not for shrimp you intend to grill.)

3. Preheat the grill. Make kebabs by threading alternating pieces of shrimp, onion, and pepper, if using, onto skewers. You should have about 3 shrimp per skewer. Brush with oil. Grill over high heat until the shrimp turn pink, turning once, 2 to 3 minutes per side. (Alternatively, you can broil them directly under the broiler's heating element.) Serve hot or at room temperature.

→ This recipe is also delicious when made with Quick Peach Jam (page 180).

PEACH BBQ MOP

Makes about 7 cups

This sauce has just enough kick to let itself be known. Use this "mop" to frequently douse the meat you are grilling. A long-handled pastry brush will do the trick, or you can use an actual miniature mop (available from most kitchen supply retailers) intended for the purpose.

INGREDIENTS

- **1½** cups apple cider vinegar
- **2** pounds peaches
- **2** pounds tomatoes
- **1** pound yellow onions, chopped
- **½** pound sweet red peppers
- **2** cups lightly packed brown sugar
- **1** habanero pepper (optional)
- **2** garlic cloves, crushed
- **1** tablespoon ground allspice
- **1** tablespoon salt, plus more for seasoning
- **1** teaspoon ground cloves

PREPARE

1. Pour the vinegar into a large nonreactive pot. Peel, pit, and quarter the peaches (see page 182), adding them directly to the vinegar as you go. Peel, core, and quarter the tomatoes, adding them to the vinegar as well. Add the onions, red peppers, sugar, habanero, if using, garlic, allspice, salt, and cloves, and slowly bring to a boil.

2. Reduce the heat and simmer until the produce is softened and the mixture has thickened, 50 to 60 minutes. Purée with an immersion blender, and season to taste with salt.

PRESERVE

⊘ **Refrigerate:** Cool, cover, and refrigerate for up to 3 weeks.

🅑 **Can:** Use the boiling-water method as described on page 20. Ladle the sauce into clean, hot half-pint jars, leaving ¼ inch of headspace between the top of the sauce and the lid. Run a bubble tool along the inside of the glass to release trapped air. Wipe the rims clean; center lids on the jars and screw on jar bands until they are just fingertip-tight. Process the jars by submerging them in boiling water to cover by 2 inches for 15 minutes. Turn off the heat, remove the canner lid, and let the jars rest in the water for 5 minutes. Remove the jars and set aside for 24 hours. Check the seals, then store in a cool, dark place for up to 1 year.

USE IT UP!

Sticky Ribs

Serves 4 for dinner or 8 as part of a buffet

I love good ribs and have been on the receiving end of some mighty fine ones, prepared with care and expertise over carefully selected smoking wood and nurtured for hours. So pit masters of the universe, forgive me when I tell you that sometimes, well, I cheat. I make ribs and I do it in the oven. And while they may not live up to tradition, they do taste pretty spankin' good and are really fun to serve at parties. Don't hate.

INGREDIENTS

2 racks baby back ribs (about 4 pounds total)
   Salt and freshly ground black pepper
2 cups boiling water
1 cup Peach BBQ Mop (see page 186)

PREPARE

1. Preheat the oven to 350°F.

2. Liberally season the ribs with salt and pepper and arrange in a large roasting pan fitted with a roasting rack. Pour the boiling water in the bottom of the pan, making sure that it doesn't fill the pan enough to touch the ribs. Cover tightly with aluminum foil and bake for 1 hour (the water may boil away during the cooking, and that's okay).

3. Remove the foil, baste the ribs with the mop, and continue roasting for 1 hour more, basting every 15 minutes.

4. Remove the ribs to a cutting board. Cut between the bones to slice them into individual portions.

PEACH MELBA COMPOTE

Makes about 4 pints

This preserve looks like a Tequila Sunrise, with a layer of ruby red berries on the bottom and an orange and peachy layer on top. You can serve it this way, in layers, or stir your jam together before you spoon it out. Either way, it tastes great!

INGREDIENTS

- **1** cup water
- **¼** cup bottled lemon juice
- **4** pounds peaches
- **4** cups sugar
- **1** pint raspberries

PREPARE

1. Combine the water and lemon juice in a large bowl. Peel, pit, and slice the peaches (see page 182), adding them to the lemon water as you go. Add the sugar, toss to coat the peaches, and set aside for 2 to 4 hours to toughen the fruit.

2. Transfer the peach mixture to a large non-reactive pot and slowly bring to a simmer. Continue to simmer, stirring gently occasionally, until the fruit is softened, but not falling apart, 5 to 10 minutes.

3. Remove from the heat. Allow the compote to rest for 5 minutes, giving it an occasional gentle stir to release trapped air; it will thicken slightly. Skim off any foam.

4. Divide the raspberries among four clean, hot pint jars. Ladle the hot peaches into the jars, leaving ¼ inch of liquid above the peaches and ½ inch of headspace between the top of the mixture and the top of the jar.

PRESERVE

Can: Use the boiling-water method as described on page 20. Run a bubble tool along the inside of the glass to release trapped air. Wipe the rims clean; center lids on the jars and screw on jar bands until they are just fingertip-tight. Process the jars by submerging them in boiling water to cover by 2 inches for 10 minutes. Turn off the heat, remove the canner lid, and let the jars rest in the water for 5 minutes. Remove the jars and set aside for 24 hours. Check the seals, then store in a cool, dark place for up to 1 year.

ENGLISH MERINGUES, *recipe on following page* →

USE IT UP!

English Meringues

Serves 4

The first time I had an English meringue I was expecting to be presented with the top portion of a lemon pie, fluffy and white like whipped cream. As I soon found out, English meringues are much different from the pie topping. They are light indeed, but they're baked to a crunch. At least that's what they are meant to be. Mine were served on a hot August day in Georgia, where the humidity kept them more on the chewy side than crunchy. Don't make the same mistake. Save your meringue baking for a dry day and they will crumble, pleasingly, with every bite.

INGREDIENTS

- **4** egg whites, at room temperature
- **¼** teaspoon cream of tartar
- **1** cup superfine sugar (or regular granulated sugar processed in a food processor for 1 minute)

 About 1 cup Peach Melba Compote (see page 188)

PREPARE

1. Preheat the oven to 200°F. Line a baking sheet with parchment paper. Wipe down all your equipment — a large mixing bowl, a whisk or the beaters of an electric mixer, measuring cups, and a flexible spatula — with a few drops of distilled white vinegar to remove any lingering oil or grease that would prevent your eggs from whipping.

2. Combine the egg whites and cream of tartar in a large bowl. Using a whisk or an electric mixer, beat the whites until foamy. Add ¼ cup of the sugar and beat until it is dissolved. Repeat with the remaining sugar, adding it ¼ cup at a time. Continue to beat until stiff peaks are formed (when you invert your whisk or beater, the meringue clinging to it will hold its shape without folding over onto itself).

3. Using a flexible spatula, gently transfer the meringue to a gallon-size ziplock bag from which you have snipped off ½ inch of a bottom corner, or a pastry bag fitted with a ½-inch tip. Pipe 2-inch rounds of meringue onto the prepared baking sheet. Bake for 1½ hours, until crisp but not colored. Turn off the oven heat and allow the meringues to finish drying in the oven for at least a few hours, or even overnight.

4. To serve, arrange three or four of the cooled meringues on a serving plate and top with ¼ cup of the Peach Melba Compote.

DUCK SAUCE

Makes about 4 cups

Duck sauce from scratch. Who knew? I didn't, until the day I found myself standing in the kitchen staring down a pile of peaches with no interest in making jam. I opened the fridge for inspiration and there it was — a sticky, icky jar of commercial duck sauce. It had a pretty long list of ingredients — some of which I am sure will make you grow a tail if eaten in any quantity — but the key ingredient? Peaches. That's where I started, and here's what I came up with.

INGREDIENTS

- **2** pounds peaches, peeled, pitted, and chopped
- **1** cup orange juice
- **1** cup distilled white vinegar
- **1** shallot, minced
- **1** garlic clove, minced
- **1** tablespoon salt
- **1** teaspoon chili powder
- **2** cups white sugar

PREPARE

1. Combine the peaches, juice, vinegar, shallot, garlic, salt, and chili powder in a large non-reactive pot. Bring to a boil, then reduce the heat and simmer until the fruit falls apart, about 10 minutes. Mash the mixture with a potato masher.

2. Add the sugar and continue to simmer until thickened, 30 to 40 minutes.

3. Remove from the heat. Allow the sauce to rest for 5 minutes, giving it an occasional gentle stir to release trapped air; it will thicken slightly. Skim off any foam.

PRESERVE

Refrigerate: Cool, cover, and refrigerate for up to 3 weeks.

Can: Use the boiling-water method as described on page 20. Ladle the sauce into clean, hot 4-ounce or half-pint jars, leaving ¼ inch of headspace between the top of the sauce and the lid. Run a bubble tool along the inside of the glass to release trapped air. Wipe the rims clean; center lids on the jars and screw on jar bands until they are just fingertip-tight. Process the jars by submerging them in boiling water to cover by 2 inches for 10 minutes. Turn off the heat, remove the canner lid, and let the jars rest in the water for 5 minutes. Remove the jars and set aside for 24 hours. Check the seals, then store in a cool, dark place for up to 1 year.

USE IT UP!

Fried Won Tons

Serves 4-6 as a cocktail nibble

What can I say? I like fried. Sometimes when we are making pot stickers and I have a few leftover wrappers, I'll make a batch of these to nibble on. Dunk them down in the duck sauce — decadent but delicious!

INGREDIENTS

- ½ cup neutral-flavored vegetable oil, such as organic canola
- At least 6 won ton skins, cut into ½-inch strips
- Duck Sauce (see page 191), for serving

PREPARE

1. Heat the oil in a medium saucepan until shimmering but not smoking. Test the oil by dropping a bit of won ton skin into it — the skin should bubble actively the minute it hits the oil.

2. Drop the skins into the oil one at time, in batches of five or six. Fry for 30 to 40 seconds, until lightly browned. Scoop out with a slotted spoon or spider, and drain on paper towels. Repeat with the remaining skins. Serve with Duck Sauce.

Pears

Check the neck. That's how to find out if your pear is ripe. It should give when gently pinched. Pears ripen from the inside out, so a fruit that is soft throughout its body may be a bit past its prime.

Pears come in brown, green, red, and shades in between. The color does not indicate ripeness. It's okay to buy unripened pears; they'll ripen if left out on your counter. Then it's best to refrigerate them or pop them in your root cellar to slow the aging process.

Of all the pear varieties, including Comice, Anjou, and Bartlett, my favorite are the diminutive Seckels. Maybe it's just their "baby fruit" cuteness, but they are great to have around for snacking — they are very crunchy — or for strewing on the holiday feast table (before feasting on them). But of course you can use any variety in the recipes that follow.

PEAR JELLY

Makes about 8 (4-ounce) jars

You want ripe, luscious pears for this recipe so that they give up lots of sweet fruit juice. Sparkling clear and pale golden in color, this jelly makes a lovely gift.

194

INGREDIENTS

- **4** cups water
- **¼** cup bottled lemon juice
- **4** pounds pears
- **2** cups sugar
- **3** teaspoons Pomona's Universal Pectin
- **3** teaspoons calcium water (from the Pomona's Universal Pectin kit)

PREPARE

1. Line a colander with a triple thickness of cheesecloth or have ready a jelly bag in its frame (see page 87), and set either device over a bowl.

2. Combine the water and lemon juice in a large nonreactive pot. Quarter the pears, but do not peel or pit, adding them to the pot as you go to prevent browning.

3. Slowly bring the mixture to a simmer over medium heat. Reduce the heat and simmer gently until the fruit is soft and falling apart, about 30 minutes. Be careful not to bring the mixture to a rolling boil, or the jelly may cloud. Pour into the prepared colander and allow to drain fully, 2 to 3 hours.

4. Combine the sugar and pectin in a small bowl and set aside.

5. Measure the volume of the drained juice (you should have about 4 cups). Bring the juice to a simmer in a large pot. Add the calcium water and stir to combine. Slowly add the pectin mixture, stirring constantly to avoid clumping. Bring to a boil, reduce the heat, and simmer for 1 to 2 minutes, continuing to stir constantly, until the sugar is completely dissolved.

6. Remove from the heat. Allow the jelly to rest for 5 minutes, giving it an occasional gentle stir to release trapped air; it will thicken slightly. Skim off any foam.

PRESERVE

Refrigerate: Cool, cover, and refrigerate for up to 3 weeks.

Can: Use the boiling-water method as described on page 20. Ladle the jelly into clean, hot half-pint jars, leaving ¼ inch of headspace between the top of the jelly and the lid. Run a bubble tool along the inside of the glass to release trapped air. Wipe the rims clean; center lids on the jars and screw on jar bands until they are just fingertip-tight. Process the jars by submerging them in boiling water to cover by 2 inches for 10 minutes. Turn off the heat, remove the canner lid, and let the jars rest in the water for 5 minutes. Remove the jars and set aside for 24 hours. Check the seals, then store in a cool, dark place for up to 1 year.

USE IT UP!

Pear-tini

Serves 1

I never had any interest in the apple-tinis that were all the rage not so long ago. Too frou-frou and too often made with liqueurs that seemed to have more artificial ingredients in them than booze. This is not that. The pear flavor is there, but it does not make you feel like you are eating a pie. And if this becomes the next great thing, well, it will come by the honor honestly.

INGREDIENTS

- **1** ounce top-shelf vodka
- **1** ounce Poire Williams (pear brandy)
- **1** tablespoon Pear Jelly (see page 194)
- **½** ounce freshly squeezed lemon juice
  Ice

PREPARE

Combine the vodka, brandy, jelly, and lemon juice in a cocktail shaker and swirl to dissolve the jelly. Add ice and shake until chilled, about 1 minute. Strain into a chilled martini glass and serve.

ROASTED PEAR PURÉE

Makes about 6 (8-ounce) jars

Roasting pears boosts their delicate flavor and brings out their sweetness without adding sugar. In this recipe I've puréed them, which gives you a rustic sauce with lots of amped-up pear flavor. Without any added sugar, this is a fruit sauce that can play on either team — sweet or savory.

INGREDIENTS

4 pounds pears, quartered

3 cups water

½ cup bottled lemon juice

PREPARE

1. Preheat the oven to 400°F. Arrange the pears in a large roasting pan, just big enough to fit them in a single layer. Add 1 cup of the water and cover with aluminum foil. Roast for 30 minutes to allow the fruit to release some of its juice.

2. Remove the foil, stir, and roast for about 1 hour, until the fruit releases all of its juice and begins to brown in spots.

3. Add the remaining 2 cups water to the pan and stir to loosen the browned juices. Roast for another 5 to 10 minutes to dissolve the caramelized juices in the pan.

4. Run the pears and liquid through a food mill, allowing the purée to mill directly into a large nonreactive pot. Stir in the lemon juice. Gently bring to a simmer and simmer until slightly thickened, 5 to 10 minutes.

PRESERVE

Refrigerate: Cool, cover, and refrigerate for up to 5 days.

Can: Use the boiling-water method as described on page 20. Ladle the purée into clean, hot half-pint jars, leaving ¼ inch of headspace between the top of the purée and the lid. Run a bubble tool along the inside of the glass to release trapped air. Wipe the rims clean; center lids on the jars and screw on jar bands until they are just fingertip-tight. Process the jars by submerging them in boiling water to cover by 2 inches for 10 minutes. Turn off the heat, remove the canner lid, and let the jars rest in the water for 5 minutes. Remove the jars and set aside for 24 hours. Check the seals, then store in a cool, dark place for up to 1 year.

USE IT UP!

Pear Soup

Serves 4

I am not a big fan of fruit soups. To me, they often just seem like melted desserts — a smoothie I have to eat with a spoon. This pear soup is very different. Its rustic nature takes over, beating the fruity notes of the pears down into savory submission. A blue cheese garnish drives the point home.

INGREDIENTS

- **2** tablespoons unsalted butter
- **1** leek, white and light green parts only, diced
  Salt and and freshly ground black pepper
- **½** pound russet or other starchy potatoes, peeled and cut into large dice
- **½** teaspoon dried sage
- **2** cups chicken stock, preferably homemade
- **1** cup Roasted Pear Purée (see page 196)
- **1** ounce blue cheese, crumbled

PREPARE

1. Melt the butter in a medium saucepan over medium-high heat. Add the leek, season with a pinch each of salt and pepper, and sauté until translucent, 2 to 3 minutes. Add the potatoes and sage, followed by the stock, and bring to a boil. Reduce the heat and simmer until the potatoes are very tender, about 15 minutes.

2. Add the pear purée and remove from the heat. Purée the soup with an immersion blender.

3. Return to a simmer and heat until warmed through. Serve garnished with a few crumbles of blue cheese.

PEAR AND HONEY PRESERVES

Makes about 4 cups

Pears have a delicate taste that can easily be overwhelmed by other flavors. I put just enough honey in this recipe to support the sweetness of the pears and give just a whiff of the round, wild flavors of good, local honey. This is a great spread to use in simple desserts that let the flavors of the preserve come through. I've also been caught sneaking spoonfuls topped with crumbled blue cheese — it's pretty great like that, too.

INGREDIENTS

- **1** cup sugar
- **2** teaspoons Pomona's Universal Pectin
- **2** cups water
- **¼** cup bottled lemon juice
- **3** pounds pears
- **½** cup honey
- **2** teaspoons calcium water (from the Pomona's Universal Pectin kit)

PREPARE

1. Combine the sugar and pectin in a small bowl and set aside.

2. Combine the water and lemon juice in a large nonreactive pot. Peel and core the pears (see steps 1 through 3 on page 200). Chop the fruit, adding it to the lemon water as you go to prevent browning.

Recipe continues on next page →

3. Bring the mixture to a boil over medium-high heat. Reduce the heat and simmer until the pears begin to break down, about 15 minutes, stirring occasionally to prevent the pears from sticking. Crush the fruit with a potato masher, leaving pea-size bits of fruit whole.

4. Add the honey and calcium water and stir to combine. Slowly add the pectin mixture, stirring constantly to avoid clumping. Bring to a boil, reduce the heat, and simmer for 1 to 2 minutes, continuing to stir constantly, until the sugar is completely dissolved.

5. Remove from the heat. Allow the preserves to rest for 5 minutes, giving the mixture an occasional gentle stir to release trapped air; it will thicken slightly. Skim off any foam.

PRESERVE

 Refrigerate: Cool, cover, and refrigerate for up to 3 weeks.

 Can: Use the boiling-water method as described on page 20. Ladle the preserves into clean, hot 4-ounce or half-pint jars, leaving ¼ inch of headspace between the top of the preserves and the lid. Run a bubble tool along the inside of the glass to release trapped air. Wipe the rims clean; center lids on the jars and screw on jar bands until they are just fingertip-tight. Process the jars by submerging them in boiling water to cover by 2 inches for 10 minutes. Turn off the heat, remove the canner lid, and let the jars rest in the water for 5 minutes. Remove the jars and set aside for 24 hours. Check the seals, then store in a cool, dark place for up to 1 year.

USE IT UP!

Mini Pear and Walnut Cheesecakes

Makes 48 tarts

I love being served a small variety of little morsels at dessert, just enough to get a taste of this and a bit of that. These make a great addition to a dessert tasting platter. You can substitute almond flour for the all-purpose flour for a gluten-free version of this treat.

INGREDIENTS

- ¾ cup walnuts, ground
- ¼ cup all-purpose flour
- ¼ cup sugar
  Pinch of salt
- 1½ tablespoons unsalted butter, melted
- 8 ounces cream cheese, softened
- 2 eggs
- ½ cup sugar
- ½ cup sour cream
- ½ teaspoon vanilla extract
- 1 cup Pear and Honey Preserves (see page 197)
- ½ cup walnut pieces

PREPARE

1. Preheat the oven to 375°F. Line mini muffin tins with paper cups.

2. Combine the walnuts, flour, sugar, and salt in a small bowl. Add the butter and stir until well combined. Scoop 1 teaspoon of the nut mixture into each cup. Using the handle of a wooden spoon, tamp the mixture down into each cup to form the bottom layer of the mini cakes.

3. Beat the cream cheese in a medium bowl with an electric hand mixer until fluffy. Then, one at a time, beating after each addition until fully incorporated, add the eggs, sugar, sour cream, and vanilla. Pour 1 scant teaspoon of cream cheese filling over the crust in each muffin cup. Bake for 10 minutes.

4. Remove the tins from the oven and top each mini cake with 1 scant teaspoon of Pear and Honey Preserves and a few walnut pieces. Return to the oven and bake for 16 to 18 minutes, until the edges begin to brown.

KITCHEN HOW-TO
Prepping & Poaching Pears

Prepping pears often involves peeling them, which is straightforward enough. Unlike apples, however, coring them takes a bit more finesse than piercing them through with a corer. The seed cluster needs to be removed, but the fibrous vein that runs upward from the seeds to the stem should also be taken out.

1. Begin by peeling your pears, and then cut each pear in half.

2. Use a melon baller to scoop out a divot around the seeds.

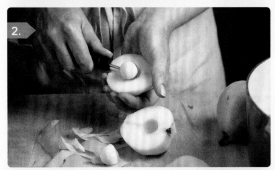

3. Then you can use a paring knife to carefully cut a small V-shaped trench to the top of the fruit to excavate the vein-like core. It's a little bit of work, but a neat job makes for really attractive fruit in the jar.

4. Arrange the fruit in a single layer in a nonreactive pot filled with poaching liquid, as indicated in the recipe. Cover with a piece of parchment. Gently heat to just below a simmer and poach according to your recipe.

PEARS POACHED IN WINE

Makes 2 well-packed quarts

I love seeing jars of these pears on my shelf. They're sort of retro — I can picture them in one of those 1950s housekeeping pamphlets, "Entertaining at Home with Sophistication and Ease." Yet their simple preparation makes them right at home with the "let the food speak for itself" farm-to-table cooking that we crave today. Timeless taste. Use pears that are still quite firm for the perfect texture in the jar.

INGREDIENTS

1 (750 ml) bottle of unoaked red wine, such as Beaujolais

1 cup sugar

1 cup water

4 pounds very firm pears

PREPARE

1. Combine the wine, sugar, and water in a large nonreactive pot. Prepare the pears for poaching, as described in the sidebar at left, and add to the pot. Gently bring the liquid barely to a simmer and poach the pears for 5 minutes, until the fruit begins to soften.

2. Using tongs, gently arrange the pear halves in two quart jars. The pears should fit snugly, but with enough room for poaching liquid to circulate. Ladle the poaching liquid over the packed pears to cover by ¼ inch, leaving ½ inch of headspace between the top of the liquid and the top of the jar.

PRESERVE

Can: Use the boiling-water method as described on page 20. Run a bubble tool along the inside of the glass to release trapped air. Wipe the rims clean; center lids on the jars and screw on jar bands until they are just fingertip-tight. Process the jars by submerging them in boiling water to cover by 2 inches for 20 minutes. Turn off the heat, remove the canner lid, and let the jars rest in the water for 5 minutes. Remove the jars and set aside for 24 hours. Check the seals, then store in a cool, dark place for up to 1 year.

USE IT UP!

Hearty Greens with Poached Pears

Serves 4

Everybody has the occasional moment in the middle of their canning session — maybe the heat of the kitchen has become a little too much, or the canning funnel is impossible to track down — when they find themselves asking, "Why am I doing this?" Then you open up the jar a few weeks or months later, and you remember why. Home-preserved food tastes so fabulous, and little gems such as Pears Poached in Wine make putting together a quick and elegant dish a snap.

INGREDIENTS

- **2** tablespoons balsamic vinegar
- **1** tablespoon poaching liquid from Pears Poached in Wine (see page 201)
- **1** teaspoon Dijon mustard
  Salt and freshly ground black pepper
- **⅓** cup olive oil
- **½** pound mixed greens, preferably including some bitter leaves such as frisée or radicchio
- **4** Pears Poached in Wine halves, cut into ¼-inch slices
- **2** ounces blue cheese
- **¼** cup walnuts, toasted

PREPARE

1. Combine the vinegar, poaching liquid, mustard, and a pinch each of salt and pepper in a small bowl and whisk together. Whisk in the oil, with a few drops initially and then in a thin stream, until emulsified.

2. Toss the dressing with the greens in a large bowl. Divide among four plates. Top the greens with sliced pears, a few crumbles of blue cheese, and the walnuts.

PEAR AND PRUNE COMPOTE

Makes about 5 cups

Macerating the fruit overnight helps it keep its shape during cooking. The result is a preserve with large chunks of fruit suspended in a thick golden syrup. I think it's too chunky for toast but love to serve it alongside spicy dishes, where the sweetness helps tame the beast of the heat.

INGREDIENTS

- ½ cup bottled lemon juice
- 4 pounds pears
- 4 cups sugar
- 12 prunes, quartered
- 1 teaspoon ground cinnamon

PREPARE

1. Pour the lemon juice into a large bowl. Peel and core the pears (see steps 1 through 3 on page 200). Cut the pears into 1-inch pieces, adding them to the bowl and tossing with the lemon juice as you go to prevent browning. Add the sugar and stir to combine. Cover with a tea towel and allow to sit at room temperature overnight.

2. The next day, give the mixture a stir (some sugar may not have dissolved, and that's okay). Drain the syrup from the bowl into a large nonreactive pot and bring to a boil. Reduce the heat and simmer until reduced by half, about 10 minutes, stirring carefully to avoid scorching.

3. Add the pears, prunes, and cinnamon, and continue to simmer until the pears become clear, 15 to 20 minutes.

4. Remove from the heat. Allow the compote to rest for 5 minutes, giving it an occasional gentle stir to release trapped air; it will thicken slightly. Skim off any foam.

PRESERVE

Refrigerate: Cool, cover, and refrigerate for up to 3 weeks.

Can: Use the boiling-water method as described on page 20. Ladle the compote into clean, hot half-pint jars, leaving ¼ inch of headspace between the top of the compote and the lid. Run a bubble tool along the inside of the glass to release trapped air. Wipe the rims clean; center lids on the jars and screw on jar bands until they are just fingertip-tight. Process the jars by submerging them in boiling water to cover by 2 inches for 10 minutes. Turn off the heat, remove the canner lid, and let the jars rest in the water for 5 minutes. Remove the jars and set aside for 24 hours. Check the seals, then store in a cool, dark place for up to 1 year.

USE IT UP!

Turkey Curry

Serves 6–8

Turkey curry is often served in England as a foil for holiday leftovers. It's so good that you might consider roasting a larger bird just to ensure that you have an excuse to make it. Creamy and spicy, but not too much so, it makes a great buffet dish. After all the glitter of the festivities has settled, invite some friends over to share a cozy plate of curry.

INGREDIENTS

- **2** tablespoons neutral-flavored vegetable oil, such as organic canola or safflower
- **1** onion, diced
- **2** stalks celery, diced
- **2** garlic cloves, minced
- **2** tablespoons freshly grated ginger
- **1–2** tablespoons curry powder (hot or mild)
- **1** (13.5-ounce) can unsweetened coconut milk, chilled
- **¼** cup raisins
- **2** apples, peeled, cored, and diced
- **2–3** cups cooked turkey meat
- **¼** cup heavy cream
- **¼** cup chopped cilantro (optional)
  Hot cooked rice, for serving
  Pear and Prune Compote (see page 203), for serving

PREPARE

1. Heat the oil in a large skillet over medium-high heat. Add the onion and celery and sauté until translucent, 5 to 7 minutes. Add the garlic and ginger and sauté until fragrant, about 1 minute. Add the curry powder and sauté for 30 seconds. Add the coconut milk and sauté until thickened, 1 to 2 minutes.

2. Add the raisins and apples, cover, reduce the heat, and simmer until the raisins have plumped, about 10 minutes. Add the turkey meat and cream and simmer, uncovered, until the sauce has thickened, 2 to 3 minutes. Garnish with cilantro, if using, and serve with rice and Pear and Prune Compote.

Plums

When I think of the word "plum," the first thing that springs to mind is not the fruit, it's the adjective, as in "What a plum job!" The saying traces back to the use of "plum" as a sweet meat or bonbon. To be given a plum was to be awarded a confection. My fascination with outdated patois aside, a plum is a pretty sweet reward.

While a mature plum will continue to ripen and sweeten a bit off the tree, an immature plum will never reach the same flavor and texture it could have if left to develop in the orchard. To ripen mature fruit, set it on a kitchen counter, preferably in the sun, for a day or more. Then refrigerate to prolong its shelf life.

Although wild plums do grow here in the United States, the most common varieties you will find in the States are damson, Japanese, and European plums. Damsons are very tart and are used predominantly in cooking and preserving. Japanese plums are round, and the largest of the three. These are the variety most often eaten fresh out of hand. European plums (including Italian plums) are smaller than the Japanese varieties and are more football shaped. But because most varieties of European plums are freestone, they are ideal for preserving.

SWEET PICKLED PLUMS

Makes about 3 pints

Pickled peaches are a classic Southern preserve. I have transferred those same flavors to this plum recipe. The vinegar definitely brings a "pickle" to the party, but the sweetness of the sugar and warm spices balance out the flavors, so it's nothing like a gherkin. I use the quick pickling method for these fruits rather than canning them, which can make the fruit too soft, even if you leave the skins on. You can nibble on these as they are, use them as a topping for ice cream, or serve them with a roast.

INGREDIENTS

- **1** cup apple cider vinegar
- **1** cup water
- **½** cup brown sugar
- **½** cup granulated sugar
- **1** star anise
- **1** cinnamon stick
- **2** whole cloves
- **2** pounds plums, halved and pitted

PREPARE

1. Combine the vinegar, water, brown sugar, granulated sugar, star anise, cinnamon stick, and cloves in a medium nonreactive saucepan. Bring to a boil, then reduce the heat and simmer for 5 minutes.

2. Pack the plums snugly, but without bruising them, into one or more heatproof containers. Scoop the spices out of the syrup and then ladle it over the packed fruit, being sure to completely submerge the fruit in the syrup. Swirl the jars to remove air bubbles.

PRESERVE

Refrigerate: Cool, cover, and refrigerate for up to 1 month.

KITCHEN HOW-TO
Pitting Plums

Freestone plums, which ripen later in the season than other varieties, have pits that are easily released from halved fruit. Just slice through to the pit, run your knife all the way around latitudinally, and then twist the two halves apart and pop out the stone.

In clingstone plums, however, the flesh "clings" or adheres to the pit, so removing the stone requires a bit more effort. Slice them in half vertically and use a melon baller or small spoon to scoop out the pits. You needn't peel plums of any variety before preserving them.

USE IT UP!

Cinnamon Rice with Pickled Plums

Serves 8–10

This rice is exotically spiced with cinnamon. You can serve it with spicy Indian dishes or even your Sunday roast, where it will be right at home with the warm flavors from the oven.

INGREDIENTS

- **1** tablespoon olive oil
- **1** onion, finely diced
- **2** teaspoons salt
- **2** cups water
- **1** (13.5-ounce) can unsweetened coconut milk, well shaken
- **1** teaspoon ground cinnamon
- **2** cups long-grain white rice
- **½** cup Sweet Pickled Plums (see page 206), drained and chopped

PREPARE

1. Heat the oil in a medium saucepan over medium heat. Add the onion and salt and sauté until translucent, 5 to 7 minutes.

2. Add the water, coconut milk, and cinnamon and bring to a boil. Add the rice, stir, cover, and reduce the heat to low. Cook until most of the liquid has been absorbed and the surface of the rice is littered with pockmark indentations, about 20 minutes.

3. Scatter the plums on top. Remove from the heat and let rest, covered, for about 10 minutes. Fluff with a fork and serve.

PLUM AND PRUNE CONSERVE

Makes about 6 cups

This was one of those recipes that sort of wrote itself, as I stood at the stove, tasting the preserves as they cooked. The pot called for more thyme and the addition of pepper and herbes de Provence like a puzzle looking for its missing pieces.

INGREDIENTS

- **2** cups red wine
- **1** cup prunes, quartered
- **½** pound shallots (about 4)
- **1** tablespoon olive oil
- **2** pounds plums, pitted and chopped
- **1** cup water
- **4** cups sugar
- **½** cup red wine vinegar
- **1** tablespoon fresh thyme, chopped, or 1 teaspoon dried
- **1** teaspoon herbes de Provence
- **¼** teaspoon salt
- **¼** teaspoon freshly ground black pepper

PREPARE

1. Preheat the oven to 400°F.

2. Bring the wine to a boil in a small saucepan. Add the prunes, cover, and set aside.

3. Toss the shallots with the oil, arrange on a baking sheet, and roast for about 20 minutes, until tender. When cool enough to handle, slip off the papery skins, trim away any leathery edges, and finely dice.

4. Combine the plums and water in a large non-reactive pot. Bring to a boil, reduce the heat, and simmer for 20 minutes to soften skins. Add the rehydrated prunes with their soaking liquid, the prepared shallots, and the sugar,

vinegar, thyme, herbes de Provence, salt, and pepper. Simmer until thickened to nearly the gel stage (see page 28), about 20 minutes.

5. Remove from the heat. Allow the conserve to rest for 5 minutes, giving it an occasional gentle stir to release trapped air; it will thicken slightly. Skim off any foam.

PRESERVE

Refrigerate: Cool, cover, and refrigerate for up to 3 weeks.

Can: Use the boiling-water method as described on page 20. Ladle the conserve into clean, hot half-pint jars, leaving ½ inch of headspace between the top of the conserve and the lid. Run a bubble tool along the inside of the glass to release trapped air. Wipe the rims clean; center lids on the jars and screw on jar bands until they are just fingertip-tight. Process the jars by submerging them in boiling water to cover by 2 inches for 10 minutes. Turn off the heat, remove the canner lid, and let the jars rest in the water for 5 minutes. Remove the jars and set aside for 24 hours. Check the seals, then store in a cool, dark place for up to 1 year.

USE IT UP!

Braised Short Ribs with Plum and Prune Conserve

Serves 4

Short ribs are magical things. They are not much to look at, but give them a few hours in the oven and "beautiful" doesn't even begin to describe them. The meat is tender, succulent, and richly flavored, and the spices in the conserve add incredible depth. This dish makes a dark, soul-satisfying sauce, so be sure to serve it with good bread to soak up every last lick. The ultimate low-and-slow feast.

INGREDIENTS

- **2** tablespoons neutral-flavored vegetable oil, such as organic canola
- **4** pounds bone-in short ribs
  Salt and freshly ground black pepper
- **1** onion, chopped
- **2** stalks celery, chopped
- **1** carrot, peeled and cut into coins
- **4** garlic cloves, unpeeled
- **1** cup home-canned tomatoes or 1 tomato, diced
- **2** cups fruity red wine
- **1½** cups chicken stock, preferably homemade
- **1** teaspoon dried thyme
- **1** bay leaf
- **1** cinnamon stick
- **1** tablespoon cornstarch
- **3** tablespoons Plum and Prune Conserve (see page 208)
  Hot cooked rice or mashed sweet potatoes, for serving

Recipe continues on next page →

Braised Short Ribs with Plum and Prune Conserve, continued

PREPARE

1. Preheat the oven to 325°F.

2. Heat the oil in a Dutch oven over medium heat. Generously season the ribs with salt and pepper, and then brown them on all sides, 2 to 3 minutes per side. Remove the ribs from the pan.

3. Add the onion, celery, carrot, and garlic, and sweat over medium heat until translucent but not browned, 3 to 5 minutes. Add the tomatoes, wine, 1 cup of the stock, thyme, bay leaf, and cinnamon stick, and bring to a boil. Return the ribs to the pan, cover, and place in the oven. Cook for 2 hours.

4. Remove the pan from the oven. Using tongs, remove the ribs from the braising liquid. Strain the liquid through a fine-mesh sieve, discarding the solids. Defat the liquid with a fat separator or by skimming over the top of it with a spoon to remove any floating fat.

5. Return the liquid to the pan and bring to a simmer over medium heat. Whisk together the remaining ½ cup stock and the cornstarch and add to the cooking liquid, along with the conserve. Bring to a simmer and whisk until thickened. Return the ribs to the pan. Cover, and return the Dutch oven to the oven to braise for another hour.

6. Remove the pan from the oven and allow to rest for at least 10 to 15 minutes. (You can prepare the dish a day ahead of time and reheat it.) Serve over rice or with mashed sweet potatoes.

KITCHEN HOW-TO

Short Ribs vs. Spare Ribs

Knowing your way around different cuts of meat can save you money and ensure that you have a great dinner. The best way to do it? Find yourself a butcher and make friends. Quality butchering is a valuable craft and one that is regaining the recognition it deserves. A good butcher can help you find delicious, economical cuts that you don't find in the grocery meat section, and he or she can introduce you to new recipes that help you make the most of your ingredients. Having a butcher is like having your own secret ingredient.

CLASSIC PLUM JAM

Makes about 4 cups

You don't see a lot of plum jam here in the States, where grape and strawberry tend to dominate the PB&J set. That's too bad, because it really is divine and makes a terrific breakfast addition for the same reason as a prune danish. You can use any variety of plum here, and your choice will be reflected in the lovely color of your finished product.

INGREDIENTS

- **2** quarts plums (about 3 pounds), pitted and chopped
- **½** cup water
- **3** cups sugar
- **¼** cup bottled lemon juice

PREPARE

1. Combine the plums and water in a large non-reactive pot and bring to a boil. Reduce the heat and simmer for 20 minutes to soften the skins.

2. Add the sugar and lemon juice and return to a boil. Simmer vigorously, stirring frequently, until the gel stage is reached (see page 28), 20 to 30 minutes.

3. Remove from the heat. Allow the jam to rest for 5 minutes, giving it an occasional gentle stir to release trapped air; it will thicken slightly. Skim off any foam.

Recipe continues on next page →

Why do you...
simmer the plums before adding the sugar?

Sugar can toughen fruit. You can use this to your advantage when you want soft fruits, such as berries, to hold their shape, by tossing the produce with sugar and allowing it to sit overnight before proceeding with your jam recipe. By simmering the plums in plain water before you add the sugar, you give the skins a chance to soften. If you skipped this step and just simmered the plums in water and sugar, the skins would remain tough.

PRESERVE

Refrigerate: Cool, cover, and refrigerate for up to 3 weeks.

Can: Use the boiling-water method as described on page 20. Ladle the jam into clean, hot half-pint jars, leaving ¼ inch of headspace between the top of the jam and the lid. Run a bubble tool along the inside of the glass to release trapped air. Wipe the rims clean; center lids on the jars and screw on jar bands until they are just fingertip-tight. Process the jars by submerging them in boiling water to cover by 2 inches for 10 minutes. Turn off the heat, remove the canner lid, and let the jars rest in the water for 5 minutes. Remove the jars and set aside for 24 hours. Check the seals, then store in a cool, dark place for up to 1 year.

VARIATION:

Classic Plum Jam with Cloves

Add 1 teaspoon cloves in the last few minutes of cooking.

USE 'EM UP!

Carrots with Plum Glaze

Serves 4 as a side dish

I love glazed carrots. Classic Plum Jam brings a little bit of tart flavor to the party, which works to balance the sweetness of the carrots and the glaze. This recipe also works wonders on parsnips — feel free to use a mix of both vegetables, if you like. This is a great dish to put on a winter buffet. Its sweet taste, with a little bit of a twist from the plum jam, will please everyone at the table.

INGREDIENTS

- **2** tablespoons unsalted butter
- **1** pound carrots or a mixture of carrots and parsnips, peeled and cut into 3-inch pieces
  Salt and freshly ground black pepper
- ¼ cup Classic Plum Jam (see page 211)
- ¼ cup water
- ½ lemon

PREPARE

1. Melt the butter in a medium saucepan over medium heat. Add the carrots, season with salt and pepper, and sauté until they are just beginning to color, 3 to 5 minutes.

2. Whisk together the jam and water in a small bowl, and add to the pan. Cover and steam the vegetables until they are nearly tender, about 5 minutes. Uncover and cook until thick and syrupy, being careful not to burn the glaze.

3. Remove from the heat and transfer to a serving platter. Squeeze the juice from a lemon half over the top before serving.

FIVE-SPICE PLUM SAUCE

Makes about 3 cups

My husband introduced me to my first moo shu on a trip to London, where he and his family have made a ritual of gathering at the Good Earth restaurant for its family-style Pekin duck for years. The table-side service of hacking and shredding the succulent fowl, the carefully prepped vegetables, and the handmade pancakes to wrap it all up in were memory-making enough. But the plum sauce, applied liberally to the wrapper with a frayed-scallion brush, is the flavor that has inspired repeat visits (it's worth the flight!) and this dish.

INGREDIENTS

- ½ cup lightly packed brown sugar
- ½ cup apple cider vinegar
- ¼ cup soy sauce
- 3 tablespoons freshly grated ginger
- 2 garlic cloves, minced
- 1 teaspoon five-spice powder (available in Asian markets)
- 2 pounds plums, pitted and chopped

PREPARE

1. Combine the sugar, vinegar, soy sauce, ginger, garlic, and five-spice powder in a large nonreactive pot and bring to a boil. Reduce the heat and simmer for about 5 minutes to allow the flavors to blend.

2. Add the plums and continue to simmer until thickened, 20 to 25 minutes. Purée the sauce with an immersion blender.

PRESERVE

Refrigerate: Cool, cover, and refrigerate for up to 3 weeks.

Can: Use the boiling-water method as described on page 20. Ladle the sauce into clean, hot 4-ounce or half-pint jars, leaving ¼ inch of headspace between the top of the sauce and the lid. Run a bubble tool along the inside of the glass to release trapped air. Wipe the rims clean; center lids on the jars and screw on jar bands until they are just fingertip-tight. Process the jars by submerging them in boiling water to cover by 2 inches for 10 minutes. Turn off the heat, remove the canner lid, and let the jars rest in the water for 5 minutes. Remove the jars and set aside for 24 hours. Check the seals, then store in a cool, dark place for up to 1 year.

USE IT UP!

Duck Moo Shu

Serves 4

Moo Shu is such a fun way to eat! You roast your duck, shred the meat, and then use it to stuff thin Asian pancakes, sort of like a Chinese burrito. Serve with plenty of garnishes, such as shredded carrots, thinly sliced cucumbers, and cilantro, so that everyone can make his or her own masterpiece. It's a fun dish for a dinner party. Everyone uses their hands to build their own pancake, so it's an instant ice breaker, too.

Duck has a lot of fat, and I mean that in a good way. I always cook a duck a week or two before Christmas so we can have potatoes that are roasted in the stuff. Save your duck fat from your roasting pan to do the same, or use it whenever you need a good, flavorful cooking oil.

INGREDIENTS

1 (5- to 6-pound) Long Island duck (also called Pekin)

½ cup Five-Spice Plum Sauce (see page 214)

12 moo shu pancakes (available in the Asian section of grocery stores) or flour tortillas

Sliced cucumber, carrot, jicama, scallions, and/or cilantro, for garnish

PREPARE

1. Pierce the duck skin all over with a sharp knife, being careful not to puncture the meat. Pat dry with paper towels, place in a baking dish large enough to hold the whole bird, and refrigerate, uncovered, for 24 hours to dry the skin.

2. Preheat the oven to 400°F. Transfer the bird to a roasting pan fitted with a baking rack. Roast the duck for 2 to 2½ hours, until it is cooked through and the fat has been rendered. (This may seem like a long time to roast such a small bird, but the fat that you are rendering keeps the bird moist.) If the drippings begin to burn, you can add ½ cup of water to the pan.

3. Carve the duck and cut away the skin, reserving it. Using two forks, shred the meat. Slice the skin into strips.

4. Serve the shredded duck and crispy skin with warm pancakes or tortillas, plum sauce, and vegetable and herb garnishes. Allow each guest to make his or her own moo shu by slathering a pancake with the sauce and then filling it with meat, skin, and garnishes.

Quince

They dined on mince, and slices of quince,
Which they ate with a runcible spoon;
And hand in hand, on the edge of the sand,
They danced by the light of the moon.
— *"The Owl and the Pussycat," by Edward Lear*

*Q*uince is one of the earliest known fruits and has earned its place in literature and mythology. The ancient Greeks found it so seductive that they dedicated the fruit to the love goddess Aphrodite, who was said to favor it and all who enjoyed it. In fact, it is believed that the golden apple Paris gave to her was not an apple at all but a quince. And the Garden of Eden? That's right, it was no apple tree that drew Eve to her doom, it was the seductive quince. To this day, quince have a wide following in South American and Mediterranean cultures, where they are enjoyed for their delicious flavor and as a symbol of fertility.

The fruit takes a little love to coax out its best nature. There are a number of varieties of quince, and most you cannot eat raw. The flesh is too astringent to sink your teeth into. You have to cook it first. But then? Sublime! Some quince, such as the popular Pineapple variety, have a texture similar to that of a potato, hard but manageable, and cook up relatively quickly, maintaining their golden color. Other varieties, such as the Champion, are much harder to prep but cook up to a gorgeous pink color.

Because the fruit is naturally high in pectin, it's easy to preserve quince as jams, jellies, and pastes. Seek some out at the farmers' market — for love of good fruit, or love alone.

POACHED QUINCE

Makes 3 (16-ounce) jars

Poaching is a traditional method for transforming quince from a pale gold, inedibly tough fruit to a tender, delectable, often vibrant pink delight. Pack these into jars, where they will be a feast for the eyes as well as the belly.

INGREDIENTS

- **2** cups sugar
- **2** cups water
- **1** (3-inch) cinnamon stick
- **2** whole cloves
- **6** whole peppercorns
- **¼** cup bottled lemon juice
- **3** pounds quince

PREPARE

1. Combine the sugar, water, cinnamon stick, cloves, and peppercorns in a medium non-reactive saucepan and bring to a simmer. Remove from the heat and add the lemon juice.

2. Core and quarter the quince (see the box on page 220), adding the pieces to the syrup as you go. Cover and let sit overnight.

3. Cut a piece of parchment paper slightly smaller than the span of the pot and lay it on top of the quince in their liquid. Slowly bring the quince to a simmer. Reduce the heat to very low — you should see just the most subtle bubbling of the syrup — and poach the fruit until just tender, 30 to 60 minutes, depending on the ripeness of the fruit. Remove the parchment.

4. Divide the poached fruit among three 16-ounce jars, leaving ¾ inch of headspace between the top of the fruit and the top of the jar. Remove the spices from the syrup, and then pour the syrup over the fruit, leaving ½ inch of headspace between the top of the liquid and the top of the jar.

PRESERVE

🄘 **Can:** Use the boiling-water method as described on page 20. Run a bubble tool along the inside of the glass to release trapped air. Wipe the rims clean; center lids on the jars and screw on jar bands until they are just fingertip-tight. Process the jars by submerging them in boiling water to cover by 2 inches for 20 minutes. Turn off the heat, remove the canner lid, and let the jars rest in the water for 5 minutes. Remove the jars and set aside for 24 hours. Check the seals, then store in a cool, dark place for up to 1 year.

Recipes

218

Lamb Tagine with Poached Quince

Serves 8–10

This low-and-slow dish is a great alternative to the more common beef stew. It's the same technique — you brown the meat well, add some braising liquid, and let a few hours on the stove do its magic. But the exotic flavors of the spices take the tagine to a whole different place. It's like a vacation for your taste buds.

INGREDIENTS

- **2** tablespoons olive oil
- **3–4** pounds lamb shoulder, trimmed of fat and cut into 1½-inch pieces
- **1** teaspoon salt
- **1** onion, diced
- **2** garlic cloves, minced
- **1** (2-inch) knob fresh ginger, grated
- **1** bay leaf
- **1** (3-inch) cinnamon stick
- **1** tablespoon ground cumin
- **1** tablespoon sweet paprika
- **1** teaspoon turmeric
- **½** teaspoon ground cloves
  Freshly ground black pepper
- **2** cups chopped tomatoes, preferably from whole home-canned tomatoes
- **1** cup chicken stock, preferably homemade
- **1** pint Poached Quince (see page 217), drained and cut into 2-inch pieces
  Hot cooked rice or couscous, for serving

PREPARE

1. Heat the oil in a Dutch oven until hot but not smoking. Season the lamb generously with salt and brown in the pan, turning as necessary to brown on all sides, 5 to 7 minutes (the meat will not be cooked through). Work in batches as necessary to avoid crowding the pan. Remove the well-browned meat with a slotted spoon and set aside.

2. Add the onion to the pan and sauté until translucent, 5 to 7 minutes. Add garlic and ginger and sauté 1 minute. Add the bay leaf, cinnamon stick, cumin, paprika, turmeric, cloves, and pepper to taste, and sauté until fragrant, about 30 seconds. Add the tomatoes and stock and bring to a simmer.

3. Return the meat to the pan, cover, and simmer over low heat until the meat is nearly tender, about 1½ hours. Add the quince and simmer for 15 minutes. Remove from the heat and let rest for 5 minutes. Use a small ladle to skim any fat off the top of the tagine. Serve over rice or couscous.

→ The tagine can be made up to 2 days ahead and refrigerated. Remove any solidified fat from the top of the tagine and reheat before serving.

QUINCE PASTE (MEMBRILLO)

Makes 1 (9- by 3- by 1½-inch) block

Quince paste, or membrillo, is a traditional preservation method for quince in South America and Spain. Fruit paste is also found in other parts of Europe, where it is called fruit "cheese." The paste is very different from jams and jellies. It is very firm and sets up in a block shape that can be sliced. It is often served for breakfast on toast, baked into pastries, or served with cheese, Manchego being the most popular pairing. My kids eat it like candy — cut into small squares and dusted with powdered sugar, it makes a nice little after-dinner sweetmeat.

INGREDIENTS

- **4** cups water
- ¼ cup bottled lemon juice
- **3** pounds quince
- **4** cups sugar
- **1** teaspoon neutral-flavored vegetable oil, such as organic canola, or vegetable glycerin

PREPARE

1. Combine the water and lemon juice in a large nonreactive pot. Core and chop the quince (see the box below), adding it to the lemon water as you go to reduce discoloration.

2. Bring to a boil over medium-high heat. Reduce the heat and simmer until the quince fall apart, 20 to 40 minutes. Remove from the heat and let cool slightly. Use an immersion blender to purée the fruit.

3. Return the fruit to the heat, add the sugar, and bring slowly to a simmer, stirring frequently to dissolve the sugar and prevent scorching. Continue to simmer, stirring

KITCHEN HOW-TO
Prepping Quince

Quince discolor very quickly once cut, so it's important to have a pot of acidulated water at the ready, as is indicated in these recipes. You don't have to remove the skin from quince — it cooks up so tender it isn't even noticeable. And that can be a very good thing, as some quince can be so hard that peeling would be difficult, if not dangerous. You do need to remove the core, however, and the fibrous thread that runs from it to the stem as you do pears (see page 200). I use a melon baller to scoop out the core, as I do for pears. Be sure to get all of the core surrounding the seeds, as it remains tough even through extended cooking. Then use a paring knife to whittle a small V-shaped trench to remove the tough membrane that runs from the core to the stem, and you are ready to proceed.

occasionally, until the mixture turns a rich, almost red color and becomes very firm, 2 to 3 hours. It should feel almost dough-like. Remove from the heat.

4. Line a 1-quart terrine or baking dish with plastic wrap. Rub the inside of the wrap with a thin coat of oil or glycerin to keep the membrillo from sticking. Carefully transfer the paste into the lined dish, and let cool completely (the paste will continue to firm as it cools).

PRESERVE

⬦ **Refrigerate:** Cover and refrigerate for up to 3 months.

HOT QUINCE PASTE IS LADLED INTO A LINED LOAF PAN

COOLED MEMBRILLO IS SLICED FOR SERVING

USE IT UP!

Romeo y Julieta (Quince Paste and Cheese)

Makes about 24 nibbles

A lot of recipes in this book pair beautifully with cheese. A quick cocktail nibble can easily and quickly be made by pairing a hunk of sharp cheese with a small dish of any chutney. It is one of my go-to snacks but not much of a recipe, so I have held back on using that card (but you should use it repeatedly — it's a great little flick of the wrist for entertaining or a quick lunch). But the Romeo and Juliet is such a classic combination that I had to lay it on the line here. I think membrillo must have been invented just for the pairing. You will find this dish at many tapas bars here and abroad, and perhaps now at your table, too. Serve with a glass of cold, dry sherry.

INGREDIENTS

- ½ pound Manchego (or any other hard, sharp cheese, such as Cato Corner's Womanchego), sliced into 2-inch triangles
- 4 ounces Membrillo (see page 220), sliced into 1½-inch squares

PREPARE

Arrange the cheese slices on a cheese board. Top with Membrillo slices. Serve as is or with crackers, if you like.

CLASSIC QUINCE JAM

Makes about 8 cups

This jam is so pretty that it's a great one for gifting, so make a few batches if you can get your hands on ripe and ready fruit. Because of the fruit's high pectin level, quince jam firms up quickly, making this a fast process even for a long-cooking jam. And — bonus — quince's powerful perfume will have your kitchen smelling like a dream.

INGREDIENTS

- **3** cups water
- ¼ cup bottled lemon juice
- **3** pounds quince
- **3** cups sugar

PREPARE

1. Combine the water and lemon juice in a large nonreactive pot. Core and chop the quince (see the box on page 220), adding them to the lemon water as you go to reduce discoloration.

2. Bring to a boil over medium-high heat. Reduce the heat and simmer until the quince are tender, 20 to 40 minutes. Use a potato masher to crush the fruit. You can leave it quite chunky or mash it to a smooth texture, depending on your preference. Add the sugar and stir to dissolve. Simmer until

the gel stage is reached (see page 28), 10 to 15 minutes.

3. Remove from the heat. Allow the jam to rest for 5 minutes, giving it an occasional gentle stir to release trapped air; it will thicken slightly. Skim off any foam.

PRESERVE

Refrigerate: Cool, cover, and refrigerate for up to 3 weeks.

Can: Use the boiling-water method as described on page 20. Ladle the jam into clean, hot half-pint jars, leaving ¼ inch of headspace between the top of the jam and the lid. Run a bubble tool along the inside of the glass to release trapped air. Wipe the rims clean; center lids on the jars and screw on jar bands until they are just fingertip-tight. Process the jars by submerging them in boiling water to cover by 2 inches for 10 minutes. Turn off the heat, remove the canner lid, and let the jars rest in the water for 5 minutes. Remove the jars and set aside for 24 hours. Check the seals, then store in a cool, dark place for up to 1 year.

VARIATION:

Ginger Quince Jam

Add ¼ cup freshly grated ginger to the simmering quince for a warm yet lively flavor combination.

Jar suitable for refrigerator storage; not approved for canning

USE IT UP!

Turkey with Quince Glaze

Serves 4

Turkey. It's not just for sandwiches and Thanksgiving dinner. You can use it in place of chicken in many recipes. After all, it shouldn't all taste like chicken. The glaze for these cutlets uses quince jam, bolstered by some warm spices that match really well with the game-bird flavor of the meat. It would also be terrific on a cut of pork.

INGREDIENTS

- **2** tablespoons unsalted butter
- **6** turkey cutlets, about 2 pounds total
- ½ teaspoon salt
- ½ teaspoon freshly ground black pepper
- **1** shallot, minced
- **1** garlic clove, minced
- ½ teaspoon ground cinnamon
- ¼ teaspoon ground allspice
- **1** bay leaf
- ½ cup white wine
- **1** cup chicken stock, preferably homemade
- ½ cup Classic Quince Jam (see page 222)
- **1** teaspoon freshly squeezed lemon juice

PREPARE

1. Melt the butter in a large skillet over medium heat. Generously season the cutlets with salt and pepper and add to the pan. Cook the cutlets until brown, about 5 minutes per side, turning once. Remove the cutlets from the pan and set aside.

2. Add the shallot to the pan and sauté until translucent, 2 to 3 minutes. Add the garlic and sauté 1 minute. Add the cinnamon, allspice, and bay leaf, followed by the wine, and cook until thick and syrupy, 1 to 2 minutes. Add the stock and jam and whisk to combine.

3. Return the cutlets to the sauce, cover, and reduce the heat to medium-low. Braise the cutlets until cooked through, about 30 minutes. Remove the cutlets to a serving platter. Raise the heat and simmer the sauce until thickened, 1 to 2 minutes. Add the lemon juice, adjust seasoning, and spoon the sauce over the cutlets.

QUINCE APPLE LEATHER

Makes about 16 fruit leather strips

"Quince? What does that taste like?" Answer your kids' questions with this recipe. Heck, you can even get them to help. It's a fun way to turn your kids on to a fruit that might be new to them.

INGREDIENTS

- **2** cups water
- **¼** cup bottled lemon juice
- **1** pound apples
- **1** pound quince
- **¼** cup sugar

PREPARE

1. Preheat the oven to 170°F. Line two 11- by 17-inch rimmed baking sheets with parchment paper.

2. Combine the water and lemon juice in a large nonreactive pot. Peel, core, and chop the apples and add to the lemon water. Core the quince (see the box on page 220) and shred the fruit on a box grater or in a food processor, and add to the lemon water.

3. Bring the mixture to a boil over medium-high heat. Simmer until the quince is very soft, 20 to 30 minutes. Remove from the heat and purée the fruit with an immersion blender.

4. Add the sugar to the purée and simmer over low heat, stirring frequently, until the mixture thickens to the consistency of baby food, about 10 minutes.

PRESERVE

▦ Dry:

1. Divide the purée between the baking sheets. Spread the purée over the sheets, tilting them back and forth to create an even layer about ⅛ inch thick. Dry in the oven for about 2 hours, until tacky to the touch. Be careful not to overdry, or the leather will become brittle.

2. Let cool to room temperature. Slide the parchment paper onto a cutting board and roll the leather into a tube. Slice the dried fruit into 2-inch strips. Store in a covered jar for up to 1 month.

USE IT UP!

Potato Stamp Seals

Makes about 28 seals

Here's a great use for Quince Apple Leather — an edible craft project. My kids were really fascinated by this one — homemade candy with their initials pressed into it. Fun to do, and even better to eat! I have set this up for two kids, but it could easily accommodate more by multiplying your ingredients.

INGREDIENTS

- **1** potato
- **4** (2-inch) strips Quince Apple Leather (see page 224)
- **½** cup chocolate morsels (white chocolate looks really pretty, but any kind of chocolate will work)

PREPARE

1. To create the stamp, cut the potato in half. Using a wooden skewer, toothpick, or other pointy implement, etch the outline of your design into the potato. Simple, clear designs with sharp edges, such as initials and stars, work best. Following your outline, use a "child safe" pumpkin carver (or have an adult use a paring knife) to cut ¼ inch down into the potato.

2. Now turn the potato on its side and cut toward the design, being careful not to cut all the way through, removing all the excess potato surrounding the shape (the shape should protrude ¼ inch from the remaining potato). Dry the cut edge of the potato with a clean tea towel.

3. To make the seals, cut the leather into 2-inch squares and lay them out on a baking sheet.

4. Melt the chocolate morsels in a double boiler (or a heatproof bowl set over a pot of simmering water) or by warming them in the microwave for 30 to 60 seconds on high power.

5. Spoon a dab of melted chocolate onto each piece of leather. Refrigerate for about 5 minutes to set up chocolate — it should be firm but still pliable. Firmly press the potato stamp into the cooled chocolate on each piece of leather to impress the cut-out shape into it. Allow to cool completely.

VARIATION:

Fruit Leather Chocolate Sandwiches

Not into so much of a project? You can just dab half of the leather squares with melted chocolate, top with the remaining squares (offsetting them a quarter turn to make a more interesting shape), and let cool until firm. These little fruit leather sandwiches look great on a cookie platter, where their jewel tones and shiny surface add a little sparkle to the tray.

→ This recipe is delicious with any kind of fruit leather.

QUINCE SYRUP

Makes about 1 cup

The next time you see quince in the market and think, "That looks and smells great, but what will I do with it?" start here. You need only about two quince for this recipe, and it cooks up quickly and leaves you with two ways to try the quince — the cooked quince and the syrup. You can serve the cooked quince for dessert with some whipped cream, and the syrup's delicate flavor will have you drizzling it everywhere maple would go and further. So buy yourself some quince; you know you want to.

INGREDIENTS

- **1** pound quince, cored and chopped
- **2** cups water
- **1** cup sugar
  Zest of 1 lemon

PREPARE

1. Combine the quince, water, sugar, and lemon zest in a small, nonreactive saucepan and bring to a boil. Reduce the heat and simmer until the quince is tender, about 20 minutes.

2. Cool and strain through a fine-mesh sieve. Reserve the cooked quince for another use — it's excellent served with roasts or topped with cream for dessert.

PRESERVE

 Refrigerate: Cover and refrigerate for up to about 1 month.

USE IT UP!

Quince Kiss Cocktail

Makes 1

This drink is a tribute to the quince's reputation for being the poster fruit of l'amour. It has a pleasantly sweet flavor that might seduce you into a second round. Serve it on Valentine's Day, birthdays, or any day that you need a little more affection in your direction.

INGREDIENTS

- **1** tablespoon Quince Syrup, chilled
- **6** ounces sparkling wine, chilled
- **1** dash Angostura bitters

PREPARE

Pour the syrup into a champagne flute. Add 2 ounces of the sparkling wine and the bitters, and use a swizzle stick or bar spoon to stir gently. Add the remaining 4 ounces sparkling wine and serve.

Rhubarb

No, that's not pink celery in the market. It's rhubarb! Technically it is a vegetable, but we use it like a fruit in desserts and savory dishes, where its bright, citrusy flavor sings.

Where I live, rhubarb is among the first produce to come to market, ringing in the flavors of spring. I often pride myself on a pretty good knowledge of seasonality and use it to judge the quality of a farmers' market. Seeing out-of-season items is a giveaway that the market is operating, at least in some regards, as a distributor for food not grown in the region. Perhaps that kind of market has its place but it's not for me — when I shop at the farmers' market, I want to support local farmers. I want to taste the region and the special things it has to offer. I was caught out one summer, though, when I saw some rhubarb in a highly regarded southwestern market. Rhubarb in July? I was used to having this plant as a spring treat so I questioned its origin. But rhubarb is one of those items that can be treated as a cut-and-come-again, being harvested continually over the growing season, depending on the climate in which it is grown. I learned something that day about rhubarb and about how important it is to talk to your farmers — they have all the answers.

RHUBARB GINGER CORDIAL

Makes about 2½ cups

This cordial reminds me of a Victorian tonic. It is tart to the point of bracing. Mix it with a little seltzer or shake it into a cocktail, and it will cure what ails you.

INGREDIENTS

- ½ cup water
- 2 pounds rhubarb, trimmed and chopped into 1-inch pieces
- 1 (2-inch) knob fresh ginger, peeled and cut into coins
- 2 cups vodka
- 1 cup sugar

PREPARE AND PRESERVE

1. Bring the water to a boil in a medium nonreactive saucepan. Add the rhubarb and ginger and simmer until the rhubarb begins to fall apart, about 10 minutes.

2. Sterilize a 1-quart glass jar with a lid, such as a canning jar, by submerging it in boiling water for 10 minutes. Add the rhubarb mixture to the jar and let cool to room temperature. Add the vodka and sugar, screw on the top, and shake to combine. Let sit for 1 week, shaking daily.

3. Strain out the solids. Wash and resterilize the jar and decant the liquid back into the resterilized jar. The cordial will keep at room temperature for up to 1 year.

USE IT UP!

Rhubarb Gimlet

Serves 1

In the summertime, the vodka gimlet is my cocktail of choice. Light and citrusy — fresh juice only, please — it's the perfect sip for an evening spent al fresco. I enjoy my martinis human-size — not the big fishbowls that are all the rage these days, but nice little 4-ounce glasses that you can sip your way through while your drink is still chilled without feeling like you are in a fraternity hazing. That's how I like this one. The rhubarb cordial makes for a terrific twist on this classic cocktail, easy and breezy and just the right size! Cue the sunset.

INGREDIENTS

- 1½ ounces Rhubarb Ginger Cordial
- ½ ounce freshly squeezed lemon juice
- ½ ounce triple sec or other orange-flavored liqueur
- Ice

PREPARE

Combine the cordial, lemon juice, and triple sec in a cocktail shaker filled with ice. Cover and shake until chilled, at least 1 minute. Strain into a chilled martini glass and serve.

FROZEN RHUBARB

Sometimes you want to have unsweetened rhubarb on hand to bake into pies and crumbles or to use in a savory recipe, such as a sauce for fish. Freezing the chopped stalks allows you stock up, which is important for those of us who see rhubarb come around just once a year.

Cooking rhubarb softens it almost instantly, so there really isn't much of a fall-off in texture in the frozen fruit. Expect to add it to dishes where softened fruit is the goal, such as cobblers and pies, and the defrosted product will not disappoint. Blanching is often recommended for rhubarb, but I find that it creates a solid "barb-berg" in the bag — the pieces, softened by the process, freeze together into a solid block. A better method is just to freeze it raw, so the pieces maintain their shape and flow freely from the bag.

INGREDIENTS

Any quantity fresh rhubarb, stalks washed and trimmed

PREPARE

1. Line several baking sheets with tea towels.

2. Chop the rhubarb into 1-inch pieces and spread on the towels. Gather up the corners of each towel and toss the fruit in it to dry the cut edges.

3. Arrange the fruit in a single layer on one or more baking sheets and freeze until solid, at least 4 hours but no more than 2 days to avoid freezer burn.

PRESERVE

Freeze: Transfer the frozen rhubarb pieces to freezer bags or containers. They'll keep in the freezer for up to 6 months.

KITCHEN HOW-TO
Prepping Rhubarb

I'm a big believer in nose-to-tail eating, even when it comes to produce. Turnip tops, beet greens — it all goes in my salad, but rhubarb leaves are an important exception. **The leaves of the rhubarb plant are poisonous! Never eat them or feed them to pets or livestock.** Trim them off and discard. The remaining stalks are what you want, and it doesn't matter whether they're red, green, or somewhere in between. Color does not necessarily indicate sweetness. Give them a rinse and they're ready for your recipe.

USE IT UP!

Rhubarb Fool

Serves 6

A light, lovely dessert full of bright, citrusy rhubarb flavor, this one is a great do-ahead. The layered cream and fruit look pretty in the glass, making it a fit for everything from a dinner party with friends to a sweet princess tea. Use the freshest cream for the best flavor — it is the key to success.

INGREDIENTS

4 cups Frozen Rhubarb (see page 229)
1 cup sugar
1 teaspoon vanilla extract
1 cup heavy cream

PREPARE

1. Heat the rhubarb in a medium saucepan, covered, over low heat until tender.

2. Add ½ cup of the sugar and the vanilla and stir to dissolve. Transfer to a shallow bowl and refrigerate until completely chilled.

3. Meanwhile, whip the cream with the remaining ½ cup sugar until it forms soft peaks.

4. Divide the cooked fruit and the whipped cream each into two equal portions. Purée half of the fruit, and gently fold the purée into half of the whipped cream.

5. Divide the remaining fruit and whipped cream among six glasses, adding them in alternating layers. Top each glass with a dollop of the rhubarb/whipped cream mixture. Serve immediately or refrigerate for up to 2 hours.

→ This recipe is also delicious when made with frozen strawberries in place of the rhubarb.

QUICK RHUBARB JAM

Makes about 5 cups

Rhubarb does not have a lot of natural pectin, so it's a good idea to add some to help it reach its gel. Without any pits or skins to remove, this is a very quick jam to make. Just a quick trim, chop, and into the pot and you're done. The color of the final jam can range from pale pink to green, depending on the color of your stalks, but it all tastes sweet and delicious.

INGREDIENTS

- **3** cups sugar
- **2** teaspoons Pomona's Universal Pectin
- **½** cup water
- **¼** cup bottled lemon juice
- **2** pounds rhubarb, trimmed and chopped into ½-inch pieces
- **2** teaspoons calcium water (from the Pomona's Universal Pectin kit)

PREPARE

1. Combine 1 cup of the sugar with the pectin in a small bowl and set aside.

2. Combine the remaining 2 cups sugar with the water and lemon juice in a large nonreactive pot and bring to a boil. Add the rhubarb, return to a boil, then reduce the heat and simmer until the fruit is tender and just beginning to fall apart, 3 to 5 minutes. Stir in the calcium water. Slowly add the pectin mixture, stirring constantly to avoid clumping. Bring to a boil, reduce the heat, and simmer for 1 to 2 minutes, continuing to stir constantly, until the sugar is completely dissolved.

3. Remove from the heat. Allow the jam to rest for 5 minutes, giving it an occasional gentle stir to release trapped air; it will thicken slightly. Skim off any foam.

PRESERVE

Refrigerate: Cool, cover, and refrigerate for up to 3 weeks.

Can: Use the boiling-water method as described on page 20. Ladle the jam into clean, hot half-pint jars, leaving ¼ inch of headspace between the top of the jam and the lid. Run a bubble tool along the inside of the glass to release trapped air. Wipe the rims clean; center lids on the jars and screw on jar bands until they are just fingertip-tight. Process the jars by submerging them in boiling water to cover by 2 inches for 10 minutes. Turn off the heat, remove the canner lid, and let the jars rest in the water for 5 minutes. Remove the jars and set aside for 24 hours. Check the seals, then store in a cool, dark place for up to 1 year.

SKILLET CORNBREAD WITH RHUBARB ORANGE SAUCE, *recipe on following page* →

USE IT UP!

Skillet Cornbread with Rhubarb Orange Sauce

234

Serves 8–10

This is just the sort of not-so-sweet dessert that I crave. It's a great finish to a summer barbecue but wouldn't be out of place on a brunch buffet, either. Use good-quality, fresh cornmeal for the best results.

INGREDIENTS

- 1½ cups fine yellow cornmeal
- 1 tablespoon sugar
- ¾ teaspoon baking soda
- ½ teaspoon salt
- 2 eggs
- 1¾ cups buttermilk
- 2 tablespoons lard or unsalted butter
- 1 cup Quick Rhubarb Jam (see page 232)
  Zest and juice of 2 oranges

PREPARE

1. Preheat the oven to 450°F. Set a medium ovenproof skillet, preferably cast iron, in the preheating oven.

2. Combine the cornmeal, sugar, baking soda, and salt in a large bowl. Whisk the eggs into the buttermilk and add to the cornmeal mixture. Stir to combine.

3. Remove the skillet from the oven, add the lard, and return the skillet to the oven for 2 to 3 minutes. Ladle the batter into the prepared skillet. Bake for 20 to 25 minutes, until golden brown.

4. Meanwhile, combine the jam, orange zest, and orange juice in a small bowl and whisk together (alternatively, you can warm the combination in a small saucepan).

5. Cut the cornbread into wedges and top with the rhubarb sauce.

KITCHEN HOW-TO
Making Buttermilk

I do not often have buttermilk in my fridge, and I hate to buy a quart, use just a little bit, and see the remainder go to waste. Here's a trick that I use: Combine 2 teaspoons white vinegar per 1 cup of milk and let sit at room temperature for at least 30 minutes and up to 1 hour. The vinegar brings its own tart flavor to the milk and will also start to curdle the milk, coagulating and thickening it. While it may not be the lip-smacking treat that my grandmother used to drink by the glass, it makes for a fine substitution for buttermilk in recipes.

ROASTED RHUBARB

Makes about 3½ cups

Rhubarb will fall apart quickly when simmered. The roasting helps it keep its shape, so that you have all the rhubarb flavor with some texture as well. Use tender, young rhubarb for this preserving method, as the larger stalks can be a bit fibrous.

INGREDIENTS

- **2** pounds rhubarb, trimmed and chopped into 1-inch pieces
- **1½** cups sugar
- **1** cup water
- **3–4** teaspoons lemon juice

PREPARE

1. Preheat the oven to 375°F.

2. Toss the fruit with ½ cup of the sugar in a 4-quart baking dish. Roast for 25 to 30 minutes, until the fruit is tender and syrupy.

3. Meanwhile, make a simple syrup by combining the remaining 1 cup sugar with the water in a small pot. Bring to a boil, reduce the heat, and simmer, stirring, until the sugar has dissolved.

4. Divide the roasted fruit among three or four clean, hot 8-ounce jars, leaving ½ inch of space between the top of fruit and the top of the jar. Top each jar with 1 teaspoon of lemon juice. Ladle the syrup into the jars, leaving ¼ inch of headspace between the top of the liquid and the top of the jar.

PRESERVE

Refrigerate: Cool, cover, and refrigerate for up to 3 weeks.

Can: Use the boiling-water method as described on page 20. Run a bubble tool along the inside of the glass to release trapped air. Wipe the rims clean; center lids on the jars and screw on jar bands until they are just fingertip-tight. Process the jars by submerging them in boiling water to cover by 2 inches for 10 minutes. Turn off the heat, remove the canner lid, and let the jars rest in the water for 5 minutes. Remove the jars and set aside for 24 hours. Check the seals, then store in a cool, dark place for up to 1 year.

USE IT UP!

Rhubarb Goat Cheese Crostini

Makes 24 crostini

Need a quick little nibble to throw together? This is it. All of your guests will want to know, "What is that on top?" Your homemade Roasted Rhubarb, that's what!

INGREDIENTS

- **1** baguette
- ¼ cup extra-virgin olive oil
  Freshly ground black pepper
- **1** (4- to 5-ounce) log goat cheese
- **1** cup Roasted Rhubarb (see page 235)

PREPARE

1. Preheat the broiler.

2. Cut the baguette on the diagonal into ¼-inch-thick slices. Using a pastry brush, lightly brush the bread slices with the olive oil and season generously with freshly ground pepper. Arrange in a single layer on a baking sheet. Broil 3 to 4 inches from the broiler's heating element for about 1 minute, until golden. Turn over and broil the other side for about 1 minute, until golden. Remove from the oven and let cool completely.

3. Spread each crostini with 1 teaspoon of the goat cheese. Top with a dollop of rhubarb and serve.

→ This recipe is also delicious with Cherry Mostarda (page 103) in place of the rhubarb.

Strawberries

*I*s there any more desirable fruit for preserving than the strawberry? Its fleeting season, seductive perfume, and gorgeous looks — no wonder we're all in love with it. A visit to your farmers' market will greet you with a number of different varieties. Though you can use any variety of strawberry in these recipes, I highly suggest a side-by-side taste test to get your bearings. And why not? I can't think of a more delightful thing to do on a late spring day than have a strawberry tasting. Some claim that the alpine variety is the most flavorful and best for preserving, but these diminutive and rare fruits can be hard to find, and their small size slows the prep down considerably, so I rarely work with them. But you will have your own opinion.

If I have the time to do it, my favorite way to stock up on strawberries for preserving is to pick them myself at the local u-pick. Strawberries ripen before it gets truly hot out, so it's always a pleasant way to ring in the sunbeams at the start of a new harvest season.

Once you've harvested your berries, you have to act fast. Unlike grocery-store berries, which are built to last, freshly gathered strawberries don't take kindly to being off the vine. You can refrigerate them for a day, but no longer, or they will start to fade.

CLASSIC STRAWBERRY JAM

Makes about 3 cups

Everybody loves strawberry jam, but some like it on the chunky side, with whole pieces of fruit in the mixture, and some prefer a smoother jam that won't leave big berries bulging in their PB&J. This recipe lets you choose the texture you prefer. Adding the sugar early in the process — way early, as in the night before — toughens the fruit and helps it maintain its shape during cooking. Adding the sugar after cooking the fruit gives the berries a chance to fall apart a bit, creating that very-berry flavor without the big berry bits. Either way you cook it, it's a classic.

INGREDIENTS

2 quarts strawberries (about 3 pounds), washed, stemmed, hulled, and halved if large

4–8 cups sugar (depending on how sweet you like your jam)

¼ cup bottled lemon juice

PREPARE

Variation 1, Chunky Jam.

1. To make "chunky" jam with whole pieces of fruit: Toss the strawberries and sugar in a large bowl and let macerate overnight to coax out the fruit's juice and "toughen" the fruit so that it maintains its shape better during the cooking process. Stir in the lemon juice. Transfer the mixture to a large nonreactive pot, and then proceed with step 2.

Variation 2, Smooth Jam.

1. To make "smooth" jam with a more uniform texture: Do not macerate the berries. Combine the berries with 1 cup water in a large nonreactive pot and slowly bring to a simmer. Cook until the berries soften and begin to fall apart, about 10 minutes, mashing them with the back of your spoon to break them down further. Stir in the sugar and lemon juice, and then proceed with step 2.

2. Bring the jam to a boil, stirring to prevent the fruit from sticking, and then reduce the heat to prevent the jam from boiling out of the pot. Continue to cook, stirring frequently, until the jam reaches the gel stage (see page 28), about 20 minutes.

3. Remove from the heat. Allow the jam to rest for 5 minutes, giving it an occasional gentle stir to release trapped air; it will thicken slightly. Skim off any foam.

PRESERVE

⊘ **Refrigerate:** Cool, cover, and refrigerate for up to 3 weeks.

🅱 **Can:** Use the boiling-water method as described on page 20. Ladle the jam into clean, hot half-pint jars, leaving ¼ inch of headspace between the top of the jam and the lid. Run a bubble tool along the inside of the glass to release trapped air. Wipe the rims clean; center lids on the jars and screw on jar bands until they are just fingertip-tight. Process the jars by submerging them in boiling water to cover by 2 inches for 10 minutes. Turn off the heat, remove the canner lid, and let the jars rest in the water for 5 minutes. Remove the jars and set aside for 24 hours. Check the seals, then store in a cool, dark place for up to 1 year.

USE IT UP!

Thumbprint Cookies

Makes about 48 cookies

These cookies are a classic, popular at bake sales, for classroom parties, and on holiday treat platters. As they should be. They are easy to make and their blast of color from the jam just makes you want to sink your teeth in. I would say you can enlist your kids to help, but you want big, grown-up-size thumbprints that can hold a lot of jam! You can't make enough. Feel free to double the batch and share.

INGREDIENTS

- ¾ pound (3 sticks) unsalted butter, softened
- 1 cup plus 2 tablespoons sugar
- 1 teaspoon vanilla extract
- 1 egg
- 3½ cups all-purpose flour
- ½ teaspoon salt
- 1 cup Classic Strawberry Jam (see page 238)

PREPARE

1. Combine the butter and the 1 cup sugar in a large bowl. Use an electric hand mixer to cream them together, until fluffy. Blend in the vanilla and add the egg.

2. Combine the flour and salt in a separate bowl. Add the flour mixture, in three parts, to the butter mixture, beating in each addition until just combined. Pat the dough into a disk, wrap in plastic, and refrigerate for 1 hour.

3. Preheat the oven to 350°F. Line two baking sheets with parchment paper.

4. Roll the dough by tablespoons into balls, arranging them on the prepared baking sheets 2 inches apart. Sprinkle lightly with the 2 tablespoons sugar. Use your thumb to press an indentation into the top of each cookie. Spoon ½ teaspoon of the jam into each indentation.

5. Bake for 20 to 25 minutes, until the cookies just begin to color on the bottom. Let cool completely before serving. Keeps in an airtight container for about 5 days.

→ Of course you can make these cookies with any of the delicious jams in this book or any other homemade jam in your pantry.

STRAWBERRY RHUBARB JAM

Makes about 6 cups

Strawberries and rhubarb are a natural pairing in the spring, when both are in season. Their flavors complement each other, with the sweetness of the berries and the tartness of the rhubarb making for a well-balanced jam. The pretty color doesn't hurt, either.

INGREDIENTS

- **2** cups sugar
- **2** teaspoons Pomona's Universal Pectin
- **1½** pounds rhubarb, trimmed and chopped into 1-inch pieces
- **1** quart strawberries (about 1½ pounds), washed, stemmed, and hulled
- **½** cup water
- **¼** cup bottled lemon juice
- **2** teaspoons calcium water (from the Pomona's Universal Pectin kit)

PREPARE

1. Combine the sugar and pectin in a small bowl and set aside.

2. Combine the rhubarb, strawberries, and water in a large nonreactive pot and slowly bring to a boil, stirring frequently to prevent scorching. Simmer until the fruit has softened and released its juices, about 10 minutes, mashing occasionally with a potato masher or the back of a wooden spoon.

3. Stir in the lemon juice and calcium water. Slowly add the pectin mixture, stirring constantly to avoid clumping. Bring to a boil, reduce the heat, and simmer for 1 to 2 minutes, continuing to stir constantly, until the sugar is completely dissolved.

4. Remove from the heat. Allow the jam to rest for 5 minutes, giving it an occasional gentle stir to release trapped air; it will thicken slightly. Skim off any foam.

PRESERVE

Refrigerate: Cool, cover, and refrigerate for up to 3 weeks.

Can: Use the boiling-water method as described on page 20. Ladle the jam into clean, hot half-pint jars, leaving ¼ inch of headspace between the top of the jam and the top of the lid. Run a bubble tool along the inside of the glass to release trapped air. Wipe the rims clean; center lids on the jars and screw on jar bands until they are just fingertip-tight. Process the jars by submerging them in boiling water to cover by 2 inches for 10 minutes. Turn off the heat, remove the canner lid, and let the jars rest in the water for 5 minutes. Remove the jars and set aside for 24 hours. Check the seals, then store in a cool, dark place for up to 1 year.

Lining a Pan with Parchment

Baking has always been a hurdle for me. I don't know why the precision and measuring of home food preservation is no problem but all the detail work of baking makes me bananas. So I have been known to, if not skip a step, at least round the corners pretty generously. One of the steps I have, on occasion, tried to leave out is lining a pan with parchment. Could it really make that much of a difference? Well, you can have only so many delicious cakes permanently cemented to their pans to know that when a recipe calls for parchment, it's not a request; it's a must.

To line a round baking pan, you need a circle of parchment just smaller than the pan. It's easy to make one that fits just right: Tear off a square of parchment bigger than your pan. Fold it in half, then in quarters, then fold that into a triangle, and continue to fold narrow triangles from the same center point until you have something that looks like a very thin wedge. Put the point of the wedge in the center of the pan, and mark the spot where the parchment comes just a bit short of the edge of the pan. Cut it at this length and then open it up. Place the parchment in the pan and smooth it down to line the pan.

To line a square or oblong pan, you simply cut a piece of parchment that is as wide as the widest part of the pan and long enough to cover the distance across the shortest sides and bottom with some overhang. Lay this "runner" of parchment on the bottom, and smooth it down. Crease it at the corners of the pan and smooth it up the sides of the pan, letting it drape over the sides a bit.

Some recipes call for buttering the pan before and after placing the parchment. If so, just butter your pan, lay in the parchment as described above, and smooth it down. Butter the top of the parchment, as indicated. Now you are totally stick-free!

USE IT UP!

Flourless Chocolate Cake with Strawberry Rhubarb Jam

Serves 8–10

This recipe is a shout-out to all of my gluten-free peeps! You can have at it and the lack of flour will never cross your mind. The cake packs a wallop of chocolate flavor, enough to sate even the most obsessed chocolate lover. And everything's better with a little jam, right?

INGREDIENTS

- **4** ounces excellent bittersweet chocolate, chopped
- **½** cup (1 stick) unsalted butter, cubed, plus enough to grease pan
- **¾** cup sugar
- **¼** teaspoon salt
- **3** eggs
- **2** tablespoons brewed coffee, cold or at room temperature
- **½** cup cocoa powder
- **½** cup Strawberry Rhubarb Jam (see page 240)
- **1** cup heavy cream, whipped (optional)

PREPARE

1. Preheat the oven to 375°F. Butter a 9-inch round baking pan, line it with parchment paper, and then butter the top of the parchment.

2. Melt the chocolate in a double boiler (or a large, heatproof bowl set over a pot of barely simmering water). Remove from the heat.

3. Whisk in the butter, one-third at a time, until the butter is melted and fully incorporated into the chocolate. Add the sugar and salt and whisk to combine. Add the eggs and coffee and whisk to combine. Sift the cocoa powder into the bowl and whisk until smooth.

4. Pour the mixture into the prepared baking pan. Bake for 25 to 30 minutes, until the top is dry and parched looking. Let cool for 5 minutes, then invert the cake onto a plate and let cool completely.

5. Serve in slices, topped with a tablespoon of jam and garnished with a dollop of whipped cream, if you like.

CHRISTMAS CORDIAL (RUMTOPF)

Yield varies according to the size of your Rumtopf container

Rumtopf is a traditional German tipple that you build over the course of the entire harvest season. It's great fun and a tribute to a productive growing season to add fruits as they ripen over the successive months, and then enjoy at the end of the year, after all the flavors have blended and the concoction is at its best. What better way to reflect back on the year's bounty than with all of its tastes in one glorious glass. Cheers, indeed!

INGREDIENTS

Fruits (see lists below)
Sugar
Rum

FRUITS TO USE

Apples, quartered or sliced
Apricots, halved and pitted
Cherries, stemmed and pitted
Gooseberries, stemmed but whole
Grapes, stemmed but whole
Nectarines, halved and pitted
Peaches, halved and pitted
Pears, cored and sliced
Plums, halved and pitted
Raspberries, whole
Strawberries, stemmed but whole

DO NOT USE

Blackberries, which are too tannic
Blueberries, which are also too tannic
Citrus, which will make it too sour
Melon, which will water down the liqueur
Rhubarb, which will make it too sour

PREPARE AND PRESERVE

1. You can build your Rumtopf in any food grade container — glass, ceramic, or even food-grade plastic will work. You can make miniature Rumtopfs in quart-sized jars but a bigger vessel, 2 to 3 gallons, allows you to use more fruit and create substantial layers that really show off their beauty. You can find specialized ceramic Rumtopf crocks that are decorated to reflect their purpose but I prefer to use a big glass jar — like a glass cookie jar — so that I can get a good look at my Rumtopf over the course of the harvest. Whatever container you use, scrub it well with hot, soapy water, rinse several times with boiling water, and rinse it out with a little of the rum and you are ready to start.

2. Add your first fruit and sprinkle sugar on top in the proportion of 1 cup of sugar for every pound of fruit. Top with enough rum to cover by 1 inch. Keep layering as fruits come into season. You can use any of the fruits listed, and the more the better. Just be sure to layer with enough liquor to cover or your Rumtopf will ferment rather than infuse. If bubbles start to appear, add a little 151-proof rum (also known as overproof rum), which will halt fermentation.

3. Allow to rest at least 4 to 6 weeks after the last fruit has been added.

4. Use a ladle to dip down into the Rumtopf to draw up your first servings. The fruit is great served on ice cream or served with roast meats, but for adults only, as it will be drenched in rum. When the liquid level threatens to go lower than the fruit, you can strain the remaining liqueur, allow it to settle out, and then carefully decant it into bottles. Leftover fruit can be frozen until ready to use.

RUMTOPF — READY TO SERVE

USE IT UP!

Boozy Parfaits

Serves 4

Yes, the hooch is the point of Rumtopf. But it comes with a delicious by-product — the fruit. Use it to top pound cake, bake into muffins, or blend into yogurt for tasty, grown-ups-only desserts. I like to use it in these big-kid sundaes.

INGREDIENTS

1 pint ice cream, softened (you can use any flavor you like, but I think that caramel/dulce de leche/butterscotch flavors go particularly well)

1 cup Rumtopf fruit (see page 244)

¼ cup Rumtopf liqueur (see page 244)

1 cup freshly whipped cream

PREPARE

In four parfait or wine glasses, layer ¼ cup ice cream, followed by ¼ cup fruit and then another ¼ cup ice cream. Drizzle with 1 tablespoon liqueur. Top with ¼ cup whipped cream and serve.

STRAWBERRY BALSAMIC GLAZE

Makes about 2 cups

It's always a hoot to come up with new recipes, particularly when they work as well as this one does. Strawberries and balsamic vinegar are a classic combination; together the two taste like they were made for each other. Try it. Drizzle a bowl of early-summer berries with some of the aged vinegar for a simple, surprising dessert. Or mix up a batch of this glaze and have the combo at the ready all year round. It's great drizzled on a salad, maybe with a few crumbles of goat cheese, basted on pork chops, or as a topping for ice cream. Truly tasty.

INGREDIENTS

- **2** quarts strawberries (about 3 pounds), washed, stemmed, and hulled
- ½ cup water
- **2** cups sugar
- **1** cup fruity red wine (such as burgundy or pinot noir)
- ½ cup balsamic vinegar
- ½ teaspoon salt

PREPARE

1. Combine the berries and water in a medium nonreactive saucepan and slowly bring to a boil, stirring frequently to prevent scorching. Reduce the heat to medium and simmer for 10 minutes, mashing the fruit with the back of your spoon to break it down and release the berries' juices.

2. Add the sugar and wine and return to a boil. Boil vigorously for 10 minutes, stirring occasionally. Remove from the heat and allow to cool slightly.

3. Strain the syrup through a fine-mesh sieve. Discard the solids, and return the syrup to the cooking pot. Add the vinegar and salt and simmer until the syrup is thick enough to coat the back of a spoon, about 10 minutes.

PRESERVE

Refrigerate: Cool, cover, and refrigerate for up to 3 weeks.

Can: Use the boiling-water method as described on page 20. Ladle the syrup into clean, hot 4-ounce jars, leaving ¼ inch of headspace between the top of the syrup and the top of the lid. Run a bubble tool along the inside of the glass to release trapped air. Wipe the rims clean; center lids on the jars and screw on jar bands until they are just fingertip-tight. Process the jars by submerging them in boiling water to cover by 2 inches for 10 minutes. Turn off the heat, remove the canner lid, and let the jars rest in the water for 5 minutes. Remove the jars and set aside for 24 hours. Check the seals, then store in a cool, dark place for up to 1 year.

USE IT UP!

Pan-Seared Pork Chops with Strawberry Shellac

Serves 4

The Strawberry Balsamic Glaze looks great in this dish, giving the chops a deep, rich color. The fact that you don't have to marinate the meat to give it great flavor makes this an easy dish for a quick midweek supper.

INGREDIENTS

- **4** bone-in pork chops, at least 1 inch thick
  Salt and freshly ground black pepper
- ¼ cup Strawberry Balsamic Glaze (see page 246)

PREPARE

1. Preheat the broiler.

2. Generously season the chops with salt and pepper and place on a broiler pan. (If you don't have a broiler pan, you can use a cake cooling rack placed over a rimmed baking sheet that's covered with foil.) Use a pastry brush to paint both sides of the chops with the glaze. Broil 3 to 4 inches from the broiler's heating element for 6 to 8 minutes per side, until browned, basting with the glaze once or twice.

3. Remove to a serving platter and let rest for 5 minutes before serving.

Tomatoes

Heirloom tomatoes are the darlings of the farmers' market. I love looking at the great expanse of varieties available when they come into season, which isn't until well into the summer where I live. But then it's a tomato rainbow — red, pink, green, yellow, even black — with tastes that range from sweet and buttery to tart and tangy. "Heirloom" gets a bad rap for sounding elitist or gourmet. It's really not. "Heirloom" just means that the seeds reproduce true — if you plant the seed of a Yellow Pear tomato, it will grow into a plant that bears Yellow Pear tomatoes. You can keep doing that on and on: plant the seed, harvest the tomato, take a seed from that tomato, plant it, and get the same variety of tomato again. You could even say, then, that an heirloom tomato is a thrifty tomato because, unlike hybrid plants that do not reproduce true, you do not need to purchase new seed season after season — you can save your seeds (and your pennies), instead.

Heirlooms are delicious and come in thousands of varieties, each with its own set of unique characteristics — not just color and flavor but drought tolerance, pest resistance, and so on, giving a garden planted with them a better shot at yielding no matter which turn Mother Nature takes in a given season. If they taste so good and are so hardy, why then aren't all cultivated tomatoes heirloom varieties? The simple answer: profit. The tomatoes you see in the grocery store are from hybrid varieties — crosses of one or more tomato varieties — that have been proven to be the most consistent. Look at them — they are all exactly the same size, shape, and color. They are picked rock hard and green (often by workers forced into deplorable conditions) and are then shipped thousands of miles to a distribution center where they are gassed with ethylene vapor to turn them red. They often have a mealy texture and are devoid of taste, but they fit very nicely into the assembly line of industrial agriculture. Heirlooms would never put up with that treatment — and neither should you!

TOMATO CHUTNEY

Makes about 7 cups

I am a fan of all kinds of chutneys, with mango, tamarind, and coconut being favorites. Their combination of sweet and savory flavors, heightened by a generous dose of spice, wakes up even the blandest of dishes. For this recipe, I usually use Amish Paste tomatoes, an heirloom variety that is very meaty and productive, and cook them down with warm spices. The result is a chutney that is a little sweet, tangy, and spicy all in one bite.

INGREDIENTS

- **4** pounds plum tomatoes, preferably heirloom, peeled, cored, and diced (see page 254)
- **1** pound red peppers, seeds and ribs removed, diced
- **½** pound yellow onions, diced
- **1** cup brown sugar
- **1** cup apple cider vinegar
- **½** cup raisins
- **1** tablespoon chopped garlic
- **1** tablespoon freshly grated ginger
- **1** tablespoon ground cumin
- **1** tablespoon yellow mustard seeds
- **1** tablespoon kosher salt
- **1** teaspoon ground allspice
- **¼** teaspoon freshly ground black pepper

PREPARE

1. Combine the tomatoes, red peppers, onions, sugar, vinegar, raisins, garlic, ginger, cumin, mustard seeds, salt, allspice, and black pepper in a large nonreactive pot. Bring to a boil, stirring frequently to prevent scorching. Reduce the heat and simmer until thickened, about 30 minutes.

2. Remove from the heat. Allow the chutney to rest for 5 minutes, giving it an occasional gentle stir to release trapped air; it will thicken slightly. Skim off any foam.

PRESERVE

Refrigerate: Cool, cover, and refrigerate for up to 3 weeks.

Can: Use the boiling-water method as described on page 20. Ladle the chutney into clean, hot half-pint jars, leaving ½ inch of headspace between the top of the chutney and the lid. Run a bubble tool along the inside of the glass to release trapped air. Wipe the rims clean; center lids on the jars and screw on jar bands until they are just fingertip-tight. Process the jars by submerging them in boiling water to cover by 2 inches for 10 minutes. Turn off the heat, remove the canner lid, and let the jars rest in the water for 5 minutes. Remove the jars and set aside for 24 hours. Check the seals, then store in a cool, dark place for up to 1 year.

USE IT UP!

Black Bean Panini with Tomato Chutney

Serves 2

It's late, the kids are just home from practice/you are just home from work, and there is a fierce hunger building within the tribe. What do you do? Paninis in a flash! This one uses the Tomato Chutney you put up over the summer to add a piquant sauce to your melty, gooey creation. You can have it as described or add any little tidbits — some leftover roasted vegetables, a few shreds of cooked chicken — that you like. It's "fast food" you can feel good about.

INGREDIENTS

- **1** tablespoon unsalted butter
- **1** small loaf ciabatta, cut in half and opened like a book
- **2** cups grated cheese (choose a good melter, such as cheddar or a nutty alpine cheese)
- ½ cup black beans, cooked or canned
- ½ cup leftover roasted vegetables or meat (optional)
- ½ cup Tomato Chutney (see page 249)

PREPARE

1. Melt the butter in a large skillet over medium heat. Place the bread in the pan, cut side down, and toast 1 to 2 minutes, until it browns slightly.

2. Flip the bread over and distribute cheese evenly over both halves. Cook until the cheese begins to melt into the crevices of the bread, 2 to 3 minutes. Reduce the heat to medium-low.

3. Top the bottom side of the bread with the beans, any tasty leftovers you care to add, and then the chutney. Cap with the top side of sandwich. Place another skillet, smaller than the one in which you are cooking, on top of the sandwich to weight it down. Cook until the bottom crust of bread begins to brown, 3 to 4 minutes.

4. Remove the top pan and carefully flip the sandwich over. Replace the top pan and cook until the top side of the bread is brown, 3 to 4 minutes. Remove to a cutting board and slice into 3-inch wedges.

WHOLE CANNED TOMATOES

Makes 1 quart for every 3 pounds of tomatoes

Canning whole tomatoes is one of the single most important processes the home food preservationist should master. Just a single afternoon of putting up tomatoes with your friends can keep you supplied with fresh-tasting jars all year long. The setup takes a little time, so it makes sense to take on this project when you have a good window of time and a good supply of tomatoes. I wouldn't do it for less than a case at a time, which is about 25 pounds of tomatoes. If you have a helpful friend and an afternoon to spend, don't be afraid to obligate yourself to doing 100 pounds at a time. It sounds like a lot, but once you get it set up, turn up the tunes and pour yourselves some lemonade: it's not a bad way to spend a summer day.

INGREDIENTS PER QUART OF CANNED TOMATOES

2 tablespoons bottled lemon juice or ½ teaspoon citric acid

1 teaspoon salt (optional)

3 pounds plum tomatoes (such as Amish Paste or Juliet), peeled, cored, and seeded (see page 254)

PREPARE

1. Add the lemon juice and the salt, if using, to each clean, hot quart jar. Pack the tomatoes into the jars one at a time, pressing firmly enough to compress the hollow core and release enough juice to cover the tomato, but not so hard that the fruit is crushed to bits.

2. Continue packing tomatoes in this manner, being careful to press out any air pockets. Tomatoes should be covered by ½ inch with their liquid. Leave ½ inch of headspace between the top of the liquid and the lid. Top with a little boiling water, if necessary, to achieve the proper headspace.

PRESERVE

🅒 **Can:** Use the boiling-water method as described on page 20. Run a bubble tool along the inside of the glass to release trapped air. Wipe the rims clean; center lids on the jars and screw on jar bands until they are just fingertip-tight. Process the jars by submerging them in boiling water to cover by 2 inches for 85 minutes (see note). Turn off the heat, remove the canner lid, and let the jars rest in the water for 5 minutes. Remove the jars and set aside for 24 hours. Check the seals, then store in a cool, dark place for up to 1 year.

→ The processing time may seem a bit excessive, but that's how long it takes for the heat to fully penetrate to the center of the cold-packed jars. If you want a recipe that processes for less time, cook up the Avalanche Sauce (see page 257).

USE IT UP!

Quick Marinara

Makes about 3 cups sauce

Marinara is my go-to quick dinner fix. It's speedy to make and takes only a few ingredients to whip up. Unlike bottled sauces, it isn't loaded with unwanted sugar or preservatives. Serve over your favorite cooked pasta or grilled foods.

INGREDIENTS

- **2** tablespoons extra-virgin olive oil
- **1** onion, diced
- **1** garlic clove, minced
- **1** quart Whole Canned Tomatoes (see page 252)

PREPARE

Heat the oil in a medium skillet over medium-high heat. Add the onion and sauté until translucent, 5 to 7 minutes. Add the garlic and sauté until fragrant, about 1 minute. Add the tomatoes to the pan, crushing each one in your hand as you go. (Alternatively, you can purée the tomatoes with an immersion blender or in a standing blender for a smoother sauce.) Simmer until thickened, about 10 minutes.

Prepping Tomatoes

Fill a cooler or your impeccably clean kitchen sink halfway with heavily iced water (about 1 quart of ice cubes for every gallon of water). Bring a large pot of water to a boil.

1. Drop the tomatoes into the boiling water, no more than six tomatoes at a time, and return to a boil. Blanch until the skins begin to loosen, 30 to 60 seconds.

2. Scoop the tomatoes out of the water with a spider or slotted spoon and plunge them into the ice water. Continue blanching the tomatoes in batches. Remove from the ice bath and drain.

3. Core the tomatoes by punching them through from pole to pole with an apple corer. This removes not only the core but also most of the seeds in one motion.

4. The skins will slip off easily for the most part; any clinging bits can be removed with a small paring knife.

SMOKY TOMATO SALSA

Makes about 4 cups

Spanish paprika is nothing like the flavorless red powder used to decorate deviled eggs, and it is even a step away from the delicious but decidedly different Hungarian paprikas. Spanish paprika is smoky and earthy — like having a little bit of wood fire in a can.

INGREDIENTS

- **1** cup distilled white vinegar
- **1** tablespoon salt
- **1** tablespoon sugar
- **3** pounds tomatoes, preferably heirloom, peeled, seeded, and diced (see page 254)
- **½** pound onions, diced
- **1** garlic clove, minced
- **1** jalapeno or habanero pepper, minced
- **1** teaspoon smoked Spanish paprika (also called *pimenton*) or other smoked dried chile powder, such as ancho or chipotle

PREPARE

1. Bring the vinegar, salt, and sugar to a boil in a large nonreactive pot. Add the tomatoes, onions, garlic, jalapeno, and paprika, return to a boil, and simmer until softened and thickened, about 20 minutes.

2. Remove from the heat. Allow the salsa to rest for 5 minutes, giving it an occasional gentle stir to release trapped air; it will thicken slightly. Skim off any foam.

PRESERVE

Refrigerate: Cool, cover, and refrigerate for up to 3 weeks.

Can: Use the boiling-water method as described on page 20. Ladle the salsa into clean, hot half-pint jars, leaving ¼ inch of headspace between the top of the salsa and the lid. Run a bubble tool along the inside of the glass to release trapped air. Wipe the rims clean; center lids on the jars and screw on jar bands until they are just fingertip-tight. Process the jars by submerging them in boiling water to cover by 2 inches for 10 minutes. Turn off the heat, remove the canner lid, and let the jars rest in the water for 5 minutes. Remove the jars and set aside for 24 hours. Check the seals, then store in a cool, dark place for up to 1 year.

Jar suitable for refrigerator storage; not approved for canning

USE IT UP!

Corn Fritters with Smoky Tomato Salsa

Makes 8 or 9 fritters

Sure, you can serve Smoky Tomato Salsa with your usual tortilla chips. It's terrific that way. But pair it with these tasty corn fritters and the salsa takes center stage. Enjoy it as a first course, or add some grilled shrimp or mushrooms to turn it into a light lunch. Brava!

INGREDIENTS

- **1** cup buttermilk (see page 234)
- **1** egg, lightly beaten
- **1** tablespoon unsalted butter, melted
- **1** cup corn kernels, preferably cut from the cob
- **½** cup finely ground cornmeal
- **½** cup all-purpose flour
- **1** teaspoon salt
- **½** teaspoon baking powder
- **1** tablespoon neutral-flavored vegetable oil, such as organic canola
- **½** cup Smoky Tomato Salsa (see page 255)

PREPARE

1. Preheat the oven to its lowest setting, to use as a warmer for the cooked fritters.

2. Combine the buttermilk, egg, and melted butter in a large bowl and whisk together. Stir in the corn kernels. In a separate small bowl, combine the cornmeal, flour, salt, and baking powder. Add the dry ingredients to the wet ingredients and whisk until just combined.

3. Heat the oil in a large skillet over medium-high heat until shimmering but not smoking. Ladle the batter in ¼-cup portions into the pan, leaving at least 2 inches between each pool of batter. Cook until the edges are dry and bubbles appear on the surface of the fritter, 2 to 3 minutes.

4. Using a spatula, flip the fritters over and cook until browned underneath, 1 to 2 minutes. Remove to a serving platter held in the warm oven. Repeat with the remaining batter.

5. Arrange two fritters on each plate and top with 2 tablespoons salsa. Serve immediately.

AVALANCHE SAUCE

Makes about 3 quarts when canned as is, less if reduced

I call this "Avalanche Sauce" because you can use it for the times when you have way too many tomatoes — when your home garden is exploding or the farmers can't move them fast enough and the markets are overflowing. It would be a crying shame to waste even one, knowing that you'll have to wait nearly another year for that sweet, authentic tomato taste to come around again. So I put together this sauce to help. The oven does a great job of breaking down the tomatoes and releasing their juices without the risk of scorching them. You can scale the recipe up or down depending on the size of your tomato trove; use it to process as many tomatoes as your equipment will hold.

INGREDIENTS

At least 10 pounds tomatoes, any variety, cored and cut into 2-inch chunks
Salt
Bottled lemon juice

PREPARE

1. Preheat the oven to 425°F.

2. Place the tomatoes in a roasting pan large enough to hold them in a single layer. Roast for 30 to 40 minutes, until the fruit is softened and has released its liquid.

3. Remove from the oven and let cool slightly. Use a food mill to remove the seeds and skins from the roasted tomatoes, milling them directly into a large nonreactive pot that will have at least 3 to 4 inches of "boiling room" left.

4. When all the tomatoes have been milled, bring the purée to a boil, reduce the heat, and simmer, stirring frequently, until thickened to your desired consistency. (You can can it "as is" for tomato juice, reduce it by one-quarter for a thin sauce, or keep simmering until it is reduced by half for a thick sauce). Add salt to taste.

PRESERVE

Can: Use the boiling-water method as described on page 20. Add 1 tablespoon of the lemon juice to each pint jar and 2 tablespoons to each quart to be filled. Ladle the sauce into the clean, hot jars along with the lemon juice, leaving 1 inch of headspace between the top of the sauce and the lid. Run a bubble tool along the inside of the glass to release trapped air. Wipe the rims clean; center lids on the jars and screw on jar bands until they are just fingertip-tight. Process the jars by submerging them in boiling water to cover by 2 inches for 35 minutes for pints, or 40 minutes for quarts. Turn off the heat, remove the canner lid, and let the jars rest in the water for 5 minutes. Remove the jars and set aside for 24 hours. Check the seals, then store in a cool, dark place for up to 1 year.

AVALANCHE SAUCE

USE IT UP!

Fish Poached in Tomato Sauce

Serves 4

This is an easy dish to prepare. I like to serve it in the fall, when the peppers are in full flush and I'm looking for something to take the chill out of the first autumn days. But you could leave out the peppers and serve it any time of year. Mashed potatoes served alongside make for a filling, comforting meal.

INGREDIENTS

- **2** tablespoons olive oil
- **1** onion, diced
- **1** bell pepper, seeds and ribs removed, sliced (optional)
- **2** garlic cloves, minced
- **1** pint Avalanche Sauce (see page 257)
- **½** teaspoon dried oregano
  Salt and freshly ground black pepper
- **1½** pounds firm, thick white fish, such as Pacific halibut (see note)
- **¼** cup parsley, chopped

PREPARE

1. Heat the oil in a medium skillet over medium-high heat until shimmering but not smoking. Add the onion and bell pepper, if using, and sauté until softened, 5 to 7 minutes. Add the garlic and sauté until fragrant, about 1 minute. Add the tomato sauce, oregano, and salt and pepper to taste and bring to a boil. Reduce the heat and simmer until thickened slightly, about 5 minutes.

2. Add the fish, reduce the heat to low, cover, and simmer, very gently, until the fish is nearly cooked through, 6 to 8 minutes. Turn off the heat and allow the residual heat in the covered pot to finish cooking the fish, about 5 minutes. Garnish with parsley and serve.

→ Check www.montereybayaquarium.org to find other sustainable fish options near you.

TOMATO GASTRIQUE

Makes 1 cup

What a useful thing to have on hand. And it's so easy to make. A little sugar, vinegar, and tomatoes boiled down to a syrup is all it takes. Try a little Tomato Gastrique in your pasta sauce to take it to a new level. You are the next Top Chef!

INGREDIENTS

- **1** cup sugar
- **¼** cup water
- **1** cup white wine vinegar
- **2** cups chopped tomatoes
  Pinch of salt

PREPARE

1. Combine the sugar and water in a medium nonreactive saucepan and bring to a gentle boil over medium-low heat. Do not stir. Cook until the sugar melts and begins to color slightly, 5 to 7 minutes, washing down the sides of the pan with a pastry brush dipped in water as necessary.

2. When the sugar begins to color, pour the vinegar into the pan, but be careful — the vinegar will hiss and spit a good bit. The caramel will harden when the liquid hits it but will dissolve again as it simmers. Simmer until reduced by about half, about 5 minutes.

3. Add the tomatoes and continue to simmer until the sauce takes on the color and fragrance of the fruit and thickens slightly, about 10 minutes.

4. Strain through a fine-mesh strainer set over a bowl, pressing on the tomatoes and working them through the sieve until only the skins remain. Scrape the pulp off of the bottom of the sieve and stir it into the strained gastrique. Finish with a sprinkle of salt.

PRESERVE

Refrigerate: Cool, cover, and refrigerate for up to 3 weeks.

Freeze: Pour into the compartments of an ice cube tray or into small freezer containers; cover and freeze for up to 6 months.

Can: Use the boiling-water method as described on page 20. Ladle the gastrique into clean, hot 4-ounce jars, leaving ¼ inch of headspace between the top of the gastrique and the lid. Run a bubble tool along the inside of the glass to release trapped air. Wipe the rims clean; center lids on the jars and screw on jar bands until they are just fingertip-tight. Process the jars by submerging them in boiling water to cover by 2 inches for 10 minutes. Turn off the heat, remove the canner lid, and let the jars rest in the water for 5 minutes. Remove the jars and set aside for 24 hours. Check the seals, then store in a cool, dark place for up to 1 year.

USE IT UP!

Roasted Vegetables with Tomato Gastrique

Serves 6-8 as a side dish

Roasting vegetables brings out their sweetness. The gastrique balances the flavor with a bright, tangy twist. You can make this dish ahead and serve it at room temperature for easy entertaining.

INGREDIENTS

- **1** pound green vegetables, such as green beans, asparagus, or broccoli, trimmed and chopped
- **1** pound root vegetables, such as sweet potatoes, parsnips, or turnips, trimmed and chopped
- ¼ cup extra-virgin olive oil
  Salt and freshly ground black pepper
- ¼ cup Tomato Gastrique (see page 259)

PREPARE

1. Preheat the oven to 425°F.

2. Arrange the green vegetables on a rimmed baking sheet and toss with 2 tablespoons of the oil and a pinch of salt and pepper. Do the same for the root vegetables on a separate pan.

3. Roast until the vegetables are tender and starting to brown in spots, about 10 to 12 minutes for the green vegetables and 25 to 30 minutes for the root vegetables.

4. Remove the roasted vegetables to a serving platter and drizzle with the gastrique.

Resources

A few key pieces of equipment and delicious food are all you need to preserve your own food. Here are some resources to help you get your hands on everything you need to put 'em up!

SUPPLIES AND EQUIPMENT

Your local hardware store probably has all that you need to preserve your own food. Shopping at these local, independent retailers is a great way to keep dollars in your community. If you don't have a store close to you, or are having trouble getting what you need, these sites are great resources. Many also offer steep discounts for bulk orders, so if you are canning in a group, some may be able to help you with volume discounts.

CANNINGPANTRY.COM

Highland Brands, LLC
800-285-9044
www.canningpantry.com

Canning Pantry is a quaint online store that caters to the home food preserving community. A good source for pectin and citric acid as well.

GOODMAN'S

888-333-4660
www.goodmans.net

Goodman's carries a large selection of canning supplies. They also offer jars in large quantity at discount prices.

JARDEN HOME BRANDS

800-240-3340
www.freshpreserving.com

Fresh Preserving is Ball's online resource for tips and equipment. You can order jars and more from them directly through this website. They carry exclusively their own brand.

KITCHEN KRAFTS, INC.

800-776-0575

www.kitchenkrafts.com

Kitchen Krafts offers a large selection of products for unique kitchen projects. They have a full line of supplies and equipment for home preservers.

LEHMAN'S

888-438-5346

www.lehmans.com

Lehman's offers a wide range of supplies including everything you need for home food preservation. A great resource for buying supplies in bulk.

S&S INNOVATIONS, CORP.

877-747-2793

www.reusablecanninglids.com

This site offers TATTLER Reusable Canning Lids, replacement gaskets, and fresh rings.

WORKSTEAD INDUSTRIES

413-772-6816

www.pomonapectin.com

Home of Pomona's Universal Pectin, this website is dedicated exclusively to this product. You can source the pectin and get more information about it here.

HOME FOOD PRESERVING COMMUNITY AND INFORMATION

There is a lot of misguided information on the web about everything, home food preservation included. If you are going to use online resources for info about food preservation, it is critical that you are gleaning your info from a reliable source. These websites are top notch. Published by folks who know their stuff, you will get delicious, safe results with their tips, tricks, and recipes.

CANNING ACROSS AMERICA

www.canningacrossamerica.com

A lovely group of canners dedicated to spreading the good word about this nifty craft. Visit their website for recipes and giveaways and keep up to date with their national and local events.

EDIBLE COMMUNITIES, INC.

800-652-4217

www.ediblecommunities.com

A national network of locally produced publications, Edible Communities can put you in touch with your local food community like no one else.

FOOD IN JARS

www.foodinjars.com

Marisa McClellan's blog is always fresh and populated with great ideas for canning and preserving.

NATIONAL CENTER FOR HOME FOOD PRESERVATION

http://nchfp.uga.edu

Funded in part by the USDA, this website offers information and recipes that are thoroughly tested for safe and successful results.

MOTHER EARTH NEWS

Ogden Publications, Inc.

800-234-3368

www.motherearthnews.com

Trust your Mother! There's a reason why this is one of the longest-lived and well-regarded resources for sustainable living. The site, as well as the printed magazines, is full of good, useful information.

PICKYOUROWN.ORG

www.pickyourown.org

This is a sweet, homespun site that is chock full of great information on home food preservation and local sourcing. A great resource for farmers and those who love them.

PUNK DOMESTICS

www.punkdomestics.com

Punk Domestics is a rich resource for deep DIY food craft. Canning, fermenting, charcuterie, even beer and wine making are covered on this site of community-sourced information.

Acknowledgments

I would like to thank my family, Drew, Thayer, and Ava, for their endless support, constant cheering, and indefatigable taste buds; my mom, Nancé, who continues to earn the biggest I-told-you-so; my agent, Lisa Ekus, and the entire team at the Lisa Ekus Group, for their excellent work and boundless enthusiasm; and everyone at Storey Publishing, particularly my insightful editor, Margaret Sutherland, for their continued efforts to bring sustainability how-to to readers everywhere. Huge thanks to Jenna Rose Levy and Eileen Katz for their skill and company in the kitchen. A shout-out to all of the farmers who continue to dedicate themselves to creating a more delicious future. And for the grace of Saraswati and all of her muses at The Joint, thank you!

Index

Page references in *italic* indicate photos.

Try this recipe from Put 'em Up!

One of more than 250 recipes in Sherri Brooks Vinton's best-selling first preserving book, Jardinière is a pickled salad that makes a great accompaniment to all kinds of sandwiches and deli meals.

304 pages. Paper. ISBN 978-1-60342-546-9.

Jardinière

Makes about 4 pints

Jardinière is the name of the pickled cauliflower and vegetable salad you often see in Italian groceries. You can use a variety of vegetables in the mix but keep the quantities consistent with those listed here to make sure you have sufficient brine to preserve them.

INGREDIENTS

- **4** cups distilled white vinegar
- **1** cup water
- **1** cup sugar
- **1** tablespoon kosher salt
- **1** tablespoon mustard seed
- **4** large carrots, peeled, trimmed, and cut into coins (about 2 cups)
- **1** small head cauliflower, leaves removed, cored, and cut into ½-inch florets (about 6 cups)
- **1** red bell pepper, seeded and chopped (about 1 cup)

PREPARE

Combine the vinegar, water, sugar, salt, and mustard seed in a large nonreactive pot, and bring to a boil. Add the carrots, cauliflower, and bell pepper, and return to a boil. Reduce the heat and simmer until the vegetables begin to turn tender, 2 to 3 minutes.

PRESERVE

Refrigerate: Ladle into bowls or jars. Cool, cover, and refrigerate for up to 3 weeks.

Can: Use the boiling-water method. Pour into clean, hot half-pint or pint canning jars, covering the solids by ¼ inch with liquid. Leave ¼ inch of headspace between the top of the liquid and the lid. Release trapped air. Wipe the rims clean; center lids on the jars and screw on jar bands. Process for 10 minutes. Turn off heat, remove canner lid, and let jars rest in the water for 5 minutes. Remove jars and set aside for 24 hours. Check seals, then store in a cool, dark place for up to 1 year.